# The Therapeutic Community Movement:

## Charisma and Routinization

NICK MANNING

Routledge
London and New York

First published in 1989
by Routledge
11 New Fetter Lane, London EC4P 4EE
29 West 35th Street, New York, NY 10001

© 1989 Nick Manning
Phototypeset in 10pt Times by
Mews Photosetting, Beckenham, Kent.
Printed in Great Britain
Billing & Sons Ltd, Worcester

British Library Cataloguing in Publication Data

Manning, Nick
    The therapeutic community movement: charisma
    and routinization.
    1. Therapeutic communities
    I. Title
    362.2'0424

ISBN 0-415-02913-9

ISBN 0-415-03057-9

Parry 6801 /13.99. 8.91

# THE THERAPEUTIC COMMUNITY MOVEMENT
# CHARISMA AND ROUTINIZATION

This book is to be retu

*By the same author*

*Therapeutic Communities*, Routledge & Kegan Paul, 1979 (edited with Bob Hinshelwood)
*Socialism, Social Welfare, and the Soviet Union*, Routledge & Kegan Paul, 1980 (with Vic George)
*Sociological Approaches to Health and Medicine*, Croom Helm, 1985 (with Myfanwy Morgan and Mike Calnan)
*Social Problems and Welfare Ideology*, Gower, 1985 (edited)

# Contents

*For Leslie, who didn't live to see its completion.*

# Tables

# Figures

# Preface

This study is about therapeutic communities. These are residential groups set up to pursue therapeutic or educational change in a manner at odds with conventional psychiatric treatment, particularly in the almost exclusive use of group experiences as the medium of therapy. The study falls into three parts. The first part, presented in chapters one and two, examines the history of therapeutic communities and their recent development both in terms of theory and practice. The second part, presented in chapters four and five, examines in empirical detail the changing nature of the leading British therapeutic community, Henderson Hospital, since the 1950s; and the effectiveness of six Australian therapeutic communities set up in the 1980s by one of the fastest growing and largest voluntary community agencies, the Richmond Fellowship.

The third part, presented in chapters three and six, reflects on the social theory available on the one hand to help inform therapeutic community work, and on the other hand to clarify the nature of the therapeutic community, both as a therapeutic technique and as a movement for social change.

Financial and institutional support has come from the Social Sciences Research Council, the Universities of York, Kent and Queensland, the Henderson Hospital, the Richmond Fellowship, and the Australian Commonwealth Department of Health. Inspiration, however, is a personal thing. In addition to the tolerance of the residents and staff at the Henderson and Richmond Fellowship communities, I could not have undertaken this work without the encouragement and scepticism (in variable amounts!) of Kathleen Jones, Stuart Whiteley, Elly Jansen, and Bob Hinshelwood. Most important of all, however, have been the ideas and work shared with Janine Lees whose interest in this area and whose vital joint work on the Australian project are reflected throughout.

# 1

# The origins of the therapeutic community

## THE RISE OF THE ASYLUM

In order to understand the origins of the therapeutic community, it is important to examine not merely what it is for, but also what it is against. This entails an appreciation of the way in which institutional confinement of the mentally ill developed, since as we shall see the failure of institutionalization was one important impetus for this innovation.

Kittrie (1971) has examined a number of deviant phenomena, such as drug addiction, homosexuality, alcoholism, and mental illness and demonstrated how such phenomena were originally regarded as moral, then legal, and now medical problems. As a result of these perceptions, particular deviants were subjected to moral, legal, and then medical modes of social control. Similarly, Conrad and Schneider (1980) conclude their review of the medicalization of deviance by proposing that

> three major paradigms may be identified that have held reign over deviance designations in various historical periods: deviance as sin; deviance as crime; and deviance as sickness. (p.27)

This religious-legal-medical scheme can be applied to an historical analysis of the social meanings associated with madness. Thus, at one time or another, it has been regarded as divine possession, possession by the devil, or possession by spirits, either benign or malevolent. Usually whether perceptions have been purely magical or religious, they have nonetheless centred around notions of good or evil, and have given rise to reward for correct behaviour or punishment for evil-doing. Different attitudes sometimes existed side-by-side: horror and adoration, indifference and admiration.

An important source of this religious view in Europe was the biblical story of Jesus casting out evil spirits from epileptic or similarly troubled people. Although other non-Christian cultures such as the Greeks, Romans and Hindus held similar views, only in Europe were they to become the basis of the systematic persecution of such deviants. Feared as a danger for a weakening church, these deviants were tackled through the Inquisition, epitomized by the manual for witch-hunters, the *Malleus Maleficarum* (Hammer of Witches), published in 1486.

With the decline in the power of the church, and the growth in power of the nation state in Europe, heralded by the Reformation and the break with Rome in England (1534), deviant minorities came to be seen in more secular terms. Rather than a theological or moral concern, they became a problem for state bureaucracies to solve rationally, either through financial support and control as in the Elizabethan Poor Law of 1601, or in new residential establishments such as the Hôpital Général founded in Paris in 1656, which at its height housed as much as 1 per cent of the population of Paris. This 'great confinement' as Foucault (1967) describes it was the beginning of the institutional segregation of mad people (often along with the poor, unemployed or elderly) which reached its greatest development in the nineteenth century. Although Enlightenment ideas provided a general alternative to theology, there were as yet no specific scientific or clinical approaches to madness.

## The golden age

The secularization of ideas in the seventeenth and eighteenth centuries thus offered no positive interpretations, and madness came to be seen as something less than human — an animal or brutish condition suitable for brutish treatment. While medical interpretations for the elite, such as George III's madness, used the humoral model of Hippocrates, the general experience of inmates in, for example, the flourishing private trade in madhouses in the late eighteenth century was equivalent to that of caged animals. And even the humoral model dictated unpleasant bouts of blood-letting or vomiting. Other medical interpretations owed more to the whim of the physician than any working theory. For example, the influential Benjamin Rush, founder of American psychiatry, who flourished in the late eighteenth century, identified such diseases as 'anarchia' evident soon after the American War of Independence:

> The excess of the passion for liberty, inflamed by the successful issue of the war, produced, in many people, opinions and conduct which could not be removed by reason nor restrained by government . . . these opinions constituted a form of insanity. (Szasz, 1971: 140)

On the other hand, Rush felt that continued loyalty to the British crown was also an illness he termed 'revolutiona'.

The real opportunity for the development of psychiatry, however, occurred as a result of what Castel (1976), and following him Ingleby (1983), have termed the 'golden age' of the asylum. This period covered the late eighteenth century to the middle of the nineteenth century, and began with the development of non-medical 'moral treatment'. From this point of view, the experience of madness was to be corrected by providing a calm and ordered life, in which the mad person was treated, in so far as was possible, a humane and respectful manner. Symbolized by the dramatic removal of the chains of the mad in 1794 by Pinel in the asylums of Bicêtre and Saltpetrière, this approach was developed by Tuke in the Retreat at York into an educational process using kindness and respect to help mad people re-establish self-control of their 'animal natures' through moral force. In *Description of the Retreat* (1813), Tuke argued that a patient's 'desire for esteem' rather than 'the principle of fear' guided the organization of treatment.

There are certain parallels between moral treatment and the therapeutic community (Rossi and Filstead, 1973; Kennard, 1983; Hollander, 1981), although they are far from identical. Indeed the therapeutic community has been termed the 'rebirth' of moral treatment (Sprafkin, 1977). Both stressed the curability of mental illness through a benign social environment, best created in a small, residential institution. Both developed through the charismatic and zealous proselytizing of committed reformers. And both aimed to resituate social control back in the individual as self-control. However, unlike moral treatment, the therapeutic community has developed within the medical profession, and with a far greater technical sophistication drawn from group psychotherapy.

Partly in response to this example, and partly in reaction to the excesses of the private madhouses revealed in parliamentary select committee reports in 1807 and 1815, a strong reform movement developed to press for the construction and regulation of public asylums. The construction of these was made compulsory in the 1845 Lunatics Act; within three years nearly three-quarters of English counties had complied, and the rest followed suit within ten years. While it might be expected that the non-medical system of 'moral treatment' would naturally be adopted in these new asylums, in fact the medical profession soon came to dominate them.

The medical profession had officially become involved with madness as early as the late eighteenth century when official (though ineffective) inspection of private madhouses was set up. In addition, many of these used medical claims in their competition for trade and were often built near infirmaries. However, the development of moral treatment at the turn of the century posed a considerable threat to such medical expansion, and it is remarkable therefore to find that by 1830 existing public asylums (built under the 1744 Vagrancy Act) mostly had medical directors, and that the 1845 Act required the keeping of medical records and encouraged medical dominance within the Lunacy Commission. An Association of Medical Officers of Asylums and Hospitals for the Insane had been founded in 1841, and began to publish the *Asylum Journal* in 1853, promoting the theory that insanity was purely a disease of the brain. The reason for this relatively rapid takeover of madness by the medical profession has been the source of some debate (Scull, 1979); but it effectively established the medical treatment of madness, and at the end of this 'golden age' the profession could look forward with hope to the successful treatment of madness in the new asylums.

## The modern age

Such optimism was to be short lived. The asylum movement drew its inspiration from not only medicine and moral treatment, but also the utopian hopes which inspired socialist and religious communards of the early nineteenth century such as Robert Owen. Yet by 1877 a Lancet Commission set up to investigate asylums recorded that 'everywhere attendants, we are convinced, maltreat, abuse and terrify patients when the backs of the medical officers are turned. Humanity is only to be secured by the watching officials' (Jones, 1972a: 166). The asylums had rapidly become overcrowded during the middle of the century, as a result both of pressure on them to take increasing numbers of admissions, and the failure of the asylum doctors to cure many of their inmates. While at the end of the first quarter of the nineteenth century there were six public asylums, of an average size of 116 inmates, this became twenty-four asylums averaging 300 inmates by 1850, and sixty asylums averaging 650 inmates by 1880 (Scull, 1979: 198). Institutions of this size, be they workhouses, prisons, public schools, or asylums tended to develop features common to what Goffman (1961) called 'the total institution', in which an inmate's entire waking life, work or leisure, was subject to surveillance and regulation such that a person's very self was stripped away. Small wonder, then, that the popular image of the asylum by the late nineteenth century was of something to be feared. Although the asylum movement had developed earlier in the century with a positive idea — literally an asylum or retreat from an increasingly stressful world — in reality the incarceration of lunatics became a sub-branch of the general nineteenth century use of institutional control. Clearly, such a place was not attractive, and in the later decades of the nineteenth century considerable concern developed about the possibility of individuals being erroneously locked away. This gave rise in 1890 to the Lunacy Act which was addressed to the proper process of admission such that mistaken confinement could not occur. Its focus on safe-guarding those outside could not be more of a contrast with the 1845 Act's intent of bringing the benefits of the asylum experience to mad people.

Despite popular fear of asylums, and a correspondingly legalistic control of them, the period since the mid-nineteenth century has come to be called the modern age since it witnessed the consolidation and eventual triumph of the medical view of madness. The opportunist involvement of doctors in the early asylum movement survived the pessimism of the late nineteenth century by repeating the claim that medicine would in time develop the right answers, as it was doing spectacularly for physical illness. It seemed not unreasonable that the success associated with the germ theory of disease (leading to vaccination, antiseptics, and so on) would spill over into the field of madness, in which the notion of diseased brains rather than troubled minds was gaining strength. By the early twentieth century, medicine had metamorphosed from an art into a science, a process epitomized in the impact of the 1910 Flexner report on medical education in the USA. This report, commissioned by the American Medical Association, concluded that a substantial number of medical schools was of insufficient standard, and within a few years about one third had closed down (Anderson, 1968).

Faith in science, including medical science, resonated with the

5

emergence of social reform around the turn of the century. Fabians (in England) and progressives (in the USA) built on imperialist concerns about the fitness of working-class military recruits to make a strong case for state intervention in working-class life. Nowhere was this argument more relevant than in the health field where it gave a further boost to the medical profession. Consequently, the final transition from medical control of asylums, to the medical treatment of mental illness, was sealed in the early twentieth century. Specifically, the successful identification of syphilis as the cause of general paralysis of the insane in 1894 and its confirmation as an infection in the nerve-cells of the cortex in 1913, and the identification of the neuroses in the early 1920s, enabled the medical profession to dominate the 1924–7 Royal Commission on Lunacy and Mental Disorder. The subsequent Mental Treatment Act of 1930, as its title implies, began to prise the control of asylum admissions away from lawyers in favour of doctors (Treacher and Baruch, 1981).

## A NEW PSYCHIATRY?

Although the problems of size and numbers were recognized in the nineteenth century, and many improvements occurred in the twentieth century in terms of staffing, food, voluntary admission, entertainment, and recreation, the buildings remained. Not until after the Second World War did the reaction to such large institutions and their custodial methods of working occur. Since it was not economically possible to rebuild enough accommodation in the 'small units' style of Bethlem or Runwell to rehouse patients from the older hospitals, the alternative possibility of re-organizing the internal administration of hospitals was developed, stimulated by war-time experience. Two distinct lines of development can be traced. The first is that of the work of the Tavistock Clinic, and its association with the Army Psychiatric Services. The second is the work of Maxwell Jones of the Maudsley hospital.

### The Tavistock influence

The prospect of war in 1939 resulted in widespread apprehension. Modern methods of warfare would inevitably involve the civilian population both in the effort to produce resources for fighting, and in the effects of air-raids and ultimately, invasion. Speculation as to the effect of war-time life was rife. Many is the story of digging air-raid shelters during the period of the 'phoney' war. By the time that such raids actually occurred the initial apprehension had passed, and the civilian population had become more accustomed to the idea of war. However the fear of panic and the recognition that public morale would be a vital factor in the final outcome guided the preparations for hostility.

In 1938 J.R. Rees, Director of the Tavistock Clinic, was appointed consulting psychiatrist to the army, and in 1939 he became head of the Army Psychiatric Services. Almost one half of the Tavistock Clinic staff moved with him. This appointment followed a Royal Medico-Psychological Association memorandum of 1938 which envisaged that the outbreak of war would result in psychiatric breakdown so widespread that the existing administration would not cope. Three to four million acute psychiatric cases were expected within six months. Indeed this prediction stimulated the consideration of other possibilities than the traditional approach of hospital psychiatry. For this reason Rees was appointed from the Tavistock Clinic, which was in an independent position — neither in mainstream psychiatry, nor in the general developments of psychoanalysis (Dicks, 1970). The very independence and unorthodoxy of the Tavistock had been chosen to deal with the special circumstances of a war which would require the development of entirely new ideas about the wider aspects of warfare. It seemed there was no great confidence that the traditional psychiatric groups could produce such new thinking; and this decision proved correct, for the war years resulted in a multitude of new concepts developed under Rees's direction.

Not only was Rees appointed, but he was also given considerable power in the rank of brigadier to pursue the direction he thought best. He records in *The Shaping of Psychiatry by War* (1945) that such importance was not attached to psychiatry by many regular army personnel, but that the application of psychiatric insights to the problems of managing men in groups successfully won over his protagonists. The power given to Rees and his staff, and the unique problems with which they grappled resulted in a fundamental shift of focus: from concern with the individual, to the larger problems of human relations in organizations, the nature of hostility, the problems of morale, and the vital need to utilize man-power effectively. This shift of focus, reflected throughout the book, meant that the war had brought psychiatry out into the world. Rees records the advances made not only within psychiatry (especially in the understanding of the neuroses), but more so within the fields of

7

psychology and sociology: group relations; selection and assessment of personnel; job analysis and placement; training; morale building; rehabilitation; resocialization; education; health promotion; sociological surveys; and psychological warfare. Many of these areas would not have been explored without the unique combination of Tavistock open-mindedness and the problems of war.

Although not directly related to the development of the therapeutic community, such work contributed to the general climate of interest in social aspects of psychiatry and co-operation between different disciplines. For instance, the Inter-Allied Study Group included sociologists, psychiatrists, and psychologists. However, certain areas of study were to be the direct forerunners of the therapeutic community. Dicks (1970) attributes much of the intellectual drive within Rees's command to his two aides, Hargreaves and Wilson. Hargreaves, as Assistant Director of the Army Psychiatric Servies, set up a Directorate of Personnel Selection. Here he developed many ideas about the use of groups for the selection of officers. This knowledge was an important element in the new ideas circulating amongst this 'invisible college' (Main, 1957) during the war. For example, both Wilson and Hargreaves were familiar with the work on groups of Kurt Lewin, then Professor of Child Psychology and Consultant to the Office of Strategic Studies in the USA.

A second product of the Tavistock-influenced army psychiatric services was the work at Northfield Hospital. Kraupl Taylor (1958) refers to two experiments at Northfield. The first was the rearrangement of the organization of the training wing undertaken by Bion and Rickman who had been drafted in to deal with 'unruly conditions'. This experiment is described by Bion in the first section of *Experiences in Groups* (1960). Bion decided that men who were so dissatisfied with army discipline would best appreciate their situation by attempting to organize themselves, and solve the problem of discipline altogether, as a community. By the time Bion left, the atmosphere of the training wing had changed dramatically, and more importantly the seeds of a new approach to hospital organization had been sown.

The second Northfield experiment involved the re-organization of the whole hospital along the lines suggested by Bion and involved Main and Foulkes amongst others (Main, 1977). The new horizons opened up by these experiences are reflected in Main's contribution to the *Bulletin of the Menninger Clinic*, volume 10 (1946), 'The Hospital as a therapeutic institution'. Here the social dimension of psychiatry is recognized in full and in particular the basis of neurosis is connected with poor social relationships which are to be revitalized through the patient's full participation in the community which is his hospital.

A third important development at the end of the war was the establishment in 1945 of an experimental Civil Resettlement Unit for ex-prisoners-of-war (Curle, 1947). By the end of the year there were twenty units in Great Britain. These were run under the direction of Wilson, who was later replaced by Main. The units drew considerably upon the experience at Northfield, and the theoretical contribution of Bion. They were designed as transitional communities to give ex-prisoners-of-war an experience of community life which would aid their re-socialization back into their familes and the wider community.

## Jones at Mill Hill

While these developments occurred within the Army Psychiatric Services amongst people connected with the Tavistock Clinic, Maxwell Jones made similar discoveries elsewhere. Jones was one of the Maudsley staff moved to Mill Hill public school which was taken over as part of the emergency medical services. Here he ran the Effort Syndrome Unit. In common with the Northfield practitioners Jones wished to change the hospital in such a way as to release unrealized positive therapeutic forces from within the organization itself. This possibility was uncovered less from a theoretical appraisal (as has happened at Northfield) than from a practical involvement in meeting the needs of the patient group with which Jones was faced. He states that when the Effort Syndrome Unit was set up (1940): 'the wards were indistinguishable from those of a general hospital . . . the nurse's traditions were largely those of the general hospital nurse' (Jones, 1952:1).

However, Jones had the opportunity to train his nurses specifically for work in a neurosis hospital, since many were conscripted and had no desire to qualify in the state examination as a mental nurse. He found that since these nurses were often well-educated and mature, training could take the form of tutorials. Direct communication developed between the nurses and the doctor without the need for liaison through a sister.

In the patient group, the symptomatology presented was the universal one of a psychosomatic complaint of 'heart disease'. Research during the First World War (Lewis, 1919) and the beginning of the Second (Wood, 1941) had established that psychological factors led to the development of effort syndrome through simple physiological mechanisms. In order to explain the nature of the

9

symptoms to the patients, it was necessary to give basic instruction in elementary physiology and anatomy. This was too time-consuming to be undertaken individually, and a 'lecture' approach was adopted. This quickly turned into open discussion, as older patients explained to new patients the pertinent facts.

Jones pinpoints as the important aspect of these group discussions their ability to bring about attitude change. Furthermore, he realized that these discussions were affecting the whole social structure of the ward. Group atmosphere and ward morale were recognized as fluc-tuating 'in response to known external stresses, while at other times mysterious unknown forces seemed to be at work' (Jones, 1952:13). These phenomena were accepted as part of the life of the unit, and linked to the use of drama as a technique in social therapy.

The developments up to this time (early 1945) are summarized by Jones in three areas:

1  Treatment was considered as a continuous process operating throughout the waking life of the patient. His reactions in the hospital were similar to his reactions outside, and the study of these real life situations gave a great deal of information about the patient's problems.
2  In order to carry out 1 effectively, a reorganised hospital struc-ture evolved: more open communication; less rigid hierarchy of doctors, nurses, patients; daily structured discussions of the whole unit, and various sub-groups.
3  A combination of 1 and 2 resulted in a reappraisal of the place of the patient in hospital, with a greater emphasis on vocational guidance to support therapeutically established changes by as smooth as possible a transition out of hospital.

It is to be noted that this description given by Jones is superficial. As in later descriptions, he gives little evidence about his own posi-tion and influence as leader. Moreover, as we shall see later, his use of the concept 'role' to examine changes in the organization is con-fused. It is difficult to distinguish between what is reported fact and what is general advice offered as a method for generating therapeutic social structures. In comparison with the activities of the Tavistock group, Jones was engaged on more specifically practical and clinical work. He developed the use of socio-drama independently of Moreno's ideas, and was concerned in particular to increase communication in his unit between staff and patients in an effort to get patients to under-stand the nature of their psychosomatic illness. Jones did not have much contact with the Tavistock group until after the war. He records in his book *Social Psychiatry* (1952) that he did not even meet Wilson (who was running the Civil Resettlement Units) until 1946, by which time Jones had moved to run the Dartford ex-prisoner-of-war unit at Southern Hospital. This may have been because of Jones's relatively junior rank during the war, and the fact that he came from the Maudsley, which, under Professor Mapother, was resolutely in disagreement with the Tavistock views.

This development of two separate lines of inquiry in the same direction is akin to the often recorded phenomenon of simultaneous independent discovery in science (Merton, 1961). In this case the common situation of an orthodox style of internal administration which was known to have deficiencies, combined with the unique pressures produced by war (staffing shortages, the rapid change and restructuring of a previously static hospital system, an influx of neurotic and psychosomatic patients, etc.) led to a similar innovation. In short, the changed objectives of senior staff resulted in the invention of new strategies, which in turn produced a qualitatively different approach to hospital administration.

By 1946 a new way of organizing certain groups of residential patients had been devised. In the following fifteen years this method was explored in many different settings and indeed reached its zenith during this post-war period. The transition from war-time to post-war setting was crucial for the growth of the therapeutic community idea.

## Transition to peace

In war time, if an officer is of senior enough status (rank) there will be sufficient authority (and therefore power) to introduce innovations to meet special needs. This combination of status, authority and power is essential to produce changes which cut across traditional methods. The military hierarchy provides the necessary power. In peace time the source of power is no longer vested in the military hierarchy as far as psychiatric practice goes. Instead power comes from both statutory provision and professional organization.

In the post-war era up to the 1959 Mental Health Act, considerable power continued to be held by a medical superintendent by virtue of the legal responsibility for every patient in the hospital and the centralized nature of administration laid down in the 1890 Act. Thus, from a statutory point of view, the medical superintendent held the reins of power.

11

From a professional point of view, the position of medical superintendent was also significant. The medical superintendent's position was a senior one in a highly professionalized body. Hence what was deemed to be the correct medical method was not challenged by more junior doctors, still in training, or limited in experience. The medical superintendent embodied the whole authority of the medical profession for the hospital, and for this reason was able to interpret medical procedures at will, orthodox or otherwise. This combination of professional and statutory power, allied with independence, made the position of medical superintendent obviously attractive to people used to power derived from the military hierarchy during the war, who were interested in new approaches to organizing and administering psychiatric hospitals.

This position was obtained by Tom Main (at the Cassel), and although Maxwell Jones did not become a medical superintendent he was appointed Director of the Industrial Neurosis Unit (Belmont), and drew his power from more influential figures such as Aubrey Lewis, then Professor of Psychiatry at the Maudsley. In effect Maxwell Jones ran the Industrial Neurosis Unit at Belmont as an independent organization, drawing on the parent hospital merely for administrative support.

This move from positions of power in the military hierarchy, to positions of power in peace time was thus affected in different ways by the two people who came to embody the emergent therapeutic community movement. Main was by far the senior man, ending the war as overall director of the Civilian Resettlement Units, and moving on into the position of medical superintendent. Jones had had to rely on the goodwill of more senior staff, particularly as he was working within the organicist stream in psychiatry, which was not sympathetic to social psychiatric ideas.

It has been argued so far that those two developments in hospital organization were the logical result of unique war-time conditions. The post-war popularity of the therapeutic community concept was a result of much more than logical strategy. The enthusiasm for the concept derived its emotional charge from a much wider desire for change.

This desire for change was a direct result of the war. The difficulties of returning prisoners of war to civilian life described by Curle (1947) highlight many of the feelings of other military personnel. In particular there was an enormous desire to change from the experience of military rule to a more egalitarian effort to get together and build a better community at home than the one that war had created. This general feeling, embodied in the massive Labour victory in the general election of 1945, also found expression in particular areas of life. Hence official support for new developments in social psychiatry included the Industrial Neurosis Unit at Belmont.

The goal of most people at this time was to tackle the task of building up the country they had fought for. War-time experiences had taught people that many old ways of living were maintained through habit rather than necessity, and that when these were challenged and changed, new developments came within reach. A social structure had never before been so altered, and this not only produced new goals to reach for, but a confidence in people's own ability to reach those goals in new ways.

The goals sought in therapeutic communities can be seen in the short paper written by Main for the 1946 *Bulletin of the Menninger Clinic*:

1 Traditional hospital practice resulted in dependent patients, who thus needed resocialisation in addition to treatment of their illness.

2 Not only must such effects be combated, but the hospital organisation itself could mobilise considerable therapeutic potential through establishing full social participation — which would be particularly valuable for neurotic individuals.

Thus there were two goals. The first was to reduce negative organization effects, and the second was to employ positive therapeutic forces resulting from full social participation — in particular encouraging increased capacity for social relationships.

Both these goals required change — change in the overall hospital organization, and in particular, change in the role of each individual member of staff and patient in this hospital. The overall organization was to become less hierarchical, with the psychiatrist as a technician involved with promoting growth and communication, rather than being a superintendent of his patients. There were to be less rigid divisions between roles amongst the staff, and decisions were to be arrived at through open group discussion amongst those concerned.

The move to such a flexible, egalitarian structure required some alternative ways of co-ordinating and integrating the organization. These problems were tackled in two ways. The first was by the emergence of strong leadership — a characteristic common to all the early therapeutic communities (and indeed to many movements for change (Weber, 1947)). The second was the development of a cohesive ideology which provided a common definition of the work and thus helped integrate staff and patients alike.

Of the war-time innovators, only Main and Jones managed to attain leadership positions with enough power and independence to pursue their new ideas for hospital organization. Foulkes and Bion were not in a position to secure such power, and had to develop their ideas elsewhere. In fact Bion moved closer to psycho-analysis, and Foulkes to group-analytic psychotherapy. Hargreaves chose to work for Unilever, and subsequently took the Chair in Psychiatry at Leeds. Wilson stayed with the Tavistock Institute until 1958, when he went to Unilever also, and finally became Professor of Organisational Behaviour at the London Graduate School of Business Studies.

Main and Jones concentrated on internal institutional reorganization and did not at the same time develop links with the outside community. The necessity to concentrate wholeheartedly at that time on internal organization arose out of the recent growth of ideas and concepts. It was felt necessary to reform social life within the institutions before expanding outside them. This concern can be seen also in the post-war activities at the Tavistock itself. Dicks (1970) comments that the professional committee of the Tavistock Clinic considered the internal restructuring of the clinic as a social experiment. He records that critics were later to point out that this 'withdrawal' resulted in missed opportunities, and allowed the 'organicists' a greater domination of British psychiatry than might have been.

## Growth of knowledge in the social sciences

Underlying the war-time and post-war factors in the growth of therapeutic community ideas was a more general development in social science knowledge. Although the war produced new ideas and concepts these were quickly assimilated into general social science, and the therapeutic community can be seen more as a specific application of these ideas in practice than as a completely new set of concepts. For instance, the therapeutic community combines two analytically distinct fields: organization theory (and in particular the interaction between structure, interpersonal process and individual behaviour); and psychotherapy (the attempt to promote personality growth through guided conversation). The therapeutic community attempted to use knowledge from the first field to improve the second. The result, though unique, is no more than the inspired use of more general knowledge.

The growth of social science knowledge is relevant in two ways. The most obvious way is to the extent that therapeutic community practitioners were conversant with that knowledge at its academic source (i.e. books, articles, lectures) and applied it specifically. The second way is the spread of ideas in a more 'popular' manner. For instance, Dicks (1970) talks of the 'invisible college' of people associated with the war-time Tavistock Institute, through which ideas were spread by word of mouth, rather than through academic study.

It is apparent from Lewin's obituary in the first volume of *Human Relations* (1947) that Bion was closely in touch with Lewin during the war. It is reasonable to suggest therefore that knowledge of group phenomena generated by Lewin was passed directly to those involved in early hospital restructuring. However, it seems that Maxwell Jones himself was not familiar with sociological ideas, from his account in *Social Psychiatry* (1952). Concepts such as leadership, power, status, ideology, which would have thrown more light on the analysis of his unit, were not mentioned at all. In fact Jones makes use largely of the single concept of 'role' in his analysis, which suggests that perhaps he was aware of some sociological concepts through their 'popularization' rather than through academic study.

The growth in social science knowledge stems really from the nineteenth century — and many of the relevant ideas can be traced back to Freud. He made revolutionary advances in thinking about the interaction between the individual psyche and its environment. Not only was he to posit the concept of the 'unconscious', but he also took an interest in collective behaviour (Freud, 1922).

In the twentieth century, interest in society turned from philosophical speculation to scientific enquiry. Durkheim's study of suicide (1952) is an early example of enquiry in the modern style. In 1908, the first book to bear the title *Social Psychology* (by E.A. Ross) appeared. Social psychology began to flourish after the First World War. Initially confined to the study of attitudes (Thomas and Znaniecki, 1918–20), social psychology rapidly developed particularly through the work of Kurt Lewin. Lewin spanned the crucial years from the end of the First World War (he had a paper published in 1917) until the late 1940s. He drew heavily on ideas developed in theoretical physics about force-fields, and held that individual behaviour was a product of the dynamic interaction between the person and his environment. A natural area for study was therefore the small group. Research on groups associated with Lewin continued up to, during, and after the Second World War, and provided an important theoretical influence on therapeutic community ideas through Bion.

The relationship between environment and behaviour was further studied by the 'human relations' school amongst students of industry

(Roethlisberger and Dickson, 1943), and in the work of G.H. Mead. Although his two major works were published posthumously (1934 and 1938), Mead was very influential in his own lifetime. Mead conceived of people as actors each possessing a self which developed through a 'reflexive process' enabling a person 'to take the role of the other'. This idea is central to the therapeutic community which attempts to place the individual in a setting in which the consequences of personal actions are made apparent, and where there is encouragement to see oneself from the other's point of view.

The penetration of these ideas into psychiatry was to a great extent through the writings of Harry Stack Sullivan. He defined personality as the 'enduring pattern of recurrent interpersonal situations which characterise human life' (1955:110–11). The knowledge that the personality develops in ongoing interaction with the environment suggested that it might develop abnormally if the environment was abnormal, and furthermore that such mal-development might be corrected by supplying a specifically therapeutic environment.

The last pre-war development in scientific knowledge to be mentioned is the discovery of new organic techniques in the 1930s and 1940s. The failure of these techniques after initially high optimism was conducive to thinking beyond the technique itself to the environment in which it was administered. Clark writes, for example, of the typical deep insulin unit:

> The staff were on easy, confident terms with one another, with private jokes and a special jargon; the patients were spoken to warmly by their Christian names, spoon-fed and encouraged; all played games together in the afternoon, patients, nurses and even doctors. But little of this was mentioned in the publications, which still discussed varieties of insulin, dosages, potentiators, frequency and depth of comas, symptomatic prognosticators and such individual 'objective' considerations. This treatment continued in vogue for nearly twenty years, despite a few critical voices. Then Bourne voiced the growing challenge, and Arkner, Harris and Oldham, in a classic study, showed that whatever the effective agent was, it was not the insulin. Attention then turned to the intensive group experiences provided in an insulin unit and the possibility of understanding and using them. (1964:6–7)

By the end of the war there was thus sufficient knowledge about the effects of the social environment on the individual, to support the use of new ideas which helped fill the vacuum left by the discarding of organic innovations. These ideas may or may not have reached therapeutic communities from their original sources, but they were certainly part of the general currency of social science knowledge in circulation.

## THE POST-WAR ERA

From the late 1940s, when both Maxwell Jones and Tom Main had found appointments in which they could develop their new ideas further, a rapid increase in these and related innovations developed on both sides of the Atlantic. Bion and Foulkes contributed little further to tackling the problems of the mental hospital which now came increasingly under the scrutiny of social scientists. This movement developed earlier in the USA than Britain, although there is evidence of a continuing, if tenuous, link between the two countries. For example, Bion and Lewin, as has been suggested, were in contact throughout the war, and until Lewin's death in 1947. Rees, as Consultant Psychiatrist to the Army, visited the USA and Canada in October-December 1943 and in October-December 1944 (Ahrenfeld, 1958). Rapoport, Parker and Rosow came from the USA to study the Belmont Unit in 1955 (Rapoport, 1960) and maintained trans-atlantic links during this period (Greenblatt, 1957).

It is important to bear in mind the different contexts and traditions of the USA. It had large hospitals of 10,000 or more beds. Britain did not. The impact of war, reducing hospital resources and personnel and precipitating neurotic breakdown in servicemen, was far more severe in Britain. Moreover the development of military psychiatry differed considerably in the two countries. Menninger (Chief Consultant in Neuropsychiatry to the surgeon general of the US army 1943–4) wrote of the USA (1947:103):

> The most severe indictment that can be made must be laid at the feet of the psychiatric profession as a whole — we permitted the military to forget almost all the lessons that we learned in the last war. As a consequence, we began this war with hospital treatment forbidden, with no plan of treatment for combat troops, no unit to provide such, no plans for training, no psychiatrist in combat divisions, and not even a psychiatrist in the headquarters when war was declared.

On the other hand, Rees (1943:1) wrote that in Britain

> we had at our disposal before the war the report of the 1922 War Office Committee on Shell-shock, and, even more valuable, Vol. X of the US Army Medical History of the last war . . . The American Vol. X on Neuropsychiatry provided us with a complete textbook on both the clinical and administrative sides of Army work, and much of the history of our Allies contained in that volume has repeated itself in the British Army in this war. There has therefore been a considerable amount of material to aid us in making plans before the outbreak of war . . .

although Churchill was rather less than enthusiastic about the use of psychiatrists:

> I am sure it would be sensible to restrict as much as possible the work of these gentlemen, who are capable of doing an immense amount of harm with what may very easily degenerate into charlatanry. The tightest hand should be kept over them, and they should not be allowed to quarter themselves in large numbers upon the Fighting Services at the public expense. There are, no doubt, easily recognizable cases which may benefit from treatment of this kind, but it is very wrong to disturb large numbers of healthy, normal men and women by asking the kind of odd questions in which the psychiatrists specialize. There are quite enough hangers-on and camp-followers already. (*The Second World War*, vol. 4, 1951:815)

In this situation, experimental methods of dealing with mental disorder could flourish in Britain without a prior analysis of the old system. In the USA, however, such encouragement was lacking and new developments could only begin at best simultaneously with or a little after the more manifest drawbacks of an institution had been described and analysed. Hence new ideas for treatment developed earlier in Britain than in the USA while the sociological analysis of institutional life developed in the reverse order in the two countries.

## Developments in the USA

Much of the relevant work in the USA at this time can be separated into two categories. In the first is contained the series of classic studies describing and analysing the sociology of the American mental hospital. Belknap in *Human Problems of a State Mental Hospital* (1956) and Dunham and Weinberg in *The Culture of the State Mental Hospital* (1960) drew attention to some of the processes and problems in American state hospitals which invited change. Although the latter study was not published until 1960, the authors had been working in the area for some time and their work was well known (for example, Bateman and Dunham, 1948).

At the same time research work was being done on the social structure and processes of smaller private hospitals. Probably the best-known study was by Stanton and Schwartz, *The Mental Hospital* (1954). In fact the hospital they studied was most unusual — a small private institution using an extensively psycho-analytic approach. However, their sustained attention brought forth some remarkably new facts about the interactions between the state of a patient's illness, and the general processes within the hospital organization. In particular they identified the link between 'pathological excitement' of patients and 'hidden staff disagreement'. This 'Stanton and Schwartz' effect has been recognized in several other studies since as a basic component of 'collective disturbance' (Miller, 1957; Caudill, 1958; Parker, 1958; Rapoport, 1960; Strauss, 1964).

This team of psychiatrist and social scientist also proved productive in the work of John and Elain Cumming. Their analysis of the social structure of a large mental hospital as 'granulated' — i.e. crosscut horizontally by caste lines, and vertically by functional autonomy — and the effect of this on communication and co-ordination within the hospital provided a sound basis from which changes could begin (Cumming and Cumming, 1956, 1957). Sustained study in this area culminated in their book *Ego and Milieu* (1962) which has had a profound effect on thinking about the interaction of the person and his social environment (Carstairs, 1974). This book draws together many of these strands into a theoretically coherent discussion, and marks the culmination of this American work of the previous fifteen years.

The Cummings had earlier contributed two articles to the 1956 Conference on the Socio-Environmental Aspects of Patient Treatment in Mental Hospitals (published in *The Patient and the Mental Hospital* (1957)). This conference was a confirmation of the extensive work being carried out in the field at that time, and included papers by many well-known workers. It epitomized the way in which social scientists had moved into the mental hospital field, and, of course, showed the substantial impact that their questions and analysis had had. The follow-ing year there were published the papers and discussion of a symposium, *Preventive and Social Psychiatry*, sponsored by the Walter Reed Army Institute of Research (1958). Although much of the symposium was concerned with non-institutional areas, one important session contained a first report from Erving Goffman of his year's participant observa-tion of St Elizabeth's Hospital, Washington, while a visiting scientist to the laboratory of socio-environmental studies at the National Institute of Mental Health. Later published in *Asylums* (1961), this report discussed the characteristics of the mental hospital as a total institu-tion, defined as: 'encompassing, to a degree discontinuously greater than the ones next in line . . . symbolised by the barrier to social inter-course with the outside' (Walter Reed, 1958:44). Now probably the most widely-read discussion of mental hospital processes, his work captures dramatically many of the effects of institution life from the patient's point of view. As a complement to the Cummings' *Ego and Milieu* (a rather technical book), Goffman provided a compelling picture to draw together the observations he and others had about the hospital system, thrust into the limelight of sociological study in the 1950s.

Goffman's work combined both an acute eye for detail in noticing the similar structures and processes in mental hospitals, prisons, monastic orders and so on, and an explicit moral condemnation of the impact of those total institutions on the lives of people in them. His argument was based on the use of ideal-types, suggested by Max Weber (1949), in that he built up a model of the total institution from a variety of empirical and literary sources. He suggested that the key process — the totality — was established by collapsing the normally separate spheres of work, home and leisure, into one monolithic social experience: a kind of 'batch living' of the kind found in factory-farmed animals. The crucial phase in this process is the entry of the patient into hospital. This process shares many similarities with the entry procedures experienced by all clients going into total institutions, from army camps to prisons and hospitals (Jones, 1972b). In essence, this amounts to the common severance of social relations on the outside and the entry into new social relations on the inside. More particularly with respect to hospitals, Goffman (1961) referred to this transition as a 'moral career'. He means by this that the changed social relation-ships resulting from movement into hospital include an important alteration in the patient's own identity, which becomes completely submerged by the requirements of the institution. Goffman identified three distinct aspects of this career in total institutions such as mental hospitals:

*Mortification of the Self.* This was achieved through the literal degrading of the person's previous status and identity, brought about by the removal of their normal social props such as clothing and personal effects, the restriction of activities and movements and the requirement to engage in various demeaning practices, such as asking permission to smoke or post a letter.

*Reorganization of the Self.* The hospital replaces those aspects of the patient's identity it has removed: hospital clothes, hospital friends, a new status as patient, etc.

*Patient Response.* Goffman was well aware that his ideal-type of total institution did not always operate fully. In particular, in his discussion of the 'underlife' of asylums, he acknowledges that there are numerous means of working the system or 'making out' within the officially-designated routines. Thus whereas some patients respond to the institution by *colonization*, or the acceptance of their new position without enthusiasm, others become positively identified with their allotted identity in a process of *conversion*, while a third response is to reject the hospital's requirements, and either become *withdrawn* or *intransigent*.

The variety of response to institutional pressures in psychiatric hospitals identified by Goffman has been viewed by some writers as throwing doubt on the validity of his general model. For example, Perry (1974) has suggested that Goffman attempts to develop both a detailed study of the mental hospital as a unique institution, and a general model of the common elements in different kinds of institutions. However, this dual project led to considerable confusion between unique and common elements, such that neither is satisfactorily portrayed. The compelling style of his analysis is achieved rather through a more literary use of metaphor and symbol: 'In Goffman's work there is an unresolved tension between sociological etiquette and metaphysical concerns (which) constitutes an important basis of (its) appeal' (Perry, 1974:353).

The final phase of this era of American sociological work on mental hospitals consists of a more detailed examination of this informal side of hospital life (Strauss, 1963). This started out from the position that what was most important, rather than incidental, was the 'underlife' of the asylum. This was *de facto* the social reality for its members, staff, and patients alike. Thus, Goffman's horrifying vision of the dominating totality of life in the asylum, and its associated moral condemnation, might turn out to be a sociological strawman in the light of the real, rather than ideal-typical, 'negotiated order'. The analysis of the hospital as a negotiated order is based on the assumption that within hospitals the official rules are rarely specific enough to guide the detailed daily or hourly interactions of people, which are therefore subject to negotiation. Thus Strauss suggests that daily life is organized around a series of bargains, struck and forgotten, or renegotiated from time to time, as desired by the individual. One of the most important notions this approach develops is of the ways in which lower-level participants within the organization, such as patients, attendants, visitors and paramedical staff, can influence the formal organization through bargaining and negotiation. An important implication of this is that lower-level members of staff have more power than would appear to be the case, given the formal structure of the hospital and their position in the hierarchy of authority. While this might appear to be a democratizing influence in the hospital, this power is frequently exercised by staff in a negative or obstructive fashion.

Negotiated order theory, although widely regarded as contributing important insights into the working of the hospital, has been criticized for over-emphasizing the fluid nature of negotiations. Bittner (1979) suggests that ordinary staff and patients do in fact adhere to some kind of formal structural description of the organization they are in. They do not necessarily believe the organization is actually like this model, but rather they draw upon such a 'scheme of interpretation' to make sense of that part of the organization out of their reach, so that they may identify with unseen actions elsewhere and gain a sense of uniform purpose.

Day and Day (1977) also point out that while negotiated order theory gets away from the idealization implicit in formal organization theory, it focuses upon only one aspect of the reality of hospital life, namely a rather low level, immediate daily experience of that hospital. Negotiations over this daily experience are then extrapolated as an explanation for the hospital order in general, under-emphasizing those considerable portions of hospital life which are non-negotiable, non-fluid and may well not be immediately symbolically meaningful. In other words, structural constraints, both political and economic, which may exist beyond the ken of the individual participants being studied or indeed beyond the control of or boundaries of the hospital, are under-emphasized. A second weakness identified by Day and Day is the idea of negotiation as the basis for social order within a hospital, which suggests that adaptation and adjustment are the key elements. It is thus difficult to conceptualize from this point of view any notion of conflict or resistance to the agreements being negotiated. This conservative bias, shared with symbolic interactionism generally, arises from focusing at a level from which it is difficult to conceptualize and measure unequal distributions of power or the sources of that power.

Whatever the theoretical adequacy of Strauss's work, it is important to note here that its practical implication is that the underlife of the asylum could soften the totalizing experience for its members sufficiently to make life at worst tolerable, and at best comfortable. For example, something akin to a 'black economy' has been noted by many observers of institutional life, such as the tobacco currency in prisons. A similar circulation of material goods amongst both staff and patients is common in mental hospitals, providing at the very least greater flexibility than the official routines allow.

The celebrated problem of 'institutionalization' thus needs some careful qualification, in so far as patients can renegotiate the negotiated order they have joined. For example, the entry of patients into hospital and their subsequent 'moral careers' include the acquisition of 'hospital time'. Since negotiations between patients and staff focus heavily upon progress towards leaving, institutionalization can be defined as a moral career that has become stuck, so that the patient no longer tries to negotiate his or her way through and beyond institutional time. This is the experience of institutionalization from the interactionist view, however it may be located in the hospital structure.

In some hospitals, patients do not, however, uniformly accept institutional time without question. As Strauss has suggested, there is room for negotiation — not merely over daily or weekly routines, such as the length and frequency of visiting hours, but, more importantly for some patients, the total amount of time they will be spending in hospital before being deemed recovered. In particular, Roth (1962) pointed out that for long-term illnesses both staff and patients often measure the depth of illness and extent of recovery in terms of time done, or to be done, and hence negotiations between staff and patients about dates of departure or home visits become highly significant and occupy a central place in the patient's identity. To the extent that staff successfully maintain uncertainty about these events they can prevent patients from making informed judgements about particular medical policies to which they are subjected. However, patients can successfully undermine such staff ploys by comparing treatments, playing off staff against each other, and so on. Indeed, as we have seen,

Goffman recognized this in his description of patient responses other than conversion (institutionalization): colonization, withdrawal, and intransigence.

The second general category of work in the USA overlaps considerably with the first, but can usefully be distinguished from it in that it is concerned with attempts to change the hospital system, whose undesirable effects had been graphically portrayed by sociological research. Of course many studies combined both analysis and programmes for change.

One of the earliest reported attempts to radically improve treatment was Myerson's (1939) 'total push' method. Although not conceived of as a form of milieu therapy, this use of many different types of staff to keep the patient active throughout the day was a forerunner of the therapeutic community's concern with the 'other 23 hours' (Stanton and Schwartz, 1954). This was a rather crude way of encouraging personal growth demonstrating at least the 'Hawthorne' effect of enthusiasm. After the war, and rather in the wake of the sociologists, reports of changes in American hospitals were published. Much concern was expressed about the problem of changing the large state hospital (Greenblatt, York and Brown, 1955; Denber, 1960), while the development of small-scale therapeutic milieux, such as the 'attitude therapy' of the Menninger Clinic remained separate (Stotland and Kobler, 1965).

The Cummings (1956), for example, had been involved in 1954 and 1955 with not only studying a large mental hospital, but also in using that analysis as a basis for organizing changes from 'chronicity to continued treatment'. On the other hand, Wilmer (1958) attempted to organize more radical changes, but on a small scale. He organized a therapeutic community in a Naval admissions ward. Although using ideas from Maxwell Jones, learned while on naval duty in England (Walter Reed, 1958:466), Wilmer had to deal with acute cases only staying for ten days. Despite such restriction, a dramatic reduction in the use of barbiturates and other methods of imposed control was effected.

These efforts at change, accelerating towards the end of the decade, were epitomized by the work of Greenblatt, York and Brown (1955) who studied changes in three hospitals in Boston. They argued strongly for using behavioural science methods in order to make effective use of the social environment of a hospital, and to improve the motivation of all personnel, both staff and patients.

Of this American work of the 1950s the sociological study of hospitals is the most notable. The development of this into practical work can be seen more clearly by turning back to look once more at Britain.

## Developments in Britain

As has been suggested, British-American links were fairly well developed in the 1950s. From the point of view of the therapeutic community movement, the American work had provided a critique of old institutional structures which strengthened the belief in the new methods already developed during the war-time emergency. In the 1950s work in Britain was more explicitly concerned with innovation. Into this filtered the American experience and towards the latter end of the decade further original research was done in Britain itself.

Although Maxwell Jones had expended considerable effort and charisma in discussing his ideas personally in the USA and in Britain (Clark, 1964), the publication of his first book *Social Psychiatry* in 1952 (1953 in the USA) marked the establishment of a trend. Though published before many of the well-known American studies mentioned, it already reflected some 7–8 year's experience of innovation. This book, discussed later at length, suffered from a lack of theoretical vigour which had been injected by social scientists into the American studies. This problem runs through many of the English studies published in this period, written by practitioners too deeply involved in their work for measured review. Goffman (1971:196) describes Jones's book as 'staid' and goes on to point out Jones's confusion in discussing the easing of status differences between patients and staff (pp. 197–8). This and other weaknesses are criticized later.

In 1953 the World Health Organization's report on Mental Health discussed new dimensions for change. This report, condensing the views of an international committee, is also rather confused and is closer to the English style than the American academic analysis. For example, it stresses how important a hospital 'atmosphere' is for the recovery of patients, but fails to indicate what the 'atmosphere' is, and how it can be monitored and changed. Such looseness of style, so typical of this period, became a major problem for the implementation of therapeutic community principles, as will become apparent in more detailed analysis later.

Towards the middle of the 1950s in Britain, the innovatory spirit then moving within hospital psychiatry spread into larger institutions. Although thereby being applied in very different circumstances these ideas descended directly from the two original strands of the

Northfield group, and Maxwell Jones. Two examples of this development may be taken as archetypal: Clark's work at Fulbourn, and Martin's at Claybury.

In 1953 David Clark was promoted from senior registrar at the Maudesley Hospital to medical superintendent of Fulbourn Hospital. Such a large step placed Clark (in his early 30s) in an advantageous position to put into practice his ideas, derived largely from Maxwell Jones (Carstairs, 1974). Clark had worked with David Henderson at the Royal Edinburgh Hospital, and Foulkes at the Maudesley, and was therefore well placed to attempt to implement therapeutic community ideas in a catchment area hospital. This situation, quite unlike that obtaining at the Belmont unit, required a very different perspective which emerged in Clark's book *Administrative Therapy* (1964). Here Clark met directly, and more explicitly than Maxwell Jones had done, the task of altering the organizational structure of a large hospital. Whereas Jones could link the style of his unit directly to therapeutic efforts, Clark attempted the more difficult task of releasing therapeutic potential at the grass-roots level, one stage removed from himself. This work was not to be completed quickly, and indeed Clark reports (1973; 1974) that the most rapid spread of therapeutic community ideas throughout the hospital was in the mid 1960s and 1970s.

Not long after Clark's appointment, Dennis Martin was appointed (in 1955) consultant at Claybury Hospital — a large traditional institution. He was also fired with enthusiasm for change, and, as had Clark before him, he acknowledged his debt to Maxwell Jones at Belmont Hospital, and the earlier Northfield experiment (Martin, 1962). In common with Jones and in contrast to Clark and Main, Martin had to rely on the goodwill and interest of the hospital's medical superintendent. This point reiterates the Cummings' observation that changes are best introduced into ongoing institutions by 'norm-bearers' rather than by 'deviants' (1957:59).

Martin reports on the changed atmosphere of the hospital as more cheerful, dynamic and purposeful. He also notes a decrease in the use of physical treatments, 'in the past . . . relied upon more than anything else for the control of the disturbed patient' (1962:140). He goes on to say that paying attention to psychological and environmental factors which provoke such behaviour '. . . has greatly diminished the occurrence of the previously very common form of disturbed behaviour'. Whether this is or is not an improvement is debatable. Critics such as Charles Perrow (1965) have suggested that the therapeutic community may be no more than a more sophisticated means of social control.

Such questions are most profitably answered by social scientific research, since speculative writing by practitioners in a field subject to so much emotional flux is rarely objective. This style of sober appraisal, apparent early in the decade in the USA, made its appearance later in Britain. By the mid 1950s some moves in this direction became evident. For example the deliberations of a research group at the Cassel Hospital published by Tom Main as 'The Ailment' (1957) record in detail the painful but thorough discussion of interactions surrounding previous experience of 'nursing failures'.

A more explicit quest for research was set up in Maxwell Jones's unit in Belmont at this time. Aware of the need for more careful work than was recorded in his first book, Maxwell Jones recruited during one of his visits to the USA a young anthropologist, Robert Rapoport, to set up a thorough study of the Belmont unit. Appointed in 1954, Rapoport spent a year familiarizing himself with the unit, its staff and patients. In 1955 a substantial grant was obtained from the Nuffield Foundation to support an ambitious programme of research into psychopathic disorder and the therapeutic community. This programme, described in detail elsewhere, produced many research papers and a book (Rapoport, 1960). Much popular knowledge of the therapeutic community process originates from this research.

By the time Rapoport's book was published a further experiment in this field had begun in Pentonville Prison. In 1957 'H' Wing was set up. This was intended to be the penological equivalent of a therapeutic community. The Morrises (1963:273) describe 'H' Wing as 'Pentonville's concession to the twentieth century'. However nowhere were its objectives explicitly stated beyond vague notions of 'reform' and 'training'. In the White Paper *Penal Practice in a Changing Society* (1959) reference is made to 'high training value' (para. 63), but with no more explanation. Lack of clear objectives, disguised by rhetoric, though more extreme here, has been a common theme in the literature of this field.

Towards the end of the decade, then, several practical efforts at innovation had occurred and some research work had been carried out. This latter activity never attained the scale in Britain that it did in the USA. Almost single-handedly Barton's discussion of negative institutional effects confirmed the sort of processes identified by Goffman and other students of institutions in the USA. Barton termed the reorganized conception of the self, which long-stay patients in psychiatric hospitals may come to accept, 'institutionalization' or 'institutional neurosis', which broadly corresponds with Goffman's notion of 'conversion'. Barton (1959) gave the following definition:

Institutional neurosis is a disease characterised by apathy, lack of initiative, loss of interest most marked in things and events not immediately personal or present, submissiveness, and sometimes no expression of feelings of resentment at harsh or unfair orders. There is also a lack of interest in the future and an apparent inability to make practical plans for it, a deterioration in personal habits, toilet and standards generally, a loss of individuality and a resigned acceptance that things will go on as they are — unchangingly, inevitably and indefinitely. (Barton, 1959:2)

However, research specifically on the therapeutic community reached its zenith with the Rapoport study.

## CONCLUSION

This chapter has documented the emergence of the therapeutic community into the world of the mental hospital. The 1950s witnessed the linking of innovations, pushed forward in the unique war-time conditions of Britain, with large-scale studies of the sociology of the mental hospital in the USA. There were interesting contrasts in the relationship between academic sociologists, psychiatric innovation and the institutional context in Britain and the USA. As has been suggested, research tended to precede innovation in the USA, while innovation tended to precede research in Britain. Which of the two processes was more fruitful is debatable. Certainly in Britain the therapeutic community was never clearly defined as a specific method even in the Rapoport study. In the USA, the problem was to change perceived institutional arrangements which may be what the therapeutic community has in fact done despite the broader claims to have introduced a 'new psychiatry'.

# 2

## The growth and spread of therapeutic communities

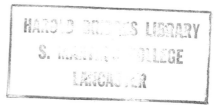

In the previous chapter, the origins of the therapeutic community were traced to a cumulative dissatisfaction with the old asylum system, the innovation of new therapeutic methods stimulated by the Second World War, and the growth of new theory and research in the social sciences. Since the early 1960s each of these influences has changed. Psychiatric practice has slowly moved its centre of gravity from the asylum to the community, and psychiatric technology has developed strongly in the areas of biochemical and physical intervention. Both of these changes would seem to have undermined the rationale of the therapeutic community, based as it is on institutional practice using social and psychological methods. Yet the therapeutic community has survived, and even flourished in response to these changes. However, its radical potential — the 'new psychiatry' envisaged by early proponents — has been unrealized. In part this has been due to the failure of its adherents to accommodate these changes in psychiatric practice; but it is also a result of their failure to develop therapeutic community ideas through a dialogue with the expansion and change in social science which has occurred since the early 1960s.

In this chapter the growth and spread of therapeutic communities will be examined, together with the theoretical and practical problems that have accompanied this development. In the following chapter, those changes in social science theory of relevance to the therapeutic community, but as yet unacknowledged in its work, will be presented.

## DEFINING THE THERAPEUTIC COMMUNITY

In chapter 1 the origins of the therapeutic community were examined, without attempting to give a tight definition of the therapeutic

29

community itself. This was deliberate, for two reasons. First, while Main had given a general definition in his 1946 paper, couched in terms of reducing the negative effects of institutions and releasing positive therapeutic forces, there was considerable variety in the way in which such work was undertaken. Second, the theoretical views used to describe the therapeutic community ranged across psychotherapy, psychiatry, sociology, and anthropology. Indeed, this bewildering variety, unified sometimes only by a general enthusiasm for change, even came to be celebrated by Maxwell Jones in the late 1950s:

> The fact is, of course, that we have as yet no single model of a therapeutic community. All that we hope to do is to mobilize the interest, skills and enthusiasms of staff and patients and give them sufficient freedom of action to create their own optimal social organisation. (Jones, 1968:115)

By this time, as Jones himself notes, the therapeutic community was already coming under attack as empty of specific content, resistent to a sufficiently precise definition for evaluative research to be undertaken, and hence in danger of losing its legitimacy in the professional psychiatric community. Indeed, the above quote has for many critical authors become itself sufficient grounds for condemning therapeutic communities to oblivion. Since the early 1960s however there has been a consistent attempt by a variety of authors to develop greater definitional precision.

An early distinction was drawn by Clark (1965) between the therapeutic community 'approach', in which Main's ideas were applied to a whole hospital, and the therapeutic community 'proper', in which a specific small ward, unit or hospital was designed explicitly to make the social environment the main therapeutic tool. The latter is exemplified in Jones's work at Henderson Hospital, examined in detail in chapter 4. A similar distinction was drawn by Crockett (1966) between the general therapeutic community in which individual (including physical) treatments were merely supplemented by community and group methods, and the 'psycho-therapeutic community' in which such methods were the exclusive means of treatment.

In an attempt to provide some empirical support for this distinction the current author conducted a small postal survey of seventeen therapeutic communities in Britain in 1975 (Manning, 1975), as part of a larger project to examine referral patterns to therapeutic communities. Nine replies were received. Questions were grouped under four main headings: characteristics of the community; sources of referral; rates of referral; rates of admission. The information from the questionnaire can be organized around two features: those characteristics shared by all or most of the sample; and those characteristics which systematically divide the sample into two consistent groups. Of relevance here is the latter situation. The eight replies used do seem to fall into two groups broadly consistent with Clark's (1965) distinction between the therapeutic community approach and the therapeutic community proper. Although not completely distinct on all points, the two groups can be divided as in table 2.1, fairly clearly.

*Table 2.1* Types of therapeutic community

| Therapeutic community approach: | Therapeutic community proper: |
|---|---|
| Acute admissions service | No acute admissions service |
| Catchment area from which most patients are drawn | No catchment area |
| Do not specialize in certain disorders/problems | Do specialize — favour neurotics/personality disorders over psychotics |
| Majority of patients are non-residential | Majority of patients are residential |
| Patients generally older (40 years +) | Patients generally younger (most in their 20s) |
| Most referrals from GPs | Most referrals from psychiatrists, special units, social services, etc. |
| Most referrers have no alternative place to refer | Most referrers could have referred elsewhere |
| Number of referrals per year is higher (400–600 +) | Number of referrals is lower (200–300) |
| Do not encourage or discourage referrals | Do tend to encourage (and sometimes discourage) referrals |

The consistency of the distinction in table 2.1 derives in part because the presence of some of the factors tends to imply the presence of others — e.g. an acute admissions service precludes much selection of patients. Despite such interaction, however, there is clear evidence here to support Clark's two-fold categorization. There seem, indeed, to be two broad types of therapeutic community which are consistently separated on a number of dimensions. These types relate to the outside world in different ways, and operate internally in different ways given their constituent characteristics.

This distinction has now become a standard categorization in discussions about the field, such as Clark (1977), Millard (1983), Bierenbroodspot (1980), Kennard (1983), Trauer (1984). However, such a simple dichotomy can be elaborated further. Logically, this can be done in three ways, each of which has appeared in the literature.

First is a large-scale survey conducted by Price and Moos (1975), which for our purposes provides an empirical basis for distinguishing the therapeutic community proper from other kinds of inpatient treatment programmes. The survey covered 144 psychiatric treatment programmes in which the social climate was measured with the Ward Atmosphere Scale (described in detail in chapter 5). This scale measures three relationship dimensions (involvement, support, spontaneity), four treatment programme dimensions (autonomy, practical orientation, personal problem orientation, anger and aggression), and three system maintenance dimensions (order and organization, programme clarity, staff control). Using cluster analysis, Price and Moos identified six programme types: therapeutic community, relationship oriented, action oriented, insight oriented, control oriented, and disturbed behaviour. The nineteen therapeutic communities identified were distinct in having high scores on relationship and treatment dimensions, but low scores on system maintenance dimensions:

> This programme cluster strikingly resembles the type of milieu therapy described by Jones (1952) as the 'therapeutic community' in that high patient involvement and a strong therapeutic orientation are emphasized, but little explicit staff control is exercised. (p. 184)

Figure 2.1 gives the scale profiles for the six programme types.

The second elaboration of therapeutic community types involves the identification of different therapeutic ideologies and corresponding clientele within the general range of programmes which identify themselves as therapeutic communities. In contrast to the Price and Moos survey, the source for these types is eclectic. First, there are several associations of therapeutic communities such as the World

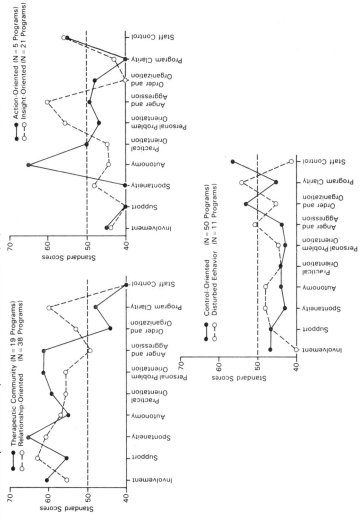

Figure 2.1 Ward atmosphere scale profiles for six different psychiatric treatment programmes

Federation of Therapeutic Communities, the Association of Therapeutic Communities, and the Planned Environment Therapy Trust. Second, is the specialist literature, such as the *International Journal of Therapeutic Communities, Hospital and Community Psychiatry*, various addiction journals, and book-length reviews (Rossi and Filstead, 1973; Hinshelwood and Manning, 1979; Almond, 1974; Gunderson *et al.*, 1983; Kennard, 1983). Most of the therapeutic communities covered are of the 'proper' variety.

The two dimensions of therapeutic ideology and client type furnish the two basic assumptions underlying most therapeutic communities. While some choose clients to match their therapeutic approach, others are committed to working with particular types of client and adopt the therapeutic method felt to work best. Often there is a combination of both. Of the range of therapeutic ideologies we can identify three broad streams, together with a miscellaneous category which, in various ways, draws upon the first three.

## The democratic therapeutic community

The first, originating in the psychiatric field, is the democratic-style psychiatric therapeutic community typically based around the Maxwell Jones model. Described in more detail in chapter 4, this kind of community is characterized by Jones (1968) as

> the way in which the institution's total resources, staff, patients, and their relatives, are self-consciously pooled in further treatment. This implies, above all, a change in the usual status of patients . . . they now become active participants in their own therapy and that of other patients. (pp. 85–6)

> The emphasis on free communication both within and between staff and patient groups and on permissive attitudes which encourage free expression of feeling implies a democratic, egalitarian rather than traditional hierarchical social organisation. (p. 86)

> An essential feature of the organisation of a therapeutic community is the daily community meeting. By a community meeting, we mean a meeting of the entire patient and staff population of a particular unit or section. We have found it practicable to hold meetings of this kind with as many as 80 patients and 30 staff; we think that the upper limit for the establishment of a therapeutic community in the sense that the term is used here is around 100 patients.

However, within this larger community there may be a number of small groups, usually of less than 10 patients which are involved in group therapy in the more conventional sense. (pp. 87-8)

The principle of expanding the role of the patient to include that of therapist is, I think, a fundamental one in community treatment procedure. What one wishes to do is to give patients that degree of responsibility which is compatible with their capacity at any one time. In no sense do the staff of the doctor in charge relinquish their ultimate authority, which thereby remains latent. . . (p. 100)

particular crises in the community offer opportunities for intensified learning, or what we call living-learning experiences. These involve the face-to-face confrontation of all the people concerned and the joint analysis of the current interpersonal difficulty. To a great extent this exchange revolves around the conscious thoughts and feelings of participants, but it may occasionally lead to an increased awareness of formerly unconscious factors. Frequent exposure to situations of this kind, if handled skilfully, can contribute to personality growth and maturity. (p. 106)

Although the Maxwell Jones model has become widely regarded as the most dominant of its types (see especially the discussion below, pp. 36-8, the tradition associated with Tom Main discussed in chapter 1 does have a distinct approach to therapeutic ideology and type of client in the use it makes of a more psychoanalytic, and less socially oriented programme. While this is insufficient to constitute a separate therapeutic community stream, since in practice the two traditions are often merged, several writers have drawn attention to this difference. For example, Crockett's term introduced earlier, the psychotherapeutic community, emphasizes the processes of psychotherapy as opposed to social learning used in more analytically inclined communities. Whiteley et al. (1972), draw a similar distinction between the Jones and Main traditions, suggesting that in the former the emphasis is on the sociodynamic exploration of patients' social actions through confrontation, while in the latter the emphasis is on the psychodynamic exploration of patients' feelings through interpretation (pp. 36-7). In a more systematic theoretical work Edelson (1970), argues that both of these emphases are important, but distinct, aspects of therapeutic community work, rather than competing methods. Defining psychotherapy as focused on the internal state of the individual, and sociotherapy as focused on the social situation of the individual, Edelson suggests that both enterprises can give rise to conflicts over interpretations of events and priorities for work, but that their careful interrelation 'in phase' (p. 23) can produce optimal results. In practice, as will be argued later, the integration of these views typically occurs in the use of group psychotherapy to bridge the individual-social, or interpretation-action distinction.

## The concept therapeutic community

The second therapeutic ideology originated in a non-professional self-help initiative generally described as a 'concept' or 'programmatic' community. These terms follow from the emulation of the original 'concept' devised in the USA by an ex-alcoholic, Chuck Dederich, who set up a group for helping addicts in his own flat in 1958, but specifically eschewed the notion of treatment, along the lines of Alcoholics Anonymous. This initiative quickly developed into a community, Synanon, with a very explicit 'programme', revolving round a highly confrontative encounter group called the 'game' or the 'stew', in which participants were exposed to the vitriolic denunciation of their personal and social defects. The game was the central element in a rigidly hierarchical structure which newcomers had to slowly ascend, suffering occasional rapid demotions at the slightest transgression of the community's rules. Synanon communities sprang up rapidly, so that ten years later there were 1200 resident members owning millions of dollars' worth of property (Kanter, 1972: 194–5). While Synanon itself remained highly insular, similar communities such as Daytop Village (Sugarman, 1974) and Phoenix House (De Leon et al., 1973), with a softer version of the Synanon concept, have also developed. By 1976, Therapeutic Communities of America was formed, with over 100 communities, and in 1980, the World Federation of Therapeutic Communities was set up to manage increasingly frequent 'world conferences' representing, De Leon (1985) estimates, over 500 programmes, mainly in the USA and Europe.

The early years of Synanon exhibited a highly zealous commitment denounced by some outsiders as little short of brainwashing. It took on all the characteristics of a religious cult, with Dederich as the messianic saviour. Public concern matched the obsessive exclusivity of the Synanon organization (Kanter, 1972: 211–12). In more recent years, with the growth of other concept communities, and federation into a national and international structure, there has been a somewhat surprising move to integrate their ideas with democratic communities; surprising because their fundamental motivation and style were so resolutely opposed to professional psychiatry, and democratic group therapy.

The integration of concept and democratic communities has been proposed on the basis of both a *de facto* merger of types of staff and clients, and the realization of many points of theoretical overlap between the two. For example, Kennard (1983) observes that British concept communities have come to accept the presence of professionally qualified staff, where earlier communities had almost exclusively recruited staff from their own ex-addict graduates. More significantly, Therapeutic Communities of America has established criteria and procedures for evaluating counsellors and certifying their competence, and De Leon (1985) reports that

> most larger and older programs incorporate the hardware and software of modern corporate organisations to facilitate operations, and they seek continued management education training. Some have developed program-based research and evaluation capability; others are participants in scientific efforts. Old issues of anti-intellectual bias have receded, as is evident in the steady recruitment of workers from all specialities to provide ancillary services to strengthen administrative operations. (p. 841)

This statement from the Director of Research at the Phoenix House Foundation, New York, now one of the leading American concept communities, is a startling contrast to the earlier combative, self-help style of Synanon, from which Phoenix has distanced itself.

Five proposals for integrating concept and democratic communities have recently appeared. Two are by Maxwell Jones, doyen of the democratic tradition, published in American addiction journals normally the province of the concept tradition. Three are from authors in the concept tradition, including Sugarman, who earlier published a notable analysis of Daytop Village in 1974, and De Leon from Phoenix Foundation — all papers published in the *International Journal of Therapeutic Communities*, normally the province of the democratic tradition. This cross-over of intellectual territory is itself significant, while the arguments of these authors are surprisingly accommodating, given the separate and at times rival development of the two traditions. The arguments are of three types. First is the identification of common elements. Jones (1979), Rubel *et al.* (1982) and De Leon (1983) suggest that, as a minimum, both types of therapeutic community are in principle democratic: members live in a residential community in which they have the right to contribute to discussions and decisions with other members as peers, but only in so far as they commit themselves to full participation in the life of the community and therefore take their share of responsibility both for themselves and for the community. In consequence both community types tend to minimize traditional client-professional relationships, and not surprisingly have shared a rather marginal place in terms of mainstream professional services.

A second argument, to be found in De Leon (1983) and Jones (1984) is that concept communities are, by virtue of widening their client types and accepting some professional expertise (such as group therapy), moving closer to the democratic tradition.

The third argument is more sophisticated. It acknowledges that while some integration may develop, there remain nevertheless great differences of emphasis between the two types, typically expressed as the use of behaviour modification on the one hand, and insight-oriented psychotherapy on the other. However, integration here is achieved through the notion of treatment as a developmental or maturational cycle which begins with the need for crude behaviour change in a relatively closed world (the special achievement of concept houses in eliminating drug use), and ends with insight-based personal change which can be sustained after leaving the community. Sugarman (1984) develops this model by reviewing eighteen components of therapeutic community structure, and suggesting that where these two community types vary sharply (for example in the strictness of controlling behaviour, or the extent of democratic decision-making) they can be seen as specializing at different ends of the developmental cycle. In short he is suggesting that in reality concept houses are mainly autocratic only for the neophyte, who gains increasing access to power and decision-making as he is promoted up the hierarchy; whereas the democratic communities are only really democratic for the longer-stay resident who has learned to participate fully in the community life but who in the early days would also have been subject to intense pressure to conform.

## The educational therapeutic community

The third general stream of therapeutic community ideology has an older tradition from the field of education, and a different client group — children and adolescents. This is in general a wide field (comprehensively documented by Bridgeland, 1971) embracing penal reformatories, mental handicap institutions, progressive education, public schools, and in more recent times the general field of maladjusted children and special education. Within this rather loose collection of concerns, however, there is a line of development which leads from Homer Lane to David Wills and the Planned Environment Therapy Trust. Lane's early working life was in various schools for deprived children in the USA, ending up in charge of the Ford Republic, modelled, like earlier boys' republics, on the American constitution. In 1913 he came to England to advise on the foundation of a similar republic, the Little Commonwealth, and stayed on to become the first superintendent. Lane claims to have drawn his ideas from Dewey, Montessori and Pestalozzi, although because he wrote little it is difficult to identify precisely what his principles were. Indeed Bridgeland (1971) observes that 'in his recorded conversations [Lane] frequently found it irrelevant to tell the literal rather than the literary truth' (p. 96). However, contemporary observers (particularly Bazeley, 1928) record his commitment to the therapeutic effect of unconditional love, crafts and manual labour, and self-respect through self-government. These principles were expressed through two central structural elements in the Little Commonwealth: the Economic Scheme and the Citizen's Court. The former required that each member pay his own way through wages earned in work within the community. If someone did insufficient work to pay, other members had to pay instead, thereby creating intense pressure to co-operate. This pressure was expressed formally through the Court which included all members over the age of fourteen. Although it heard complaints, and discussed policy and where necessary punishments, Bridgeland (1971) notes that it was 'One of the main agencies of therapy in the community through which self-analysis through group criticism of one another would become automatic' (p. 108).

These are familiar ideas to modern therapeutic community practitioners and, given Lane's widely acknowledged influence over subsequent pioneers such as A.S. Neil, Lane can perhaps be acknowledged as their actual originator, despite their apparent reinvention by both Maxwell Jones and Chuck Dederich. Nevertheless the ideas remained within the education field and came to be most vigorously expressed by David Wills. Wills, like many earlier leaders in this tradition, was associated with several different educational communities until his retirement in 1968. Unlike Lane, he wrote numerous books about his experiences. Nevertheless, the most systematic expression of his principles has been through the Planned

Environment Therapy Trust (PETT), set up in 1966 by Franklin, a key founder of Wills's first community, the Hawkspur camp.

In the first volume of *Studies in Environmental Therapy*, published by PETT in 1968, Wills writes:

> Planned Environment Therapy, as I see it, is a form of treatment, preferably residential, aimed at helping people who have hitherto, for whatever reason, found themselves unable to adjust happily in society. It seeks to provide experience of loving social relationships in an egalitarian setting, through all sharing in the responsibility for the administration of day-to-day affairs. (p. 107).

In the same volume (pp. 99–100) Marjorie Franklin echoes this definition, emphasizing Planned Environmental Therapy's work on the here-and-now, the continuous influence of the environment, and the focus on the current reality of social relationships encouraged through children taking shared responsibility for their community experience. Subsequent volumes in this series in 1973 and 1979, however, offer little further in the way of specific definitions either of theory or structure, although it is apparent from much writing in this field that psychoanalytic ideas are heavily drawn upon.

While happy to use the prestige of the early pioneers, especially Homer Lane, to lend legitimacy to their current work, proponents of Planned Environment Therapy have been sensitive to the fact that their ideas have been poorly articulated, and in consequence feel overshadowed by more successful intellectual entrepreneurs such as Maxwell Jones. For example, Bridgeland, author of the basic guide to this educational field (1971), has recently complained (1985: 179) that the publisher's blurb on Maxwell Jones's latest book (1982) is 'unnecessarily effusive' in its presentation of Jones's work as of relevance to schools and other institutions, since Jones has virtually ignored his educational precursors.

Nevertheless, PETT has reluctantly come to acknowledge the intellectual vigour of writing stemming from the democratic therapeutic community tradition, in a manner reminiscent of the intellectual crossover observed above between the concept and democratic streams. For example, volume three (1979) of the *Studies in Environmental Therapy* was devoted to an integration of PETT and democratic therapeutic community ideas. In the introductory paper, Righton is critical of the Franklin/Wills model as 'short on theory sufficiently extensive and rigorous to yield convincing explanation and accurate prediction of outcome' (p. 12). In particular, he points out that insufficient attention has been paid to 'external social systems and forces to which they relate, and which to a significant extent control and limit what they can effectively achieve' (p. 13).

Moreover, Righton points out that although PETT celebrates the environmental view of disorder and treatment, it has

> assumed that personality is the dominant variable, and taken too readily on trust that apparent favourable changes in a resident's personality brought about during the course of a therapeutic regime will last him for the rest of his life . . . . Recent research, however, gives little support to this view, and in a particularly interesting study Mischel (1968) has shown that a detailed knowledge of a person's current socioeconomic environment provides a substantially more reliable basis for predicting his behaviour than a detailed description of his 'personality traits' derived from his past history. (p. 14–15)

These are criticisms to which we return in the next chapter.

This crossover of democratic community ideas into PETT has been matched by the recent inclusion of a special issue on therapeutic educational establishments for children and adolescents in the *International Journal of Therapeutic Communities* (1985), normally the home of the democratic tradition, edited by Bridgeland and Rose. In the editorial, Bridgeland points out that

> Maxwell Jones's work might be viewed as the culmination of the work undertaken in therapeutic environments for disturbed and disordered children and adolescents within the context of education and child care during the previous century. Not only would pioneers such as Homer Lane, Russel Hoare, A.S. Neill, David Wills, J. Edward-Seel, Otto Shaw and others responsible for pre-war therapeutic educational communities, have been quite happy with the goal attributed above to Maxwell Jones, but many of them also pioneered those principles and structures more specifically associated with psychodynamic therapeutic communities. (p. 179)

Thus, while there has yet to be an attempt at full theoretical integration of PETT and democratic community ideas, there is clearly an agreed common overlap.

The fourth group of therapeutic communities is miscellaneous, in which most communities appear to be drawing on elements from one of the above three streams. The Maxwell Jones model has been influential in a range of therapeutic settings. Not surprisingly his ideas have been used more or less directly in a number of day hospitals, day centres and psychiatric wards (including acute admissions units) (Kennard, chapter 4). There have also been limited applications in prisons (Briggs, 1972; Gunn, 1978). The half-way house movement providing hostels for ex-psychiatric patients has also found the Jones model useful, particularly the extensive network of hostels run by the Richmond Fellowship, discussed in detail in chapter 5.

The therapeutic education tradition also encompasses a number of communities for the mentally handicapped, the best known being the Camphill communities based on the ideas of Rudolph Steiner. Steiner's ideas embraced a range of philosophical and religious notions which stressed the spirit as trapped in a disturbed or handicapped body. Sharing a certain imprecision already noted in other PETT ideas, Steiner nevertheless stressed 'fraternity in the economic life of the community, equality in the need for mutual cooperation between community members, and liberty in the need for individual privacy within the community' (Bloor *et al.*, 1988: 27). Bloor records that the Camphill movement now covers seventeen countries and approximately 8,000 community residents. A similar movement, L'Arche, established initially by Jean Vanier in 1964, now has sixty communities spread across fourteen countries.

A final group of therapeutic communities is loosely structured on anti-psychiatry ideas elaborated by R.D. Laing and David Cooper in the 1960s. These are typically anti-medical and based on a naturalistic household arrangement in which residents are helped to regress and regrow their inner selves. There are few contemporary examples of these communities working, although the Philadelphia Association and Arbours Association (Berke, 1982) are well known in London, as is Soteria House in the USA (Gunderson *et al.*, 1983).

The third way in which we can try to bring greater precision to the definition of therapeutic communities is to examine variations in their social organization. Some of the possible dimensions of relevance have already been examined. The Price and Moos (1975) survey showed how the quality of social relationships in therapeutic communities differed from other settings. The discussion of democratic, concept, and educational communities also suggested variations in the level and kind of professional training of the staff, variations in the size and physical setting of communities, and variations in the extent and manner of patient/resident participation.

There are few systematic comparative studies of therapeutic communities in the literature, as opposed to the many descriptive single-case studies to be found. Nevertheless, we can draw on those that are available to examine some variations. First we can look at the extent to which therapeutic communities approximate some unitary ideal. The current author and others (Crockett *et al.*, 1978) conducted a small survey of thirty-six British communities in 1977 to look at the extent to which such communities felt themselves to be like the 'therapeutic community as generally understood by psychiatrists and other helping professions' (p. 13), and the extent of the weekly programme devoted to groups of various types. Of the twenty communities which replied, it was found that the use of community meetings (most residents and staff present) and smaller groups on at least a daily basis was universal. However, beyond that minimum there was a fairly even spread from 3 hours to 20 hours a week in community meetings, and from 6 hours to 30 hours a week in smaller groups. It was hypothesized that this variation in the use of groups, often seen as the *sine qua non* of the therapeutic community, would be closely related to the extent to which communities identified themselves as like the ideal therapeutic community. This was measured using a visual analogue (VA) scale varying between '*like* the therapeutic community as generally understood' and '*not at all like* . . . .' The range of response was fairly well spread, with three quarters of the sample in the ideal half of the scale. Ranking the samples on each of these dimensions, gives the correlations (Spearman's R) set out in table 2.2.

*Table 2.2* Rank order correlations between the use of groups and the ideal therapeutic community

| | | |
|---|---|---|
| VA scale x time in community groups | | R = 0.45 |
| VA scale x time in smaller groups | | R = 0.51 |
| VA scale x total number of groups | | R = 0.61 |
| VA scale x total time in groups | | R = 0.64 |

It appears from these data that there is both a range of time devoted to groups in therapeutic communities, and that the amount of time devoted to groups is related to the closeness of the community to the ideal therapeutic community. The gap between ideals and the daily practice of therapeutic communities may arise for a number of reasons.

43

Three studies are suggestive here. First, Bell and Ryan (1985) compare the treatment environment of three therapeutic communities, using a version of the Moos Ward Atmosphere scale, introduced earlier and in chapter 5. They use it to measure both the ideal environment (the ideal form), and the existing environment (the real form). In two of the communities, there is a noted discrepancy between the ideal and real results, although all three more or less agree on the ideal form, as shown in figure 2.2. Bell and Ryan conclude that the ideal-real gap has opened up because two of the communities are simultaneously pursuing other treatment aims: one psychoanalytic psychotherapy; the other an activities-based programme and some biologically-based treatments. Consequently the leaders of these two communities have other research and didactic interests, devolve therapeutic community 'work' onto lower status non-medical staff, and are less tolerant of patients' misdemeanours. In the third community, pursuing rehabilitation aims, no such conflicts were apparent.

In a second study, Wilmer (1981), identifies two aberrant types of therapeutic community in which practice varies from the ideal, which he terms respectively communities of the 'left' and the 'right'. Using case studies from the literature, he suggests that communities of the left 'manifest extremes of permissiveness, patient government voting, and attitudes that often result in chaos, even anarchy, on the wards' (p. 97). Moreover, such communities, he suggests, become immune to criticism or to inconvenient facts, difficulties or contradictions. Communites of the right on the other hand

staunchly abide by a theoretic concept of treatment enshrined in a single ruling theory [which] dominates the community by elaborate rituals; alternative methods or hypotheses are seen as intrusive, are bitterly resented as contamination and always are interpreted in light of the ruling theory. (p. 97)

Communities of the centre, however, are flexible, responsive and balanced, Wilmer suggests. We shall see elements of both his aberrant types clearly illustrated later in this chapter when discussing the collapse of the Paddington Day Hospital (p. 63).

A third study was conducted by the author to examine the relative problems of young and old therapeutic communities in implementing their ideals in practice (Manning & Blake, 1979). Comparing just two communities, it was observed that the young community faces the

*Figure 2.2* Ideal and real ward atmosphere scale profiles for three therapeutic communities

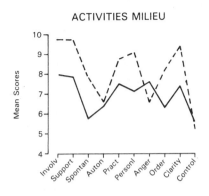

ACTIVITIES MILIEU

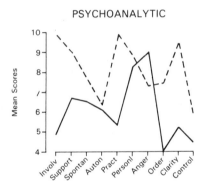

PSYCHOANALYTIC

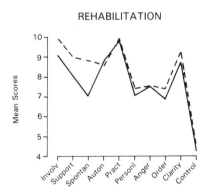

REHABILITATION

difficulty of setting up and sustaining a therapeutic community culture, unfamiliar to new staff, patients, administrators, and referers, and containing a number of internal contradictions and difficulties which can be routinely handled in more mature communities. On the other hand, the older community suffers from the dangers of structural atrophy in which it is difficult to sustain initiative and zeal in the face of, for example, staff concerns over long-term career prospects. A number of models which throw light on such difficulties were elaborated, and these are discussed in more detail in chapter 4.

A final comparative study of eight communities (Bloor *et al.*, 1988), focuses explicitly on the nature of the work done in therapeutic communities: 'We have treated medical work in therapeutic communities as redefinitional work, the transformation of mundane events in the light of some paradigm of therapy' (p. 192). At the end of their study, Bloor *et al.* seek to identify the

> Common properties of therapeutic work. These common properties do not have fixed values: they are not some lowest common denominator of diverse practices, or a residuum of similarity surrounded by a mass of diversity. Rather they are (with one exception) common dimensions of variability, universally present while differentially extensible. The different extensibility of these common properties allow us to map different approaches to therapeutic work in different settings. (p. 193)

The common properties identified surround a single core notion: reflexivity. This refers to the observation that therapeutic community work is basically the construction and reconstruction of social reality for and with the residents — therapeutic utterances actually constitute the reality that they describe. While this *is* a common attribute in that all therapeutic communities exhibit it, Bloor *et al.* then outline five further properties of this core therapeutic activity which do vary between communities: the breadth and depth of *interpretations*; the confrontation or reconstruction of behaviour through specific *intervention*; the extent of *dominance* through power or authority; the *selection* of different aspects of daily life for therapeutic attention; and finally the extent to which *habituated* or standard therapeutic manoeuvres develop. These are not explicitly knitted together into particular types in the Bloor study, although it is not difficult to see how they would vary in the context of the three therapeutic community streams identified earlier. Concept houses are extensively dominant and confrontative, for example, while democratic communities use interpretation both widely and in depth, and educational communities (often with the greatest length of stay) aim for long-term behavioural reconstruction amongst other things.

This lengthy discussion of the definition of therapeutic communities has been undertaken for the obvious reason that we must be as clear as possible about the phenomenon under study. However it is also clear that some confusion about the nature of the therapeutic community exists amongst both proponents and critics of the idea. We can conclude from the review that, first, therapeutic communities are distinct from other therapeutic practice in terms of theoretical aims, organizational structure and process, and self identity. Second, there are three broad originating streams of therapeutic community work which are beginning to converge towards one general type, most clearly represented by the democratic community. Third, that there is nevertheless, and not surprisingly, variation around this common core in terms of therapeutic ideology, client type, and the purity with which therapeutic community principles are put into practice.

## THE THERAPEUTIC COMMUNITY MOVEMENT

In the previous chapter we gave an outline of the development of the therapeutic community movement in Britain and the USA up until the late 1950s. Earlier in this chapter, in discussing democratic, concept, and educational communities, some indication of the size, spread and federal organization of communities was given. In this section a more detailed analysis of this growth will be presented. The most detailed discussion will centre on the democratic stream, for reasons of space, information availability, and, as has already been argued, the predominant influence of this stream in terms of conceptual development and, to the extent that it is occurring, conceptual integration.

By the early 1960s there was a pervasive sense in the psychiatric literature that the democratic therapeutic community fad was on the wane. This was caused by two interconnecting sets of factors, one relating to internal developments within therapeutic communities, and the other relating to the context within which therapeutic communities operated.

Internally, therapeutic communities had failed to bring about some of their more inflated claims to be founding a new social psychiatry. Main (1946) had argued for a complete reconstruction of the internal

47

relations of the psychiatric hospital. Yet most therapeutic communities had developed as specialist units, or wards, within hospitals. Jones's Belmont unit became a hospital (Henderson) in its own right. While celebrated and much visited for its specialist work, most mental health workers came to see it as a referral resource, rather than a model for reconstructing their own hospitals (see chapter 4 for evidence of this).

While such units had in earlier years justified their work on an innovative and experimental basis, little conventional research had been published to justify the efficacy of this new method. Indeed it became apparent that conventional research methods, such as the controlled trial, were difficult to apply to such a method (see chapter 5 for a detailed discussion of this point).

Externally, the psychiatric professions were also becoming less receptive to this kind of innovation. While the therapeutic community was essentially an attempt to transform the old asylum into a genuinely therapeutic agency, using a new socially informed theory, and a new technology based on the social environment of group life, mainstream psychiatry began to move in quite a different direction. A key development was the invention of the psychoactive drugs in the late 1950s. Whether or not these are now considered to be thoroughly efficacious, they enabled psychiatrists to deploy both symbolically and technically the kind of scientific treatment that general physicians had already successfully used to establish widespread public credibility. In addition, the asylum became displaced as the centre of psychiatric practice; as with medicine in general, psychiatric practice began to move out into the community through general practice, out-patient departments, ordinary general hospitals, social work and psychological counselling and, more recently, into mental health centres (Miller and Rose, 1986).

This process of psychiatric displacement not only left the therapeutic community seemingly reconstructing yesterday's asylums, but it also reinstated much of the professional authority which the therapeutic community had aimed to redistribute to the community and the group (hence the title of Rapoport's (1960) study of the Henderson, *Community as Doctor*).

Yet the therapeutic community did not disappear. A review of the evidence about therapeutic community activities since 1960 will suggest why the therapeutic community survived. This evidence is of two types. First is the visibility of the therapeutic community concept in terms of the specialist literature. Second is the extent of therapeutic community activities, both in terms of the number of communities, and the extent of their collective organization.

An initial measure of therapeutic community interest can be gained through the frequency of articles cited in *Index Medicus*, and the *Social Science Citations Index*. Both journals have established therapeutic community sections, but usefully neither includes the *International Journal of Therapeutic Communities* (established in 1980), so that they indicate the frequency of articles produced other than in this specialist journal. The annual number of citations is given in figure 2.3. During the early 1970s *Index Medicus* recorded an annual production of between twenty and thirty articles per year, and since 1976, both journals have recorded an annual production of around twenty articles per year, averaging 19.3 for the SSCI and 27.6 for *Index Medicus*. *Index Medicus* also recorded on average an additional 6.9 articles per year in foreign language journals.

A further indication of continued interest in therapeutic communities is given by the steady publication of books explicitly centred on the area. Since 1970, twenty-one major books have been published, evenly spread across the years (Edelson, 1970; Schoenberg, 1972; Whiteley *et al.*, 1972; Rossi and Filstead, 1973; Almond, 1974; Clark, 1974; Foudraine, 1974; Sugarman, 1974; Kreeger, 1975; Jones, 1976; Hinshelwood and Manning, 1979; Whiteley and Gordon, 1979; Jansen, 1980; Toch, 1980; Jones, 1982; Kennard, 1983; De Leon and Zeigenfuss, 1986; Shenker, 1986; Baron, 1987; Hinshelwood, 1987; Bloor *et al.*, 1988). In addition Routledge & Kegan Paul have, since 1980, established a book series focusing explicitly on therapeutic communities.

Some survey evidence about the interest of psychiatric professionals in therapeutic communities would also be useful. This is lacking for Britain, but such a recent survey has been undertaken in Australia. Clark and Walker (1984) surveyed fifty-two state and regional psychiatric directors, and psychiatric superintendents of hospitals to ascertain the extent to which the respondents considered the democratic therapeutic community concept important for both service delivery and treatment, which kind of professionals favoured it, whether the concept was gaining or losing ground, and the number of units fully or partly using the concept. Over 80 per cent of respondents considered that the concept was of some influence on both service delivery and treatment, 50 per cent felt it was of considerable importance to service delivery, and 25 per cent felt it influenced treatment approach to a great extent. The majority of respondents felt that while staff and patients mostly perceived the concept positively, policy-makers did not. Consequently there were mixed views as to whether the concept was gaining or losing ground, two thirds suggesting that it was

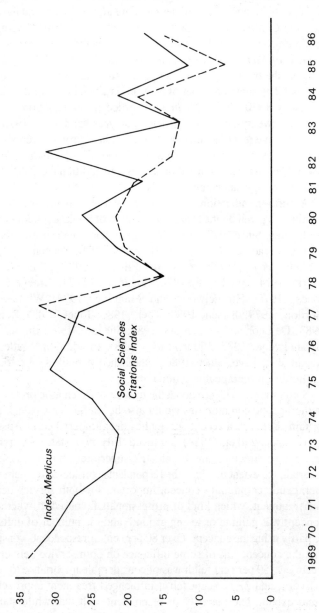

*Figure 2.3* English language therapeutic community articles cited in *Index Medicus* and *Social Science Citations Index*. 1969–86

*Figure 2.4* The growth in the number of therapeutic community units in Australia, 1963–82

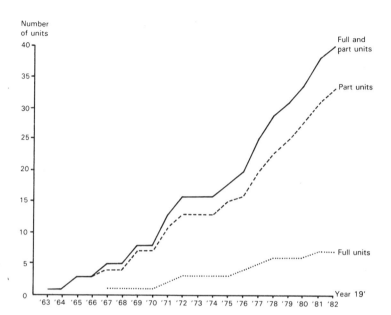

unchanged or gaining ground, and one third suggesting that it was losing ground. Nevertheless, the evidence as to the number of units partly or fully using the concept, reproduced in figure 2.4, clearly indicates steady expansion since the 1960s.

The second kind of evidence about the continued existence of the therapeutic community concept is in terms of the extent of its practice. We have already noted (figure 2.4) the steady growth of democratic therapeutic community units in Australia. In Britain, the best evidence is the size of the individual and group membership of the Association of Therapeutic Communities (ATC), formed in 1972, given in figure 2.5. In the early years of the Association, membership grew rapidly, with a substantial turnover from year to year. Since the late 1970s, membership and turnover has stabilized. Individual members are those most active in the field, while group membership represents the interests of therapeutic community staff, often at more junior levels. The Association published a *Directory of British Therapeutic Communities* in 1986, which contained ninety-three entries, with a total of 2,000 places. Assuming a typical staffing ratio of 1:3, this indicates a national staffing level of around 700, spread across hospitals, hostels and schools.

51

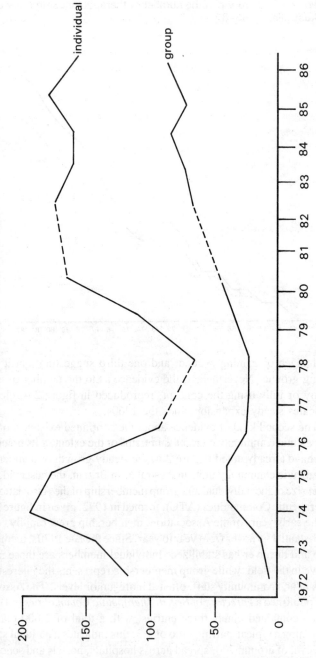

*Figure 2.5* Individual and group membership, Association of Therapeutic Communities, 1972–86

*Source:* AGM minutes, ATC Bulletin and Newsletters, 1972–87

Overlapping the ATC membership in Britain, but not overseas, we have already noted earlier in this chapter that the Camphill movement covers seventeen countries, with approximately 8,000 residents, L'Arche covers fourteen countries with sixty communities, and the World Federation of Therapeutic Communities includes over 500 concept programmes in the USA and Europe. In addition, the Richmond Fellowship reported in 1984 that it ran seventy-two therapeutic communities spread across the USA, Europe and Australasia.

In addition to the sheer volume of therapeutic community practice, there is evidence about the extent of its corporate organization. Each of the three streams of therapeutic community work it was noted has organized a corporate association to represent its interests, exchange and develop ideas, and to develop the therapeutic skills of its practitioners. The British Association of Therapeutic Communities has been most active in each of these respects. The ATC arose out of

> a meeting at the Henderson in July 1969. That meeting was called because we at Henderson were in some difficulty and wanted to discuss different methods of working, other ideas about the therapeutic community and what direction we should take, etc. We simply invited people known to us as having formulated ideas about the therapeutic community and hoped for a purely task oriented meeting. It has subsequently become clear that despite something of a move back towards physical methods of treatment there is still a great deal of interest in therapeutic community work. (Whiteley, 1972: 5)

This extract is from a document circulated as a call for the formation of the ATC in April/May 1972. In July of that year the ATC was formed with Whiteley, consultant psychiatrist at the Henderson, as secretary (a post he held until 1978). The aim of the ATC, adopted directly from Whiteley's contribution to the April/May document, had

> the prime task of furthering therapeutic community work by the exchange of ideas in meetings, large and small, in publications, for the promotion of research into the method and the installation of a training programme into therapeutic community technqiues. (*ATC Newsletter*, no. 10, August 1973)

In the early years of the ATC there developed some heated exchanges between members who favoured an activist, political approach to pushing therapeutic community ideas within, for example, the National Health Service, and those members who conceived of the ATC as a more conventional professional association (see for example *ATC Newsletter*, no. 7, February 1973). However, the ATC has in general taken the latter course, becoming a registered charity in 1982, and on the whole has pursued the aims originally outlined by Whiteley. To this end the association has developed a fairly elaborate structure, centred around a national conference held three times a year, and at one of these conferences an AGM in which members exercise their basic decision-making powers. In between conferences, various elected officers such as chair, secretary, treasurer, conference organizer, membership secretary, journal and news letter editors meet regularly in a steering committee to carry out ATC work. In addition, various sub-groups, with elected convenors, meet to discuss and organize training, research and supervision.

Apart from conferences and sub-groups, the substantial work of the ATC has developed in four areas. First has been the proselytizing of therapeutic community ideas in relevant government and professional arenas. This has also included the vigorous defence of therapeutic communities under threat of closure. Second has been the publishing of a newsletter, bulletin and, in 1980, a formal academic journal, the *International Journal of Therapeutic Communities*, with Human Sciences Press. Third has been the development of various training courses, in particular a formal Certificate in Therapeutic Community Practice run since 1986 jointly with the Institute of Advanced Nursing Education, at the Royal College of Nursing. Fourth has been the organization of various research projects.

It is clear, then, that neither the idea nor the practice of the therapeutic community have disappeared as seemed possible in the early 1960s. The most likely reasons for this can be found by returning to the factors outlined earlier which seemed to spell their demise. Internally, specialization has been counteracted by the spread of therapeutic communities into new areas such as hostels, drug and alcohol programmes, and residential care generally. Furthermore, while research is still equivocal with respect to outcome evaluations, the continuous publication of specialist articles has produced a body of supportive evidence. The data reported later in chapter 5 also suggest one method for a more complex modelling of therapeutic outcomes. Externally, the psychiatric profession has begun to entertain doubts about the success of organic and particularly drug treatments, and it has become clear that while indeed the population of psychiatric hospitals has contracted, there are still many patients in hospital residence, and increasing numbers in community residential settings.

## THE THERAPEUTIC COMMUNITY TODAY: THEORY, CRITICISMS AND PROBLEMS

Theory typically develops in two ways. Kuhn (1970) suggests that normal science is the process of filling in dominant theoretical paradigms by illuminating specific regions of ignorance, and resolving anomalies thrown up in the practical use of theory. Normal science, however, is occasionally interrupted by periods of revolutionary theoretical upheaval, when old theories become hopelessly overwhelmed by internal contradictions, inability to handle ignorance, or failure in practical application. As will be discussed in greater detail in the final chapter, early therapeutic community practitioners felt that they were the heralds of such a revolution in psychiatry. This now seems ambitious. However, therapeutic community theory has in its own field exhibited many of the features of normal science since the 1940s. That is, there has been an elaboration of theory to deal with a number of theoretical and practical problems.

At the level of the whole community, therapeutic community writers have tried to develop theory which can explain what the community is and how it works. We have already seen, in discussing definitions of the therapeutic community, that there are two general approaches. One examines the therapeutic community as a social system, the other as a psychological system. Each approach has been developed to elucidate and overcome various problems and criticisms associated with therapeutic community work.

There are four social system approaches which have appeared in the literature. The first, reported in Rapoport (1960) and discussed in detail in chapter 4, focuses on the community as a therapeutic culture. Rapoport identified four cultural themes (democracy, permissiveness, communalism, and reality confrontation) which he suggested permeated the Henderson Hospital's work, and acted as a basic guide to therapeutic practice and the nature of community life for both staff and patients. He showed how the complex structure of groups in the Henderson's programme was designed to realize these cultural themes, but also noted that there were problems in that some of the themes had loose or unspecified limits, and came into conflict with each other. Two related studies have also broadly used the kind of cultural or anthropological approach adopted by Rapoport. Almond

(1974) suggests that therapeutic communities are a sub-set of a more general type which he describes as 'healing communities'. Comparing a psychiatric-ward therapeutic community with various non-western healing cults, sects and societies, he suggests that

> the healing community is characterised by the following: (1) an internal sense of specialness attributed both to individuals in their relations to one another (healing charisma) and the group as a whole (communitas); (2) translation of this specialness into charismatic roles and into behaviour norms that reflect the cohesiveness of the community and its espousal of a specific set of beliefs and practices; (3) devotion of much attention to healing activities and derivation of much sense of individual and group effectiveness through the positive results of healing efforts; (4) a varied pattern of relations between healing community and its culture, characterised universally by a boundary between members and non-members. (pp. 319–20)

Shenker (1986), in a parallel study, suggests that therapeutic communities are a sub-set of a more general type which he describes as 'intentional communities'. Comparing therapeutic community hostels of the type analysed in chapter 5 with Hutterite religious communities, and Israeli kibbutzim, he argues that

> intentional communities share certain features with organisations, sects and social movements, yet are none of these. An intentional community is a relatively small group of people who have created a whole way of life for the attainment of a certain set of goals. The two elements of the term are of equal importance. They are *intentional* communities in that they are not . . . developed spontaneously . . . [and] they attempt to create an entire way of life, hence, unlike organisations or social movements, they are intentional *communities*.
>
> Their being communities has two further qualities: they are characterised by face-to-face relations and they embrace communalism as an ethical end in itself. (p. 10)

Both Almond and Shenker are more concerned with elaborating the nature of therapeutic community work, than confronting problems and criticisms (and to this extent offer additions to the literature on definitions considered earlier), yet they nevertheless indicate the crucial and problematic place that boundaries and commitment have in therapeutic community work.

A second approach to therapeutic communities as social systems has been the use of organization theory. Perrow has examined the therapeutic community as a hospital organization, for which he uses a variety of sociotechnical analysis (Silverman, 1970, chapter 5):

> organisations are influenced by three factors: the cultural system which sets legitimate goals; the technology which determines the means available for reaching these goals; and the social structure of the organisation in which specific techniques are embedded. (Perrow 1965: 912)

Perrow is specifically critical of therapeutic communities on the basis of the three factors he highlights in this quote. First, that psychiatric institutions are necessarily required to sustain custodial practices, that bureaucratic and professional structures are very resistant to change, and most pertinently that while a new technology (such as drugs, one might suppose) could be powerful enough to change such custodial goals and existing structures, therapeutic communities quite definitely have not found such a technology:

> The technology was not sufficient to sustain the structure; the structure broke down periodically and did not foster the anticipated relationships. In a sense, an ideology was mistaken for a technology. Social scientists have endorsed and encouraged that ideology, and though they can hardly be said to be responsible for it, they are responsible for the mischief it can do in the field of complex organisations. Without an adequate understanding of the role of technology in organisations — the work done on the material which is to be altered — they will fail to understand goals and structure. (Perrow, 1965: 945)

As we shall argue below, however, therapeutic community practitioners have tried to specify this technology, and increasingly turn to group psychotherapy to do so.

With regard to Perrow's conviction that custodialism is the bottom line legitimation of psychiatric practice, neither therapeutic communities which almost universally take voluntary patients, nor the new mood of community care abroad in the 1980s, support this view. However, it is true that democratizing bureaucratic and professional structures is difficult. Wilson (1979) and Punch (1974) both note that therapeutic communities are attempting, Canute-like, to stem the tide in this respect, in that as Punch puts it there is an inevitable paradox about institutionalizing the 'anti-institution', or making a basic rule that there are no rules, or at least that all rules are negotiable.

This issue is central to a third approach which focuses on the exercise of power and authority in therapeutic communities. A frequent criticism of therapeutic communities is that they are merely pseudo-democracies. Indeed, in an earlier quote (p. 35) we saw that Maxwell Jones acknowledged that ultimate authority was not to be relinquished by the staff. An influential model of the nature of power and involvement in organizations has been developed by Etzioni (1975).

Etzioni is concerned with the question of how members of the organization are persuaded to accept the rules and conditions (including technology) of their work. Etzioni explains the nature of this compliance by separating Weber's concept of authority into two variables of power and involvement (table 2.3). Etzioni suggests members can accept or reject the power position to which they are subjected. Those who reject their position are subject to coercive power; those who accept their position at a price are subject to remunerative power; and those who positively accept their position are subject to normative power. Members of an organization consequently develop a positive or negative emotional commitment giving rise to three related kinds of personal involvement: alienative if their commitment is negative; calculative if their commitment is neutral; and moral if their commitment is positive. Etzioni suggests that hospital patients or doctors are likely to have a positive involvement or moral commitment to their organization. Etzioni also suggests that hospitals are most effective when their members (staff and patients) both accept the power exercised over themselves and in addition have a positive moral involvement. However Etzioni provides no criteria by which effectiveness is to be judged and merely assumes that willing compliance by hospital staff and patients to the system of authority is best — an assumption that has been questioned particularly with regard to psychiatric hospitals.

Almond (1983) has extended this model slightly to suggest that in 'pure' therapeutic communities normative power is exercised by a horizontal or community influence of peers, and that moral involvement is a positive commitment to the common set of beliefs and behaviour of those peers.

Table 2.3 Typical compliance relations in organizations

| | | Kinds of involvement | | |
|---|---|---|---|---|
| | | Alienative | Calculative | Moral |
| Kinds | Coercive | Prisons | | |
| of power | Remunerative | | Factories | |
| | Normative | | | Hospitals (therapeutic communities) |

Source: Etzioni, 1975, p. 12

The implication here is indeed not that therapeutic communities are pure democracies but that the exercise of authority, and the consequent distribution of power and involvement, is achieved through a negotiated consensus of community members. However, in a study of the management of conflict in two therapeutic communities Grove (1985) suggests that such a notion of negotiated consensus is naïve. Grove attempts to analyse his communities through Strauss's (1978) 'negotiated order theory'.

The analysis of the hospital as a negotiated order was introduced in the previous chapter (pp. 21–3). One of the most important notions this approach develops is of the ways in which lower-level participants within the organization, such as patients, can influence the formal organization through bargaining and negotiation.

However, as noted before, Day and Day (1977) point out that negotiations over daily experience are extrapolated as an explanation for the hospital order in general, under-emphasizing those considerable portions of hospital life which are non-negotiable, non-fluid, and may well not be immediately symbolically meaningful. In other words structural constraints, both political and economic, are absent. Moreover the idea of negotiation as the basis for social order within a hospital suggests that adaptation and adjustment are the key elements. It is thus difficult to conceptualize from this point of view any notion of conflict or resistance to the agreements being negotiated.

These criticisms were borne out in Grove's study in which he found that staff made considerable efforts to manipulate the discussions taking place in community and group meetings in order to divert attention from their exercise of authority, and from splits or disagreements within the staff group. Whereas Grove expected that negotiated order theory should apply to therapeutic communities, which ostensibly proclaim their commitment to democratic and open communication and decision-making, he found in fact that external intolerance of a community, or internal splits between staff, lead rapidly to the suspension of genuine negotiation with and between community members. To the extent that the therapeutic process involves members learning how to take responsibility for themselves and participate in the genuine exercise of power, Grove suggests that 'practitioners should consider which conditions promote real negotiating and which promote manipulation and pseudo-negotiation' (p. 346).

The fourth approach to therapeutic communities as social systems takes a rather different focus than the previous three in that it analyses the therapeutic community as a social movement. The current author, Manning (1976), argued that both sociological and practitioner accounts of the therapeutic community have made the basic assumption that it remains a technical or scientific innovation within psychiatry. While the sociology of science has much to say on this aspect (discussed in detail in the final chapter), it cannot account for the grander aspirations of earlier practitioners, nor the general trajectory that the concept has experienced since the 1940s:

> In addition to innovation and professional advocacy, the therapeutic community called for more fundamental social change. It included hopes for changing the whole institutional structure of the mental health services. It developed values which challenged the supremacy of the psychiatrist and the dependency of the patient. . . . From this point of view, the therapeutic community not only treats mental disorder but does so in a particular way, which incorporates wider social and political values. Staff who work in therapeutic communities tend to share these values and apply them to their own working conditons, which they would like also to be democratic, permissive and communal. Inevitably, considerable blurring ensues between what is considered technically useful for correcting patients' disorders and what is valued in itself as a good way of working. (pp. 274–5)

Manning argues that therapeutic communities, as a social movement, exhibit typical characteristics such as wide ideological slogans, and charismatic leadership. Consequently the fate of therapeutic communities can be analysed in terms of the general sociology of social movements. Two typical processes are firstly what Weber (1948) described as the 'routinization of charisma', whereby, after an early stage of unrest and dissatisfaction with existing social conditions, charismatic leadership mobilizes and popularizes social changes, which is followed by attempts to routinize and institutionalize the changes. However, such routines carry the danger of goal displacement and stagnation as charisma gives way to the process of standardizing the reproduction and implementation of the original innovation. The formation and expansion of the British Association of Therapeutic Communities is cited as evidence of this.

A further influence on the natural history of a social movement is the fact that its

> external development depends crucially on the role of advocacy of a movement amongst the wider society, and whether it is consciously encouraged or repressed by the prevailing power structure. And at a less conscious level the movement's growth will be enhanced to the extent that it can attract general support by resonating with other emergent social groups or values in the wider society. (p. 277)

On these grounds Manning argued that with the move towards organic treatments in psychiatry, and the expected demise of the asylum, the therapeutic community movement in the early 1970s was 'nearing the end of its life'. However, as noted in the previous section, this prediction now seems premature, as will be discussed in more detail in the final chapter.

More recently, similar observations have been made with respect to the American concept-based communities by De Leon (1985):

> The uniqueness and strength of the TC lay in its fundamental elements of self help and community as healer. Its original form and, perhaps, its fate resemble those of its historical prototypes. These quasi-religious groupings spontaneously arose among the disaffiliated as responses to societies which failed to help, and then disappeared, usually through dilution or assimilation. . . . bureaucracy, accountability and professionalisation (and the increased distance from its first generation roots) are factors which could radically change the self-help character of the TC. These institutional attributes, which assure its survival, could pollute its humanistic ecology and devitalise its community dynamic.
>
> Nevertheless, this phase of the TC experiment may yet prove to be the most exciting. Its essential 'curative' elements — community, self-help, individual commitment, role modelling

and social learning — may be transmittable forces mediated more through attitude, conduct, values, and vision of the people involved in the process than through its institutional framework. Thus, the TC can remain immune from the potentially dehumanising influences of technology, professionalisation, management and bureaucracy by utilising the advantages of these in the service of its purpose, the positive transformation of human lives. (p. 841-2)

The second general approach to the therapeutic community has been to analyse it as a psychological system. This kind of analysis has typically been undertaken by practitioners applying psychological and especially psychoanalytic ideas used in their daily practice. A typical approach has been to take the psychodynamics of the individual, and apply them as a mode of explanation to the community as a whole, as if the community were a single personality. Examples of this kind of analysis have been typically prompted by practical concerns in terms of the pathology of the community.

Drawing on his experience at Bethlem hospital, Hobson (1979) has analysed the 'therapeutic community disease' whereby a dedicated and charismatic leader pursuing an ideal becomes idealized by the community:

An idealization involves a splitting between 'illusory good' and 'illusory bad'. The leader and his colleagues collude in an idealisation of himself and of the UNIT (now spelt in very large capital letters), which is often personified. The good UNIT is engaged in a battle with the powers of darkness: the 'badness' outside, which is embodied in the rest of the hospital, the traditional psychiatric hospital, or the world at large. The unit is under attack. (p. 233)

Hobson suggests that this disease, unchecked, moves from this initial stage of 'the coming of the messiah' through 'the enlightenment' to 'the catastrophe' when the unit collapses and disintegrates, sometimes along with the leader. The cure, he suggests, lies in applying, as to an individual patient, careful and appropriate analysis and interpretation. A similar analysis, also couched in terms of the community suffering from the process of splitting, has been suggested by Main (1957) in another aptly titled piece, 'The Ailment'.

A second example of this kind of analysis comes from Crockett (1985) in his discussion of the troubled history and final closure of the Paddington Day Hospital (PDH) therapeutic community during the 1970s. PDH occupied the ground floor of a three storey building, which also housed other psychiatric units, with which it shared some resources and professional and administrative links. Threatened with closure in 1972–3, it successfully fought off administrative attack, and in the process developed a powerful solidarity which slowly metamorphosed into the kind of disease described by Hobson, with an idealized leader and a staff group intolerant of any but the correct interpretive therapeutic work. Eventually, with the backing of the chairman of the whole Paddington centre, a group of patients complained and succeeded in initiating an enquiry which resulted finally in the dismissal of the medical director leading the community, and several years later, in the closure of PDH. Crockett's analysis used a different psychological mechanism from Hobson's:

> By describing what happened as 'acting-out' I hope that I convey to the technical reader the essence of the problem in the Day Hospital and in the Centre. The actual events, hour by hour, day by day, week by week and month by month amounted to no more than elaborations and ramifications of this basic behavioural mechanism, although admittedly carried to quite extraordinary lengths. (p. 112)

A third example which analyses the therapeutic community as a psychological system can be found in a series of papers which explicitly identify the 'community personality' in an analysis of the Marlborough Day Hospital (MDH) therapeutic community, once again during a period which was to lead eventually to the closure of the hospital. In this case the problem to be addressed was the development of a split community in which the community meeting was

> functioning with what might be described as the large group syndrome, i.e. long silences, staring out of the window, no proper exchanges. This was becoming so depleted that it was even mooted that perhaps we should abandon using the large group syndrome since so few of us felt there was any therapeutic value attached to it. . . . Hand in hand with this large group syndrome came the awareness of the proliferation of small specialised groups. These groups appeared to have an autonomy from the main life of the community and seemed to detract from it. The connection between these two aspects, that of the large group syndrome and the

peripheral splintering, was quite remarkable, and in fact leads us to propose a direct correlation between the two. (Hinshelwood and Grunberg, 1979:246)

This situation was analysed as if the community was a single personality in which splits had occurred between good and bad parts, with the good parts being projected into peripheral activities. The solution was an attempt to restructure the community in order to reintegrate these split-off parts.

The development of these kinds of structures, Hinshelwood (1978) argued following Menzies (1960), results from the attempts of the community and its individual members to defend themselves against painful or uncomfortable experiences. The desire for structure is the desire for defence. However, it is one of the characteristics of therapeutic community groups that such structures are deliberately fluid so that defensive processes can be identified as they come to be expressed in structure. Thus, for example, Main (1975) shows how large group experiences commonly involve a sense of depersonalization:

In *large* unstructured groups — with memberships of over 20 or so — projective processes may be widespread and can lead to baffling, even chaotic, situations, which can bring the group's work to a standstill. The members will sit in long uneasy silences with even the most resourceful apparently lacking the capacity for contributing usefully. It seems that many individuals at such moments actually do not have their full thinking-capacities at their own disposal. For various reasons . . . they have denied, split off and projected much of their mental vigour outside themselves. (p. 60)

Following this connection between groups and thinking, a third paper in this series on the MDH shows how the resolution of the large group syndrome, achieved through reintegrating the split-off parts, seemed to be evidence of the community personality thinking for itself. Whereas initially the staff reserved to themselves the key activities of interpretation, planning and so forth, these were gradually given to and dispersed amongst the community as a whole, not as a conscious decision by the staff, but through the gradual evolution of a new structure over a period of three years which integrated the patients into these activities. In fact, Grunberg (1979) here suggests an analogy with Kleinian theory:

> To have thoughts and then to think originates in the experience of feeding. The development of thought has a great deal to do with the development of the mother and baby relationship . . . with the satisfaction of mothering (i.e. containment and maturation), the baby learns to wait (if there is a sufficient toleration of frustration) and to take on the capacity to contain and understand his anxieties himself, and this process involves introjection (Bion, 1962). So the two significant processes which have to occur before the infant can begin to think are: (1) the satisfactory development of the mother and baby relationship through the process of projective identification; and (2) the introjection of this mechanism. (p. 258)

Grunberg suggests that an analogous development explains the growth of the community's capacity as a whole to think for itself over the three year period.

These theoretical elaborations of the therapeutic community as a whole have been matched by a great deal of work on activities and processes within the community such as the nature and function of large groups, the effectiveness of group psychotherapy, the nature of leadership and the perennial question of the emancipatory or social control effects of therapeutic intervention in the lives of patients. While some of these issues will be taken up in the final chapter, much of this work is not unique to therapeutic communities, and will not be considered in detail here.

Rather the question to be addressed at this point is whether the problems thrown up in therapeutic community work since the 1940s, and the kind of theoretical elaborations and practice innovations which have occurred to deal with them, have lead the therapeutic community to develop in any particular direction, and the likely consequences of this. The social and psychological models discussed raise between them a number of common problems, and suggest a number of related solutions.

The common problems are, first, how to set up and sustain a structure which both demarcates the community from the outside world and orders the internal life of the community so that therapeutic work can take place; and, second, how to orchestrate commitment to this structure, both externally so that the community has the legitimacy to gain resources (referrals, staff, finance) and internally so that staff and patients actively engage in therapeutic work. Main and Jones, in their original proposals, had little to say on these problems. In fact, as several observers have noted, these problems were managed through charismatic leadership. We have seen in reviewing earlier the three streams of therapeutic community work that in each case powerful leadership was crucial to the early initiation and sustenance of communities. However, in Perrow's terms, the question arises of identifying an appropriate technology so that subsequent generations of therapeutic community workers can sustain the structures and commitment necessary. One way of course is to organize charismatic succession. But this is clearly a precarious solution, although communities do still emerge and, more importantly decline, in relation to the strength of their charismatic leadership.

What of the rest? The only alternative to charismatic authority in this field is to draw on another widespread form of legitimate authority, namely science-based professional knowledge embodied in, for example, clinical psychology and psychiatric medicine. The problem here as we have seen is that psychiatry has been moving away from social and psychological methods towards organic treatments. However, in recent years there has emerged a technology which increasingly commands legitimate support both theoretically, and in terms of empirical research, namely group psychotherapy.

Group psychotherapy can overcome many of the problems identified. It can provide a clear boundary and structure for the community both internally and externally, and perhaps even more importantly it can command external legitimacy and internal commitment, in Almond's terms of 'specialness', both in relation to individual patients and the group as a whole. Not surprisingly, therefore, many communities have adopted this therapeutic method as the heart of their therapeutic work, although it was not such a necessary or central feature to the early innovators. Some evidence for this shift is provided in detail in chapter 4. This is particularly significant, since the Henderson Hospital is arguably still the flagship of the democratic therapeutic community fleet, which, as we have argued, is itself increasingly the dominant therapeutic community stream.

The relevance of group psychotherapy to the therapeutic community is well illustrated by Bloch and Crouch's (1985) review of therapeutic factors which have been identified theoretically and empirically as central to group psychotherapy. Basing their study on a wide review of published theoretical, clinical and empirical work. Block and Crouch suggest ten factors:

1. *Acceptance* — the patient feels a sense of belonging and being valued (cohesiveness).
2. *Universality* — the patient discovers that he is not unique with his problems (universalization).
3. *Altruism* — the patient learns with satisfaction that he can be helpful to others in the group.
4. *Instillation of hope* — the patient gains a sense of optimism about his potential to benefit from treatment.
5. *Guidance* — the patient receives useful information in the form of advice, suggestions, explanations and instruction.
6. *Vicarious learning* — the patient benefits by observing the therapeutic experience of fellow group members (spectator learning, identification).
7. *Self-understanding* — the patient learns something important about himself, usually through feedback or interpretation (insight, intellectualization).
8. *Learning from interpersonal action* — the patient learns from his attempts to relate constructively and adaptively within the group (interpersonal learning, interaction).
9. *Self-disclosure* — the patient reveals highly personal information to the group and thus 'gets it off his chest'.
10. *Catharsis* — the patient releases intense feelings which brings him a sense of relief (ventilation). (p. 246)

In reviewing the relative effectiveness of these factors on outcome, and in terms of patients' perceptions of helpfulness, Bloch and Crouch suggest some tentative patterns: self-understanding (insight) is the most effective factor in all groups; acceptance is important also for short-term and in-patient groups; learning from interpersonal action and self-disclosure are also important for long-term and out-patient groups.

Whiteley and Collis (1987) have examined these factors for Henderson patients, asking them to record recent important therapeutic events. Their findings concur closely with Bloch and Crouch, shorter-stay patients exhibiting the short-term pattern, and longer-stay patients exhibiting the long-term pattern. While Whiteley and Collis claim that the therapeutic community 'addition' to normal group psychotherapy is vindicated in that half of the 'important events' occurred in the community but not in formal groups, it is apparent on close inspection of their paper that this finding was most strongly exhibited by shorter-stay patients upon whom one might expect the general, and unfamiliar, community setting to have most impact. For longer-stay patients, however, who in most studies are likely to exhibit the greatest therapeutic gains, the relative preponderance of formal groups over the general community as the source of important therapeutic events begins to show.

## CONCLUSION

In this chapter a detailed review of the definition and development of therapeutic community work has been undertaken, together with the identification of theoretical elaborations of the original ideals in the light of areas of continuing ignorance, and problems and criticism surrounding practice. It has been shown that the therapeutic community is a distinct type of therapeutic work that varies in practice around core notions which, while originating in the democratic stream of work, have become focused on group psychotherapy as the central therapeutic method.

It has been argued that this focus has to a certain extent moved the therapeutic community away from Main and Jones's original emphasis on the totality of relationships within the community. This shift in emphasis remains relatively unacknowledged in therapeutic community writing and raises two unanswered questions: first, the extent to which the therapeutic community remains as distinct from the provision of residential group psychotherapy as some authors, such as Whiteley and Collis (1987), would wish to argue; second, the question of whether theory is available to rescue the therapeutic community from this position, which comes close to a fairly conventional psychiatric aim of reconstructing the patient's internal state. While Whiteley in particular has continued to emphasize what Edelson (1970) termed the sociotherapeutic aspects of therapeutic community work, that is dealing with the social situations of patients, it is not clear that therapeutic community practitioners have an adequate theoretical grasp of this dimension, in comparison with psychotherapeutic concepts, and nor is it clear that the Henderson itself has managed to avoid this drift in practice, as is documented in chapter 4. A review of recent and potentially relevant social science theory which might help to replenish therapeutic community theory is undertaken in the next chapter.

# 3

# Social theory and the
# therapeutic community

The aspiration of the early therapeutic communities was to introduce radical changes in psychiatric practice at two levels, necessarily interlinked. The Northfield experiments and Mill Hill innovations described in chapter 1 combined both a new social structure, and a new technology of psychiatric treatment. In this chapter, theory about the nature of persons relevant to therapeutic communities will be discussed.

In the 1940s therapeutic community practitioners drew on a limited range of theory to understand the way in which the individual patient and their social environment interacted. In chapter 1 it was noted that Freud, Lewin, Mead and Sullivan provided the developmental and environmental theory which underpinned both a social view of psychological disturbance, and a social view of personal change.

Since that time there has been relatively little new theory taken up by therapeutic communities to examine the therapeutic process. The literature reviewed earlier in chapter 2 indicated that there has been little work on any theory of 'residential functioning' (Millard, 1983), and that in practice theories of group psychotherapy have become, *de facto*, a substitute for therapeutic community theory. As will become apparant in the next chapter, this parallels the emergence of the small psychotherapy group as the symbolic heart of the modern therapeutic community. However, there is a convergence in current social science theory from a number of directions on the problem of understanding the individual and their immediate social environment which can be developed both to re-examine the nature of the therapeutic process, originally the focus of the therapeutic community, and to revitalize the radical potential of the therapeutic community which has been overshadowed by group psychotherapy.

This new theory focuses on two basic problems: what is the

nature of the individual and their social environment, and how do these two entities interact? Traditionally social science has conceptualized the individual and the social as two distinct types of reality which, while closely interwoven, were to be understood as ontologically separate and self-contained. This dualism has now come under critical scrutiny in the search for continuities rather than discontinuities between the individual and the social, both on theoretical and empirical grounds. We can present this new work most succinctly in terms of two typically separate arenas of academic work. The first is conventional academic study in the disciplines of sociology, and psychology (especially the subfields of social and developmental psychology). The second is the more radical tradition associated less with specific disciplines than the commitment to individual emancipation to be found in marxist, feminist, and neo-Freudian work on subjectivity and ideology, particularly associated with French social theory.

## DEVELOPMENTS IN SOCIOLOGY

As we have seen in chapter 1, Jones (1952) and Rapoport (1960) used the traditional sociological approach to understanding individual-social interaction, the concept of role. This was classically formulated by Linton (1936) as the active component of a basic element of social reality, status, which he observed to be the 'presence of patterns for reciprocal behaviour between individuals or groups of individuals' (p. 346). Thus he proposed that

> A role represents the dynamic aspect of a status. The individual is socially assigned to a status and occupies it with relation to other statuses. When he puts the rights and duties which constitute the status into effect, he is performing a role. . . . Status and role serve to reduce the ideal patterns for social life to individual terms. (p. 347)

This decidedly deterministic view of the social constraints on the individual was subsequently softened through theoretical elaboration which stressed the multiple and overlapping set of roles available which necessarily gave rise to potential and actual conflicts between roles (Merton, 1969). Consequently, the argument ran, a gap could be opened up between the self, and role requirements:

Just as social structure presents massive forces which influence the individual from without towards certain forms of adaptation, so does personality present massive forces from within which lead him to select, create, and synthesize certain forms of adaptation rather than others. Role-definition may be seen from one perspective as an aspect of personality. It represents the individual's attempt to structure his social reality, to define his place within it, and to guide his search for meaning and gratification. (Levinson, 1969: 305)

The logical extreme of this argument was reached in Goffman's (1971) 'dramaturgical' analysis of the way in which role performance is regionalized between 'front' (public) and 'back' (private) areas, both literally and metaphorically, such that

When a performance is given it is usually given in a highly bounded region, to which boundaries with respect to time are often added. The impression and understanding fostered by the performance will tend to saturate the region and time span, so that any individual located in this time-space manifold will be in a position to observe the performance and be guided by the definition of the situation . . . it will be convenient to use the term 'front region'. (p. 109)

However such a public role performance becomes in Goffman's view something quite distant from the real self, since

When one's activity occurs in the presence of other persons, some aspects of the activity are expressly accentuated and other aspects, which might discredit the fostered impression, are suppressed. It is clear that accentuated facts make their appearance in what I have called a front region; it should be just as clear that there may be another region — a 'back region' or 'backstage' — where the suppressed facts make an appearance. (p. 114)

And, it seems, it is these 'suppressed facts' which constitute the real self. However, such a radical separation of back and front regions raises rather than solves the problem of individual — social interaction, since there is a danger of the front region becoming thereby an empty performance, a social world bereft of people, while the back region is inhabited by a-social individuals beyond the influence of others. Clearly back regions are in reality still pervaded by social influences: time, language, and cultural values are not left behind. Even such intimate matters as sex or pain are socially structured. Similarly front regions exhibit the authentic commitment that individuals bring to social roles, otherwise such performances would be empty of content and the motivations and defences ordinarily displayed in public life would be inexplicable.

The difficulty of fruitfully interpreting this dualism has been taken by Giddens as the key focus for his reworking of sociology in terms of a new synthesis, called 'structuration theory'. He has developed this in the course of a prolific output over the last fifteen years covering the whole range of sociology. His work is in the grand tradition of drawing together prior theoretical tendencies and insights into a new synthesis which attempts to provide consistent explanation across a wide range of social phenomena.

Giddens's search for a synthesis begins with the collapse of American structural functionalism (to which the concept of role was central) in the early 1970s, and the consequent upsurge of interest in previously 'excluded' theory, such as marxism, phenomenology, psychoanalysis, and symbolic interactionism. He argues that common to these newer theoretical currents are three important themes: an emphasis on the active, reflexive character of human conduct; a fundamental focus on language and other cognitive faculties; and a recognition that the philosophy of social science now implies not that natural science is the ideal model of empirical investigation, but that empirical investigation itself in both natural and social science can no longer stand apart from the significance of language, and the interpretation of meaning. From this basis Giddens (1985) develops the argument that the dualism that has plagued rival social theories, between the individual and the social, between the subjective and the objective, must be 'reconceptualised as a duality — the duality of structure' (p. XXI). In particular he rescues Marx for social theory, not as a marxist, but as a theorist: 'This book, indeed, might be accurately described as an extended reflection upon a celebrated and oft-quoted phrase to be found in Marx. Marx comments that "Men (let us immediately say human beings) make history, but not in circumstances of their own choosing" ' (p. XXI).

Giddens suggests that the dualism can be dissolved by conceptualizing both individual and society as constituted by social practices which are recursive. In other words social phenomena are continually recreated, rather than created, by people as a result of the very way in which people express themselves. Ordinary people are of course more or less aware of this process, and Giddens stresses the importance of paying attention to people's accounts of their own motives and reasons for doing what they do. However in this respect he makes a crucial distinction between discursive and practical consciousness. The former being people's ability to articulate their accounts of social practices, the latter being the inarticulate but much larger stock of knowledge we all need to be able to continue in the routines of daily life. Both of these are to be distinguished from a more or less Freudian notion of the unconscious, created through repression and early pre-language experiences.

For Giddens, however, it is practical consciousness which he wishes to elevate to a greater status than has been the case in previous social theory. He argues simply that daily life is more important than is usually thought, especially as it is crucial to the fusion of the individual and the social: 'Ordinary day-to-day life — in greater or lesser degree according to the context and the vagaries of individual personality — involves an ontological security experiencing an autonomy of bodily control within predictable routines' (p. 50). The concept of routines is crucial for it provides the key link between the continued existence of a secure personality (Giddens leans heavily on Erikson's ego psychology here), and the reproduction of structured institutions in society. Both depend on routines, as can be easily appreciated when daily-life routines are radically interrupted by some kind of emergency, and personal security and institutional structure begin to crumble. It is interesting, in the present context, that Giddens chooses to illustrate this point through discussing critical situations in which either the social context for routines is radically altered (Nazi concentration camps; a residential unit for parolled prisoners), or the individual's performance of routines breaks down (mental illness).

Finally, Giddens notes that the material of which such routines are constructed consists of two elements — rules and resources: what to do and what to do it with. Rules, Giddens suggests, do not specify particular actions, but they are 'techniques or generalizable procedures applied in the enactment/reproduction of social practices' (p. 21). They are at the very heart of the practical consciousness which enables people to continue their daily lives, indeed they are what distinctively characterizes human beings.

We can now return to the problem of reconceptualizing the dualism of 'individual-social' in terms of a duality of structure. Giddens suggests that the rules and resources ordinarily drawn upon in daily life are structures which in operation reproduce and create the wider structures of the social system. In other words the structural properties of individuals in daily life, as he outlines it, are both constrained by and recreate wider and more enduring institutional structures, also conceptualized as rules and resources sedimented over time and space.

Of course much of this discussion seems rather abstract, and Giddens has tried to show how it can be used in empirical research. He chooses to examine Willis's (1977) research to illustrate how the duality of structure is helpful in understanding the daily life of schoolchildren, and the relationship between this and the wider institutions of school, work, and government (Giddens, 1985: chapter 6). Willis's study followed a group of schoolchildren who became progressively opposed to the official expectations and requirements of school routines towards the end of their school careers, seeing little hope for themselves as successful graduates moving into good jobs in adult life. Rather the 'lads' actively participated in their own disengagement from the dominant school culture, moving naturally on leaving into unskilled and unrewarding jobs. The point Giddens wishes to draw out from this study is the way in which the 'lads' consciously see through the authority relations in school in a highly perceptive manner, as the basis of their opposition to it. Ironically however this leads them into jobs situated in a shop-floor culture which actually quite resembles the school and which in effect they have learned to tolerate. Consequently their successful penetration of the school culture actually leads them to perpetuate the social conditions to which they were opposed. We see then how these children's practical consciousness is a sophisticated and subversive use of rules and resources in the routines of school life, which in the end contributes to the reproduction of very general structures such as factory-work relations.

The relevance of all this for therapeutic communities lies in the twin problem of the nature of psychological disorder and the process of therapy. In chapters 1 and 2 it became apparent that therapeutic communities aim to achieve personal change in a social context, that is they operate on both sides of the traditional dualism of individual and social environment. However it seems that therapeutic community work has lapsed into an over-determined view of the nature of the person, and hence of the possibilities of therapeutic intervention. I mean by this that the unconscious on the one hand, and social structures on the other, are given too much importance in determining the nature of the patient's psychological disorder. Therapy has been reduced to the privileged work of intensive group psychotherapy (to work on unconscious material), in a communal setting, while the social structures impinging on the patient outside in the real world are felt to be beyond reach.

Giddens's stress on the routines of daily life achieved through practical consciousness suggests first that psychological disorder is manifested in not only the unconscious disruption of practical consciousness, but in its *incompetence*: either rules are misunderstood, or resources are too impoverished for the patient to achieve ordinary daily routines. This leads, Giddens suggests, to the exhibition of 'situational improprieties' in face-to-face conduct. Second, the implication from Giddens is that greater competence in practical consciousness ripples outwards into the recursive nature of social reality, since social phenomena are continually recreated as daily life goes on. Clearly therapeutic communities are in a good position through their principles of permissiveness and reality confrontation to work much more intensively on educating the patient in the ways of practical consciousness, and hence slowly recreating the patient's social context. This is in essence what Maxwell Jones's model of 'living-learning' aimed to do, but which has been eclipsed by preoccupations with group psychotherapy.

## DEVELOPMENTS IN PSYCHOLOGY

Despite their early commitment to mobilize the total social resources of a hospital, we have seen how therapeutic communities have in practice stepped back from Main's (1946) conception of 'full social participation' to a more familiar psychiatric presumption that the patient has a disordered personality which can be treated through group psychotherapy. This location of a fairly fixed disorder in the patient is based on a traditional view in psychology of the personality as consisting of a collection of permanent, stable and fixed set of traits:

> Each of us, through the vagaries of chance and the determining influence of heredity and personal experience, develops a distinctive set of enduring dispositions to respond to other people in characteristic ways. These dispositions — here called interpersonal response traits — play the same kind of central explanatory role for the social psychologist that psychodynamic personality traits play for the clinical psychologist. Interpersonal response traits help us to describe social man, to understand his behaviour, and to predict his actions. (Krech, Crutchfield and Ballachey, 1962: 103)

The relationship of the concept of trait to personality theory is much like the relationship of role to sociological theory, and has been subject to similar criticism. Just as the notion of role came to be seen as over-determining of social life from which individuals could 'take distance', so the idea of fixed personality traits has also been attacked, again on both empirical and theoretical grounds. Just as sociologists accumulated observations which threw doubt upon the extent to which individual behaviour accorded with role prescriptions, psychologists have found that character traits in practice seem to vary markedly according to different social situations. As early as 1928 Hartshorne and May found that children exhibited little consistency on tests of such traits as honesty and deceitfulness in different situations, unless those situations themselves were similar. A more recent study, in which the settings could be more closely controlled (Gumpe *et al.*, 1957), showed definitively that the social interactions of boys on summer camp were more consistent within than between settings. And similar results were available from other studies only tangentially related to this problem, for example in Lewin's study of changing group atmospheres as determinants of the behaviour of children in an after-school activities' club (White and Lippitt, 1960).

These and similar findings lead eventually to a general questioning of the adequacy of trait theory by Mischel (1968), who concluded in a review of the literature that there was a ceiling in correlation measures of cross-situational consistency of behaviour of no more than 0.3. Such a low level suggested that new theory was required to explain situational behavioural variance. Such theory has developed in two directions, again showing some similarity to sociological work on roles. The first has been to try to 'add in' social situations to trait theory, arguing that it is the interaction between personality traits and the social environment which can more adequately explain behaviour. In a review of studies of this type, Argyle (1976) concludes that indeed situations are more important than traits in accounting for behaviour, but that the most powerful effect is a third variable, namely the interaction effect of personal traits with situations, having a variable impact depending on different situations and persons:

I conclude that PxS variance studies can usefully be carried out if (1) attempts are made to sample persons and situations equally widely, (2) overt behaviour is used, and (3) two-way analyses are performed. Samples of studies which approximate these conditions show that person variance falls in the range 15–30 per cent, situation variance 20–45 per cent, and PxS variance 30–50 per cent. (p. 151)

However, the measurement of situations (or the social environment) has proved much more difficult than the measurement of traits. Moreover since in ordinary life people choose and change situations, and different kinds of behaviour (other than a limited range of universals such as the amount of talk or eye-contact) occur in different situations, it has proved impossible in general to satisfactorily apportion variance between traits, situations or their interaction. Consequently psychologists have begun to look to new theories of behaviour, just as sociologists dissatisfied with attempts to 'add in' notions of the self to social roles have reconceptualized the dualism of self and social context.

We can approach some of these new theories through the psychological sub-fields of social psychology and developmental psychology. In so far as the dualism of self and social situation has proved difficult to integrate, the obvious strategy has been to reconceptualize both in common terms. For example, work associated with Tajfel (1982) on the nature of social groups has sought to define both social groups and the self through the notion of social categorization. Turner (1982) suggests that:

individuals structure their perception of themselves and others by means of abstract social categories, internalise these categories as aspects of their self-concepts, and social-cognitive processes relating to these forms of self-conception produce group behaviour. The first question determining group-belongingness is not 'Do I like these other individuals?', but 'Who am I?'. What matters is how we perceive and define ourselves and not how we feel about others. (p. 16) (see also Turner, 1987: chapter 3)

Rehearsing the trait theory debate we have already discussed Turner suggests that the self is composed of both a personal and a social identity, and that the latter is both a product of the categorization of social groups, and in turn the source of social groups created through categorization. While this provides a useful conceptual continuity between the self and social groups, it does so at the expense of hiving off a part of the self as personal identity, separate from the social environment. In other words the self-society dualism is reproduced as a split *within* the individual, reminiscent of Mead's distinction between the 'I' and the 'me'.

This unfortunate reappearance of the self-society dualism has been the subject of some debate in developmental psychology, particularly

77

in two key works edited by Richards (1974, 1986). In the earlier work traditional developmental psychology was criticized for focusing on individuals, neglecting social and cultural contexts, and denying the relevance of human agency in psychological development. However attempts to correct these weaknesses by 'adding in the social' nevertheless failed to transcend the split that was one of the objects of criticism. This failure is a major focus of the more recent book. In it, 'social constructionism' is proposed by various authors as a strategy to:

> break down the individual/society dichotomy via the following two-stage argument. First, human thought, perception and action must be approached in terms of meanings; secondly, the vehicles of 'meaning' are codes (especially language) whose nature is inherently intersubjective. Therefore, mind is an intrinsically social phenomenon. And if psychology is the science of mind, then the object of psychology is not individuals, but (to put it rather ineptly) what goes on in the space between them: that is the codes which structure action. (Ingleby, 1986: 305)

The best sources for the systematic development of this theory are the various publications of the Oxford philosopher Rom Harré. Harré has argued for a complete revision of social psychology, away from a positivist natural science project towards an 'anthropomorphic' theory in which individuals and social situations are reconceptualized in terms of human action:

> Regularities in human behaviour may be explained according to several different schemata. Two extremes are: (1) the person acting as an agent directing his own behaviour, and (2) the person as an object responding to the push and pull of forces exerted by the environment. . . . self-directed and self-monitored behaviour has been generally neglected in behavioural science, is the prototype of behaviour in ordinary daily living, and we believe it to be the main factor in the production of specifically social behaviour. (Harré & Secord, 1972: 8–9)

It followed from this position that the main task of social psychology in explaining social behaviour was the identification of meanings which individuals ascribe to social situations in the course of their own self-monitoring. These would give rise to sets of rules used by individuals in their accounts of their own and others' behaviour, and to the hidden structures of sequences of social episodes. Central to this approach was the idea that language was particularly important in two respects. First, the meaning which guided people's behaviour in social situations was best excavated through their own accounts or descriptions expressed in ordinary day-to-day language. Second, social behaviour could itself be conceptualized like a language in the sense that, as with speech while no particular action (utterance) could be predicted, the general rules (grammar) for action could be identified. It was not surprising that positivist models in psychology had failed to predict behaviour reliably, since no linguist would even attempt, in the analogous situation, to predict particular utterances.

Individuals nevertheless did vary in their relative grasp of the rules and structures of social situations, and hence their competence in social performance. Indeed the acquisition of such competence was at the heart of a person's biography (Shotter, 1976). This brings us on to the question of individual differences or personalities. Harré suggests the term 'persona' to indicate the 'resources upon which a person draws in giving form and meaning to his actions as social performances. These resources are the basis for what one could call his social competence' (De Waele and Harré, 1976:193). However he immediately stresses that

> personas are unities perceived in creations of the moment, called forth by the recognition of situations, i.e., by the endowment of contingent environments with meanings. . . . The persona presentation of human beings cannot be examined in isolation from an examination of the situations which a particular culture recognises as distinct and the capacity for the creation and recognition of which has been acquired by many of its members. (pp. 194–5)

Before presenting some practical illustrations of this approach, and its relevance to therapeutic communities, it is worth noting at this point the marked similarity of Harré's theory to that of Giddens discussed earlier. Coming from two different traditions, they have arrived at remarkably similar positions. Both reject the natural-science model, and emphasize as an alternative the importance of self-conscious human action, in which language is given a central significance. Both try to overcome the dualism of individual and social worlds by reconceptualizing both in common terms. For Giddens, social practices and practical consciousness grow out of the routines of everyday life, based on rules and resources. For Harré, social behaviour and accounts of meaning grow out of the episodes/ situations of daily life, based on rules and competencies. One is tempted to suggest that only the terms are different!

Some practical applications of Harré's ideas are presented in Argyle's review of trait theories. He proposes a 'generative-rules approach to PxS interaction' (1976:174 ff.), focusing on social situations as the source of rules for social behaviour. He stresses both that situations are discrete, discontinuous entities which are thus difficult to dimentionalize, and also that people vary in their choice of situations, in the way in which they group situations (eg. in terms of the social skills required), and in their knowledge of the relevant situational rules. Argyle then shows how these ideas can be used to explain, for example, inter-cultural misunderstandings, in that apparently equivalent situations in different cultures (eg. market bargaining) may have quite dissimilar rules. A related example he discusses is the way in which people from different cultures may be differentially sensitive to equivalent situational demands. A further example, closer to our concerns in this book, is the treatment of neurotic patients who complain of anxieties or inadequacies in certain situations. Therapy can involve both the education of patients about the relevant situational rules, thus increasing their competence, and the identification of particular elements or classes of situations which patients can learn to avoid or minimize through active choice. This kind of management of social episodes is quite different from the more conventional psychiatric project of reconstructing the patient's personality through therapy.

The relevance of these developments in psychology for therapeutic communities can once again be addressed through the twin issues of the nature of psychological disorder and the process of therapy. In a comprehensive reconstruction of psychological theory Harré (1979) argues that the basic problem for a person in a society is to be recognized as of worth, and as such to be producing meaningful actions and speeches (p. 167). Since human social activity consists of two main kinds of performance, the performance of acts in socially-recognized episodes, and the speaking of accounts so that acts are given certain meanings — particularly that they are seen to be the products of a rational being (p. 163) — it follows that intelligibility is the key criterion around which mental disorder is manifested, either with respect to recognized actions, or with respect to meaningful accounts:

Problems of intelligibility are solved as a continuous day-to-day achievement by the use of two main techniques. We attain intelligibility most readily if we draw upon standardized solutions to the specific social problems our social and physical environment presents us with. These solutions involve a standardised, integrated personal style appropriate to each type of problem-situation. There is a local typology of personas available to draw upon. . . . Human beings have a further resource for achieving intelligibility required of their actions, namely accounting. Accounting is speech which precedes, accompanies and follows actions. Actors give accounts to ensure the twin goals of intelligibility and warrantability, that is, the meaningfulness and propriety of their actions. (Harré, 1979:169)

However, Harré notes that there may be deficits in an individual's cognitive resources such that knowledge of the appropriate style of self-presentation or of the rules for successful action in a situation, and consequently the possibility for contemplation and correction by self-monitoring and self-control, may be lacking. There is clearly some similarity between this position, and that of Giddens noted above which stressed the problems of incompetence in practical consciousness leading to 'situational improprieties'. Consequently the potential of therapeutic communities to remedy these deficits, as noted before, is significant, through the construction of a rich and varied set of social situations for the patient combined with a continuous feedback through reality confrontation. In Harré's terms, patients are encouraged to learn how others develop standardized solutions to making acts in social situations intelligible, and how intelligible accounts of such actions can be constructed.

The potential strength of the therapeutic community's twin focus on individuals and social situations can be seen quite clearly in an earlier paper by De Waele and Harré (1976) where they observe that:

On the ethogenic view, however, situation definitions being an integral part of the cognitive matrix through which interactive performance and problem-solving express themselves, the study of situations, their possible requirements and meanings are inseparable from the study of an individual personality. . . . So, the personality investigation always has to start from the largest possible sample of social situations in order to discover which ones are particularly relevant to that individual (pp. 232–3).

81

They then observe that one fruitful setting for this kind of assessment is:

> the highly complex social structure of institutions like the army, a prison, or a hospital. In the latter case the assessment situation is directly influenced by the institutional structure of which it is but a subordinate part, so that investigations have to include every possible aspect of the conduct-in-situation which the individual may exhibit while residing in the institution. While this kind of day-to-day observation by trained participant observers can be organised without too great difficulties, its interpretation has to face the difficult task of having an institution studying itself from within (p. 233)

and conclude that:

> the social enquiry has to work from the description and commentaries furnished by the individual who is being studied and when it has been completed he has once again to be confronted with its results, since their social reality consists only in the meanings he gives to them and which can be negotiated with those with whom he is presently interacting (pp. 234–5).

These are without doubt views which Main and Jones would have endorsed as central to therapeutic community work.

## DEVELOPMENTS IN CRITICAL THEORY 1: (MATERIAL BASIS FOR SOCIAL LIFE)

The rules and resources identified in the above sections in sociological and psychological theory still require further theoretical elaboration with respect to two key problems. First is the identification of the material basis for social life, both in terms of the resources available for individuals to become socially competent, and in terms of the constraints on what is socially possible. The production of the means to satisfy needs is not a mere background to social life, but a central aspect of daily life, namely the competence for, and requirement to, work (Doyal and Gough, 1984: section 5). Second is the elaboration of the source and nature of language, and particularly the ideas and knowledge which go to make up practical and discussive consciousness, and which shape the typology of standardized personas and accounts of meaning used in social life.

Recent work which can help with the first problem returns to the ideas of Marx as a key theorist of material life. In the 'young' Marx, writing before 1845, there is a clear humanist concern for the individual within nineteenth-century capitalism. In the early 1840s, Marx's main concern was to understand why the system of capitalism could at the same time produce both an abundance of wealth, and misery and poverty: 'We shall begin from a contemporary economic fact. The worker becomes poorer the more wealth he produces . . . . The devaluation of the human world increases in direct relation with the increase in value of the world of things' (Marx, 1961:95). He tackled this issue by elaborating the concept of alienation, borrowed from Hegel and transformed by Feuerbach. Feuerbach argued that Christianity was a result of the 'natural fetishism of human activity' whereby human relationships were projected onto non-human agencies, such as God. Marx argued that this insight could be extended to other super-human agencies, such as the state, wealth, money, and so on, which are similarly regarded as things which affect people but are beyond their control. This experience was literally the alienation of human relationships.

Marx argued that in capitalism this process of alienation was significantly multiplied through the development of wage-labour. The worker produced things which were owned by the employer and hence

the object produced by labour, its product, now stands opposed to it as an alien being, as a power independent of the producer . . . the more the worker expends himself in work the more powerful becomes the world of objects which he creates in face of himself, the poorer becomes his inner life, and the less he belongs to himself. It is just the same as in religion. The more of himself man attributes to God, the less he has left in himself. (Marx, 1961:95, 96)

The significance of this process is underlined by Marx's belief that labour is the central activity of people:

the whole of what is called 'world history' is nothing but the creation of man by human labour, and the emergence of nature for man; he therefore has the evident and irrefutable proof of his self-creation, of his own origins. (Marx, 1961:26)

Marx was keen to understand the problem of labour and alienation to be found at the heart of capitalism's success: the creation of
wealth. He emphasized that alienation, a social process, created a
person's estrangement from himself, from his own potential, by
depriving him of his own products. The individual then was damaged
and constrained under capitalism by the environmental constraint to
work, but in a context through which he reproduced his own alienation (Arthur, 1980).

Having arrived at this position, Marx proceeded to ask himself
what it was about the nature of capitalism that so distorted the
fundamental attribute of human beings, labour, as to create not self-
fulfilment, but misery. While his concern was for humanity, his
theoretical argument led him naturally towards an understanding of
political economy. This is commenced in 1845 in *The German
Ideology*, and his *Theses on Feuerbach*, but finally gave rise to the
volumes of *Capital* more than twenty years later.

The line of argument now taken up is significant for our concerns
here about person/environment interaction. Starting with a reitera-
tion that 'the first historical act is thus the production of the means
to satisfy needs, the production of material life itself', it followed that
'definite individuals who are productively active in a definite way enter
into definite social and political relations. The social structure and
the state are continually evolving out of the life-processes of definite
individuals' (Marx, 1961:197). Therefore, the essence of being human
'is not an abstraction inherent in each single individual but in its reality
. . . [it] is the ensemble of social relations' (Marx, 1951:366). Thus,
being human is the result of social relations generated by human
labour, not their cause:

> here individuals are dealt with only insofar as they are the
> personification of economic categories . . . . My standpoint can
> less than any other make the individual responsible for relations
> whose creature he socially remains, however much he may sub-
> jectively raise himself above them. (Marx, 1976:92)

Many writers have seen this last, and seemingly highly determinist,
position as radically different from the early humanist concerns —
a difference celebrated by Althusser as a clear epistemological break
(Althusser, 1979; see also Molina, 1978). However as Geras (1983)
has convincingly demonstrated this is achieved only by heavily
emphasizing the determinism implicit in *Capital*. Séve (1978) has more

correctly emphasized the continuity between the young and mature Marx, on the argument that *Capital* does not, as is generally thought, abandon a concern with the early concept of alienation, but rather is a necessary theoretical detour in order to understand the system which required the kind of labour which generates alienation. In our concern here, too, with the person, the individual, and his personal alienation, we must also be prepared to follow such detours in getting to grips with the social environment we see as important. But the origin remains alienation (Walton and Gamble, 1972).

However, it is true to say that Marx never finished his theoretical detour. He never had time to return to developing a theory of the human individual, the human subject, who could both be a creator through labour, and whom could be created through the 'ensemble of social relations'. This project has been resurrected in various places in the twentieth century: in the development of a 'humanist' Marxism; in the integration of Marx and Freud; and in the construction of new psychology on the basis of the concept of labour. The first two, as exampled by the work of Lukacs (1971), and the critical theory of the Frankfurt school (see, for example, Jacoby, 1975; Slater, 1977; Held, 1980), are outside the concerns of this chapter. This section and the next will be confined to two more recent French writers, who themselves take into account the attempts of Lukacs and the Frankfurt school, and in doing so develop some concepts remarkably similar to those in the earlier sections on the sociological and psychological approaches to personality and environment.

Séve (1978) is concerned to build a science of personality directly on the basis of Marxist theory, rather than importing some other system (e.g. psychoanalysis). He starts with Marx's point that since people and their history are founded upon labour and 'the existence of men is their actual life-process' (Séve, 1978:78), the primary concept in the scientific theory of personality is that of an 'act'. Ingleby (1972), drawing on a similar approach, puts it succinctly: 'What constitutes a person is here defined as a collection of meaningful actions' (p. 78). Séve argues that since an act is simultaneously both an act of the individual and of a determinate social world, we can see the possibility of contradictions and hence movement and change. The determinate social world is, as has been argued, first and foremost a world of social labour; and we must make an important qualification of it by separating concrete and abstract labour.

Under capitalism, Marx observed, workers do not sell their labour directly (i.e. the things they make) as commodities, but rather their potential labour (their labour-power, or time), and it is up to the capitalist to persuade them to actually produce things (hence the need for foremen, managers, etc.). Marx distinguished a worker's labour 'for himself', or concrete labour (e.g. do-it-yourself), from labour 'for capital', or abstract labour (e.g. factory work). The latter, as we observed above, is the source of alienation, since a worker's products are not his own, since he has sold his labour-power for his wage. This process in which labour-power becomes an abstract commodity, from which labour must be extracted with factory discipline, generates relations typical of capitalist society: isolated individuals subject to the anarchy of the market, the satisfaction of needs through commodity consumption, and so on.

Following this definition of labour, and in so far as acts are part of a social world, we can similarly distinguish concrete acts and abstract acts; or acts for oneself and acts for others; or personal life and social labour. However, we must remember that abstract acts (social labour) are determining under capitalism. Not only do they fill the greater part of the day, but a considerable proportion of our personal lives are also in effect abstract acts in so far as they constitute the reproduction of our strength and ability (our labour-power) to perform social labour.

A second essential concept which follows from the above is Séve's notion of 'capacities', or the ability to carry out an act. Clearly, in the world of social labour labour-power is the capacity to perform abstract labour, or abstract acts. Capacities then, like acts, can be both concrete and abstract. Furthermore, there is an intimate connection between capacities and acts in that capacities are developed through acts, while at the same time making them possible. Indeed, a theoretical distinction can be made between those acts which develop capacities further (learning — sector I in figure 3.1) and those acts which merely produce some 'desired effect' (sector II). Many acts do both.

A third concept must of course be centred upon the nature of this 'desired effect'. This is divided by Séve between needs and products. Need satisfaction is the object of an act, while production is what the act achieves. As before, we can distinguish concrete needs and products, and abstract needs and products (e.g. the heavily promoted trivia of mass consumption).

Séve suggests that the general unit of measurement should be time, or more correctly, use-time, which the individual has available for allocating between various activities, concrete or abstract, for development or need satisfaction. Hence the shape and development of the personality may be measured in terms of the time used on different

*Figure 3.1* General topology of personalities produced within capitalist forms of individuality

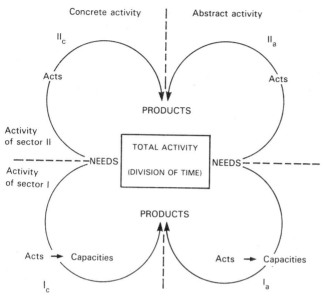

*Figure 3.2* Hypothetical examples of the real use-time of particular personalities

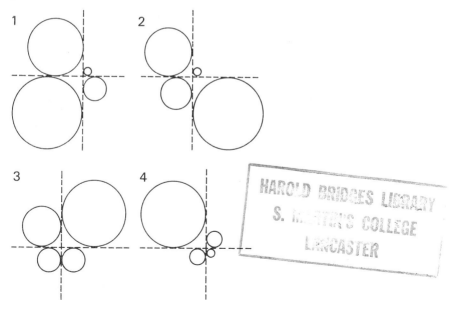

activities. Séve presents this diagrammatically as in figure 3.1.

Séve pictures different personalities of individuals by representing their distribution of use-time. Thus in figure 3.2, 1 represents a child, 2 a student, 3 a worker, and 4 a retired person. It is interesting to note that since these are measures of time used, they also indicate the kind of personality encouraged by a certain distribution of activities, such as the structure of time in different therapeutic communities. For example, 1 might be a typical distribution for analytically oriented groups and communities, whereas 2 might be more typical of a programme oriented towards social therapy. This distinction is similar to that drawn between sociotherapy and psychotherapy (e.g. Whiteley *et al.*, 1972:37).

These maps indicate what Séve terms the 'infrastructure of the personality' and he admits that, in addition, it is necessary to develop an analysis of the superstructure of controls, for which he suggests 'There is a case for investigating the psychoanalytic concept of unconscious controls' (p. 350). But he favours the view that

> this inclination or disinclination [to act] is the immediate expression of the quasi-ideological intuitive evaluations of the *general* relationship of needs to products, *and* the relationship of needs to products of the use-time of the activities in question. (p. 350)

It is clear that Séve's model bears several similarities to ideas in the earlier sections on sociological and psychological views of personality and the environment. His focus on action, capacities, and perceived needs could have been drawn respectively from Harré, Mischel, and Argyle.

We can conclude this section by drawing out Séve's basic position in relation to therapeutic community work. First of all, it must be said that it is a theory located chiefly at the level of the conscious, although he does not deny that the unconscious exists. However, the main, and very fruitful, point is that Séve relates his theory of personality to the central aspects of social life under capitalism: the distinction between concrete and abstract labour, and the social relations this implies. By carrying this distinction through all his concepts, Séve sets up a significant continuity between his analysis of the individual, and the political economy of capitalism; or between personality and environment.

This implies two very crucial things for therapeutic communities. First, that the conditions surrounding a patient's labour activity should be a central focus. Second, the relationship between, and extent, of a patient's capacities, and the expenditure of use-time in developing them, are important. While of course staff cannot control the position of a patient in the labour market very much, they can reappraise their view of work-groups (which after all were a key part of the early Maxwell Jones regime), and second, they can pay attention to what is more conventionally called social-skills training. This emphasis is decidedly away from sophisticated psychodynamic counselling and toward the relationship between the patient and his work environment (his social determinants).

## DEVELOPMENTS IN CRITICAL THEORY 2: (IDEOLOGY AND LANGUAGE)

The second general problem identified at the beginning of the previous section concerns the sources of knowledge which go to make up practical and discursive consciousness, and which shape the typology of standardized personas and accounts of meanings used in social life.

Critical theorists have traditionally tackled this problem either through 'humanizing' Marx, drawing particularly on the early works on alienation, or through a rapprochement with Freud. Indeed, frequently these have been developed together. However, this has mostly been at the expense of either or both theoretical approaches, a point forcibly argued by Althusser for Marx (Althusser, 1979), and Jacoby for Freud (Jacoby, 1975).

What these writers are suggesting is that many twentieth century reworkings of Marx and Freud have tended to massage away the awkward, uncomfortable and threatening aspects — to humanize both, and hence bring them closer together. However, such integration is bought at a high theoretical price. For example, Habermas suggests that Marx frequently cheated, in that in his concrete empirical work 'he adopts a concept of the system of social labour that contains more elements than are admitted to in the idea of a species that produces itself through social labour' (Habermas, 1972:52), and proceeds to suggest that 'technology and science become a leading productive force, rendering inoperative the conditions for Marx's labour theory of value' (Habermas, 1971:104). Another example is where Marcuse reinterprets the necessary place of instinctual repression in Freud's model of human development into the relativistic notion of surplus repression generated by our particular historical period, which he argues is rendered increasingly unnecessary with economic growth (Marcuse, 1966).

Such revisionism, we have seen, was not the basis of Séve's work. This is equally true of Jaques Lacan who has become of central importance to critical theorists concerned to identify the way in which the individual develops as a social being. Lacan achieves this through the use of structural linguistics. The main significance of his work for this book is that he provides a link between psychoanalytic development stages and the social world via language, or more correctly, symbols. And these, it can be argued from Marx, are the result of social labour. This connection is a considerable advance on Freud's model in which development within the family is analysed without reference to social labour.

Lacan argues that the ego is not autonomous, but subordinated and alienated to the objects (people and images) with which it has identified during its development. This takes place in two key phases. First, in the mirror phase (6–18 months), the child comes to see itself as a whole, rather than fragmented, by identifying with its image of itself. However, this is direct, unmediated, asocial. The second, and social, phase is more crucial. Here the child enters the symbolic order — the symbol has intervened between things. This is classically the Oedipal crisis, but here repression comes to mean the acceptance of a new interpretation of the self, a symbol provided by language. It is at this moment that the subject, the individual, is born by splitting and repression. The subject literally is the symbol provided in language, or as Lacan puts it 'a signifier represents a subject for another signifier' (Lemaire, 1979:71). Thus the subject or individual becomes what he is represented as in language; what is not thus represented equals the unconscious.

The significance of this model is in the question of who supplies the representation, or the symbol. Under capitalism, it can be argued that embedded in language are certain ideological representations which belie the true (i.e. materialist) nature of reality. For example, according to Coward and Ellis (1977)

> the individual is treated as a consistent subject in control of his destiny, able to act . . . a subject can represent itself as free, homogeneous and responsible for its actions because the social relations of capitalism are exchange-relations. For the social practice of wage-labour to continue, these exchange-relations must presuppose such a free subject. (pp. 75, 77)

But, in reality, Althusser points out that

what is represented in ideology is . . . not the system of real relations which govern the existence of individuals, but the imaginary
relation of those individuals to the real relations in which they live
. . . the existence of ideology and the hailing or interpellation of
individuals as subjects are one and the same thing. (Molina,
1978:255)

It follows from this that the sense of coherence of the self is illusory.
The self is 'decentred' on entering the symbolic order, and hence,
Lacan argues, 'Man's being cannot be understood without reference
to madness nor would he be man without carrying madness within
as the limit of his freedom' (Turkle, 1981:145).

Once again there is, in this work, a similar development to that
outlined in the section on psychological approaches to personality and
environment — in this case, Harré and Argyle's use of linguistics
to understand the generative rules which link individuals and situations. But again, the notion is dealt with more satisfactorily here. In
this case, Lacan's model of the symbolic order both bridges the
person/situation gap (the personality is the symbol) and explains its
own origins (the social relations within capitalism).

However the ideological nature of the symbolic order is heavily
stressed by critical theorists. Just as material needs are shaped and
fulfilled in particular ways within modern capitalism, giving rise to
both concrete and abstract acts and capacities so the symbolic order
is structured or distorted in certain ways which, following Lacan, are
embedded in the consciousness of individual subjects. The most
vigorous and original discussion of ideology is to be found in Marx's
writings. His work was developed in two distinct phases, in relation
to Feuerbach's materialism initially and later through his analysis of
the commodity in volume 1 of *Capital*, as we argued briefly in the
previous section.

Marx focuses explicitly on the way people's lives, their social practices, give rise to consciousness — to the way that they understand
their lives. However this is ideological to the extent that their lives
contain contradictions; for example the fact of class dominance in a
formally free and democratic society cannot be resolved through conventional social practice. That is, formal parliamentary democracy
cannot be translated into real economic democracy within conventional social practice. Ideological consciousness serves to mask such
a contradiction Marx suggests by enabling people to imagine that they
are free to resolve conflicts as equal citizens in the political system.

However this of course helps to deflect criticisms away from class dominance and is therefore clearly to the advantage of the dominant class.

However, Marx at this stage (the 1840s) has no more precise an analysis of the key elements of people's 'life process'. His mature thoughts on Feuerbach's problem of the 'natural fetishism of human activity' appear much later in volume 1 of *Capital* where he sets out to analyse the key elements of the life process of modern society, i.e. capitalist production, by starting with its central element, the commodity. In a remarkable continuity of analysis he examines not the fetishism of religion or the state, as before, but the fetishism of commmodities:

> A commodity appears at first sight an extremely obvious trivial thing. But analysis brings out that it is a very strange thing . . . the enigmatic character of the product of labour . . . arises from . . . the measure of the expenditure of human labour-power [as] the value of the products of labour . . . and the relationship between the producers [as] a social relation between the product of labour. (Marx, 1976:163–4)

Thus Marx suggests that commodities are special in that the effort to produce them is measured in terms of their market values, not the real effort; and that the producers of commodities do not relate together directly but through the medium of apparently independent things — commodities:

> The commodity-form, and the value-relation of the product of labour within which it appears, have absolutely no connection with the physical nature of the commodity . . . the definite social relation between men themselves assumes here, for them, the fantastic form of a relation between things. (Marx, p. 165)

Harking back to Feuerbach's concerns, he therefore suggests that

> to find an analogy we must take flight into the misty realm of religion. There the products of the human brain appear as autonomous figures endowed with a life of their own, which enter into relations with each other and with the human race. So it is in the world of commodities. (Marx, p. 165)

While Marx starts his analysis at the heart of the capitalist 'life process', the commodity, his use of fetishism can be extended to other relationships in society. Of particular note is the way political conflicts between people become displaced in an exactly similar way, to assume the 'fantastic form' of a relationship within the conventions of the state. For example Cohen (1978) argues that in our capitalist society class antagonism appears to us in a falsely autonomous and separate political realm of parliamentary democracy, which takes on the form of political conflict as a natural, inevitable fact of life. Rather, Cohen suggests, such conflict is peculiar to class-divided societies, and would not appear in classless societies.

Wells (1981) extends this idea further to suggest that the connection between commodity, state and other possible fetishisms is the fundamental ideology in capitalist society of dissolving the real relations of dependency and group identity amongst people into isolated abstract individuals who are endowed with natural (usually selfish) propensities which must be curbed by another isolated and abstract entity, society. Real relations thus appear to be combinations of separate things — individuals and societies. Wells points out that this explains the commonsense view of the necessity of an autonomous 'thing' — the state — as minimally the upholder of the rules of fair play between (selfish) individuals, and maximally the helping hand for those unable to survive in the game as it is seen to be played.

While Marx's discussion of ideology is very helpful, its development in terms of fetishism can be criticized on two counts. First it is a rather reductionist account of consciousness. By this we mean that ideology is conceived of as an automatic element in antagonistic class society, which can be reduced to the basic principles of capitalist economic relations — it is an almost mechanical necessity of the society of which it is a part. In this respect although ideology is an essential part of class conflict, since it masks reality to the advantage of the dominant class, it is conceived of without reference to the conscious activities of the dominant class itself in creating and manipulating ideas. Moreover, since ideas are essentially determined, any criticism or discussion is pointless.

A second criticism of Marx is that his faith in what is reality and what is appearance requires considerable scientific arrogance. The possibility that, as Mannheim suggested, all thought is potentially ideologically biased, and hence in principle contestable, is brushed aside by Marx's self assurance that he has quite definitely arrived at 'the truth'.

In relation to these criticisms, twentieth-century developments of

Marx's work place political struggle rather economic logic at the centre of the analysis. From this point of view ideology cannot be reduced to a necessary element in a commodity-producing society, but is rather contingent upon the balance of political forces. This approach is more akin to the earlier formulation Marx used in *The German Ideology* where he suggested that consciousness arises out of social practice. The notion of fetishism was built upon the social practice of commodity production — for the worker the experience of the 'dull compulsion' to work in order to live. However Marx also stressed a different kind of practice, which also produces consciousness, but of a different kind from fetishism. Gouldner (1980) has elaborated the difference between these two social practices in a project which tries to trace the development of modern Marxism:

> There is, then, a tension between Marx's dismissal of idealism and his call to change the world. . . . This ambiguity is reproduced in his conception of 'praxis'. Marx had two tacitly different conceptions of praxis or, as I will usually call it here, of practice: Praxis[1] is the unreflective labour on which capitalism rests, the wage labour imposed by necessity which operates within its confining property institutions and its stunting divisions of labour. While this labour inflicts an alienation upon workers, it also constitutes the foundation of that society, reproducing the very limits crippling workers. Here workers are constrained to contribute to the very system that alienates them. This conception of praxis is congenial to Scientific Marxism. In the second, more heroic concept of practice — Praxis[2], more congenial to Critical Marxism — emphasis is on a practice that is more freely chosen, most especially on political struggle. If Praxis[1] is the constrained labour that reproduces the status quo, Praxis [2] is the free labour contributing toward emancipation from it. In undertaking the first form of labour or practice, persons submit to necessity; in the second, however, they undertake a deliberate and Promethean struggle against it. (Gouldner, 1980:33–4)

From this perspective, then, ideology also arises out of the struggle to resolve antagonisms. It becomes not the counterpoint, in disguise, of truth, but the world view of groups in struggle. Gramsci develops this idea. In modern capitalist societies ideology does not merely emerge automatically, but rather depends on whether the dominant class can organize a system of beliefs to which the general public freely submits. Observing the failure of the Russian revolution to spread to western Europe, Gramsci argued that the dominant classes in the west were able to exercise hegemony over other classes by using ideology as a kind of social cement. However, there is a danger here of adopting a conspiracy theory of class dominance which requires an overly passive model of the public as cultural dopes. But Gramsci overcomes this problem by acknowledging that ideology is not just about an organized system of ideas for understanding social issues; just as important is the place of commonsense and folklore which comprise significant portions of the public's consciousness: 'It is not possible to separate what is known as "scientific" philosophy from the common and popular philosophy which is only a fragmentary collection of ideas and opinions' (Gramsci, 1971). Class dominance, or hegemony as Gramsci calls it, is thus also the subtle organization of commonsense to naturalize ideas and possibilities which are in the interests of the dominant class.

Mechanisms surrounding the development of ideological forms in the struggle for and against hegemonic closure by one class or group over another include areas of discourse such as the conversations between professionals and clients found throughout the welfare state. Here we are beginning to move away from the orchestration of the commonsense level of ideology, to Gramsci's other level, of formal philosophies. Hc placed great significance on the role of 'intellectuals' in the development and circulation of ideologies. In particular he argued that 'organic' intellectuals were those who significantly organized ideologies which expressed the interests of particular classes and genders. While of course journalists can be organic intellectuals with respect to ideologies at the level of public opinion or commonsense, we are here thinking more in terms of doctors, teachers, lawyers, social workers, academics and so on.

Probably the most influential notion which studies of the representation of ideas by these organic intellectuals have recently drawn upon is Bernstein's (1971) distinction between elaborated and restricted linguistic codes. He demonstrates that working-class language leaves many meanings implicit, relying on shared and mutual knowledge between people to fill in gaps. Middle-class language on the other hand makes meanings more explicit, and elaborates the contents of communication, freeing it from context. The difference is similar to the different language usage by intimates as compared to strangers. Many writers (including Bernstein himself) have been quick to realize the political implications of this observation, since restricted codes are available to all classes but elaborated codes are only available to the middle class: elaborated codes may make explicit the meanings (ideologies) in the interest of dominant groups in a way working-class interests are not elaborated. Since public debate takes place in elaborated code, working-class meanings tend to be excluded.

While Bernstein's work had been criticized for its elevation of the difference between language use into a hierarchy of preferred language use (Rosen, 1972), he nevertheless opened up a debate about class and language which has developed to include gender and language (Spender, 1980), and race and language (Reeves, 1983). All of this work shares a concern about the way political interests are constituted in, and to a certain extent actually determined by, language. Familiarized as the 'Sapir-Whorf' hypothesis in which world views of pre-industrial societies were understood as embedded in their languages, this notion has been given a critical usage with regard to differential language use by groups in conflict within a society since

A major function of sociolinguistic mechanisms is to play a part in the control of members of subordinate groups by members of dominant groups. This control is effected both by regulation and by constitution: by explicit manipulation and by the creation of an apparently 'natural world' in which inequitable relations and processes are presented as given and inevitable. Power differential provides the underlying semantic for the systems of ideas encoded in language structure. (Fowler, *et al.*, 1979:2)

This is particularly the case where working-class clients interact with organic intellectuals operating within a dominant elaborated code. Thus for example studies of doctors (Strong, 1979) and social workers (Baldock and Prior, 1981) as well as teachers (by Bernstein himself) illustrate clearly the use of language which directly or indirectly structures assumptions about appropriate conduct expected from patients, clients, and pupils. In other words there is a restriction of legitimate meanings to the *status quo* which Marcuse (1964) classically expressed in terms of 'one-dimensionality'.

What is the justification for such a long detour into relatively unfamiliar territory in relation to therapeutic communities? Language and the symbolic order, we have argued throughout this chapter, are central to understanding persons and their social environments. But these are not neutral processes. Studies of ideology suggest that language is a reality in which social situations and social relations are presented in particular ways which disguise or highlight certain aspects at the expense of others, whether in dominant or oppositional forms. Gramsci's concept of hegemony sensitizes us to the ways in which both commonsense and intellectual sense are shaped to naturalize certain social competencies, or practical consciousness, in the interest of dominant classes, genders or other groups. In attempting to reshape definitions of mental disorder, and modes of therapy, the therapeutic community is affected by such processes, knowingly or unknowingly. More specifically, it seems clear that Lacan's views can provide an important addition to Séve's model. The key point is that it can continue the categories derived from social labour, which Séve employs, right into the developmental sequence of early life before the child ever has to allocate use-time between concrete and abstract activity. To use Séve's terms in place of Lacan's, it can be said that the subject/individual is an abstract self literally created by the symbolic order. For example, the child learns its name as its father's name, and acquires its label as a legal 'subject' of the state. Simultaneously, the concrete self is repressed, becomes unconscious. Individualism, a key part of capitalism, is here thrust upon the child in the very awakening of its consciousness.

In so far as therapeutic communities operate within a world of person-environment interaction, this Lacanian perspective usefully joins together both concepts without reducing either to an undifferentiated category. It thus integrates person and environment without violating the internal differentiation of either, developed separately in Freud and Marx. This is a theoretical advantage. Does it have any practical suggestions? Lacan himself was apparently a therapeutic pessimist. However, linked with Séve's model, it can be suggested that Lacan's views support the suggestions outlined earlier in this chapter and, in addition, strengthen the therapeutic community process: the 'free occurence of real interpersonal reactions' (Whiteley, 1972) generates a specific cultural and symbolic order, however temporary, in which it may be possible to literally re-present the subject to himself in a less abstract and more concrete mode. However, the source of Lacan's pessimism — that the symbolic order is determined by capitalist social relations — must be remembered: however sophisticated these theories, members ultimately leave their community and return to pressures of the outside world.

## CONCLUSION

In this chapter recent theoretical debates about the nature of the individual and their social situation have been reviewed for their relevance to therapeutic community work. It has been argued that while therapeutic community writers have an extensive knowledge of psychodynamics, appropriate to the therapeutic community's drift towards group psychotherapy as its central method, they have not utilized new theory which might inform their work on the social situation of patients, which was more strongly emphasized in original formulations about the totality of social relations in therapeutic communities.

In particular five authors, Giddens, Harré, Séve, Lacan and Gramsci have been examined for their ideas. It appeared that there was a noticeable convergence amongst these authors on the notion of the personality as socially structured through language and social labour, which in turn were inextricably linked to the material and ideological factors associated with capitalist industrial society. This theory implies that the totality of social relations in a therapeutic community would include not only the psychotherapeutic reconstruction of patients' intra-psychic states, but also the ideological assumptions embedded in staff and patients' language, and the material circumstances of both groups.

From these arguments we would conclude that therapeutic community practice should work with problems of social labour (e.g. work groups, and relationships to work), and problems of symbolic identity. To the extent that, for example, work groups have become eclipsed by the more fashionable preoccupation with psychodynamics (as Christian and Hinshelwood (1979) have argued), the therapeutic community places inappropriate weight on the individual in isolation, and in the past.

# 4

# The therapeutic community at Belmont

In the previous chapters we have examined the origins and development of the therapeutic community in general. In this chapter we look at the leading British community in greater detail. It is an important central strand in that historical development; but it is also a continuing influence on therapeutic community workers both by way of practice, and in terms of the kind of research it has sustained.

The survey of the therapeutic community literature in chapter 2 made it less, rather than more, easy to isolate the main concept. Certainly a knowledge of various applications and modifications of the idea is vital to its understanding. However, the most useful approach to understanding the therapeutic community seems to be to trace the career of one specific community, probably the best known, in order to look at its response to changing internal and external pressures over the years. With this aim in mind, the ideas of Maxwell Jones embodied in the unit established in 1947 as the Belmont Hospital Industrial Neurosis Unit will be followed. In the first chapter it was shown how conditions surrounding war-time psychiatry in England encouraged innovation in hospital organization and concepts of treatment. Maxwell Jones developed these ideas in three different units during the 1940s — at the Mill Hill Emergency Hospital Effort Syndrome Unit, the Southern Hospital ex-prisoner-of-war Unit, and finally at the Belmont Hospital Industrial Neurosis Unit. He was appointed director of the latter in 1947. In 1952 with his associates he reported on his experience, and offered an appraisal of their aims, structure and process.

At the beginning of the description of the Belmont unit, Jones lists five aims:

1   to study a sample of (hard core unemployed) and as far as possible to understand its clinical characteristics.

2  to give appropriate psychiatric treatment.
3  to decide on the most suitable job (for the patient).
4  to arrange resettlement, preferably while the patient is still in hospital.
5  to test the effect of these procedures by carrying out an adequate follow-up study. (Jones, 1952:25)

Jones briefly describes a typical day as centred around two work sessions (10–12 a.m., and 2–4 p.m.) and the morning community meeting (9–10 a.m.). He identifies the crucial task as changing attitudes towards work, and to tasks in general, whether they be vocational, social, recreational. He states that mainly supportive psychotherapy is given, along with 'all known physical methods of treatment'.

At this point some themes begin to emerge. The first of the five aims indicates the extent to which this unit was considered experimental, also noted elsewhere (Wiles, 1949; Lewis, 1952; Freeman, 1952). This aspect permeates the changes which the unit underwent throughout the 1950s, such as the slow relaxation of the authoritarian regime initially set up as result of anxieties about extremely antisocial patients.

Second, it is apparent that although Jones and his team were concerned to move into the area of 'social disability', they were still using the traditional paraphernalia of physical psychiatric treatment.

Jones's book has throughout it an atmosphere of contradiction. Medical psychiatric perceptions of patients alternate with a sociological approach to the description of the unit, but there is very little theoretical linkage of the two areas. Indeed, whenever Jones moves beyond description his ideas become inconsistent, containing a large degree of prescription. This is most clearly demonstrated in his chapter on the 'social structure of the Industrial Unit', which he bases entirely on one concept — role. This will be examined in greater detail below.

A third theme is associated with the last of the five aims. Research was a duty from which the unit did not shrink. Indeed, starting with Jones's book, there has been a considerable tradition of research associated with the unit since the 1950s.

## CRITICISMS OF JONES'S MODEL

Jones uses the concept of role first in the introduction where he defines the condition of being out of work as 'absence of a work role'. He states that the units he has run have attempted to provide 'social and vocational roles' for patients. In describing the changes developed at Mill Hill, Jones notes that at first the nurse's role was not clearly defined, but that in time she came to play a 'leader role'. While arguing for a clarification of roles, Jones also approves the 'greater social penetration between doctors, nurses and patients' (p. 14), which seems to mean more overlapping of roles. At Dartford, the main aim is stated as 'to try and find social and vocational roles for patients in the local community' (p. 16). This activity sometimes 'amounted to nothing more than a spectator role' (p. 17).

Having thus used the concept of role extensively, Jones briefly introduces chapter 3 by reference to the concept itself. He argues that to understand the structure of the staff group, it is necessary first to study and clarify the roles of the various categories in the group. A role is defined as 'a set of legitimate expectations of behaviour'. Jones then looks at four groups of people — nurses, doctors, disablement resettlement officers, patients — in terms of their roles. The subsequent discussion is vague. Not only is there little theoretical discussion about how roles help us to understand the relationship between personality and social structure, but more seriously the use of the term 'role' is haphazard and inconsistent.

Role theorists (Gross, 1958; Levinson, 1969; Banton, 1965; Jackson, 1972; Holland, 1977) suggest that a role is both the expectations and behaviour associated with a social position (status). Jones mixes up status with role. Moreover, his idea of role is too elastic to be meaningful. It is stretched from specifying what a nurse should do when a rule is broken by a patient (p. 36) to her role as a transmitter of unit culture to patients (p. 38). A solution to this problem has been offered by Banton (1965) through a scale of role specificity. Without such awareness, Jones's discussion becomes difficult to follow. For example, nurses are said to have three types of role: authoritarian, social, and treatment. This classification is broadly an intuitive appreciation of the processes of social control, informal co-ordination and task attainment. However, doctor's roles are classified into five types: social, supportive, by example, activating, interpretive. These refer to the doctor-patient relationship almost exclusively. Any recognition of the activity of the doctor as unit leader, external co-ordinator, or holder of statutory responsibility is not found here. Furthermore this five-fold classification contains in the last four categories an elaboration of the single nursing-role category of treatment. No reason for this elaboration, with respect to doctors but not nurses, is given.

Early role theory tended to stress the close fit between structurally given demands, a person's conception of his position, and the resultant actions of the person. However Levinson (1969) notes that this tendency restricts our understanding of organizational dynamics and change which is to be found in the contradictions in and between these three aspects, rather than in their congruence. In this context, where Jones wishes to look precisely at organizational change, his use of role theory is inadequate. Rather than separating social position, associated expectations, actual role performance, and relevant sanctions, in order to catch the subtle interplay of these factors in contributing to the final shape of the unit, Jones provides a simplistic description using an arbitrary classification.

The attempt to circumscribe the role-set of each official status (nurse, doctor, patient), although begun, is unfortunately not continued to cover all types. The absence of the further step of specifying the 'status-set' (Merton, 1968) for each individual leads Jones to miss out some vital aspects of the unit, such as his own status as leader, and the various role performances associated with that position. For example, in the introduction to Jones (1952), Aubrey Lewis notes that:

> what he has not demonstrated so clearly, though it can be inferred from what he has accomplished and is known to those in touch with his work, is the unremitting energy, sustained purpose and enthusiasm which he has put into this difficult task.

Rapoport (1970) makes a similar point. Without an adequate knowledge of possible role and status sets, Jones falls into the position of considering the relationship of staff to patients almost exclusively, whereas some of the most vital clues to the changes in the unit are in the relations inside the staff group and between the staff group and the outside world. Indeed, the organizational changes in the unit appear to be appended almost as an afterthought to chapter 3, when Jones briefly states that the initial authoritarian style of the unit is beginning to relax. He says no more on this vital point.

In summary, Jones's description suffers from theoretical simplification. This leads to a loose description which misses out important areas about the social dynamics of the unit. Furthermore, Jones does not link psychiatric practice to sociological analysis clearly, and as a result tends to state what has happened or should happen with little differentiation between the two, and little explanation. It is difficult to draw out from this his ideas of the essential nature of the therapeutic community.

## THE RAPOPORT STUDY

As we noted in chapter 1, R.N. Rapoport, an anthropologist, was appointed in 1953 to look at the social structure and process of the unit. The following year, the Nuffield Foundation provided a substantial grant to support a research team at the unit under his direction. During the subsequent four years many papers were published, and the major findings combined in a book, *Community as Doctor* (Rapoport, 1960).

Rapoport and his co-workers set out initially to study the phenomenon of 'psychopathy'. An elaborate design was developed which would look at: ecological data to ascertain likely causes of the disorder; the ways in which the disorder came to be recognized in families; the process involved in treatment (especially the Belmont Social Rehabilitation Unit); and finally, the outcome of patient care on return to the home environment (Jones and Rapoport, 1955). This integrated design was abandoned for two reasons. First, it soon became apparent that it was too difficult to locate enough suitable subjects for study in the community before treatment. Second, the members of the research team could not agree on the variables to be studied in the search for aetiological factors.

The strategy subsequently adopted centred on the (now renamed) Belmont Social Rehabilitation Unit itself. Only there could there be found sufficient patients to be studied. Moreover, each research worker worked on the study of his/her choice which was not systematically related to any other. These studies ranged from the intensive analysis of twenty families of patients, to a broad look at referral sources. The heart of the study focused on the social rehabilitation unit itself, however. In particular, Rapoport and Parker looked at the ideology of the unit, the social structure and processes it encompassed, and the way patients reacted to treatment.

It is important to remember that the type of patients referred to the unit provided its activities with certain opportunities and limitations. Very few psychotics (9 per cent) and neurotics (8 per cent) occurred in the population, which consisted predominantly of personality disorders (81 per cent). 'Medical' treatment seemed less relevant than one based on sociological principles. Moreover, the high degree of anti-social acting out posed considerable problems, particularly for administration. This unusual population, in so far as it was problematic to traditional psychiatry, invited new approaches of the social type, and thus fitted well with the therapeutic community concept.

Rapoport's study was of crucial importance in that it described in considerably more detail and with considerably less bias than previous work (in particular by Maxwell Jones) the way in which the ideology of a therapeutic community operated in practice. The rationale of the therapeutic community had been set out frequently by practitioners in the late 1940s and 1950s (Main, 1946; Jones, 1952; Schwartz, 1957). However, these ideas were seldom set in perspective, or subjected to a dispassionate appraisal in operation. This appraisal initially described the ideology before evaluating it (pp. 34–69). Trained in anthropology, Rapoport viewed the place of ideas and cultural themes as a vital part of his subject matter, and hence the key to an understanding of the cohesion in the unit. Rapoport distinguished three propositions held by the staff at the time as fundamental: 'Everything is treatment'; 'All treatment is rehabilitation'; and 'All patients (once admitted) should get the same treatment'. He then abstrated four cultural themes which underlay these propositions: democratization; permissiveness; communalism; reality confrontation.

Democratization means that each member of the community should share equally in the exercise of power in decision-making about community affairs. Permissiveness means that the unit should function with all its members tolerating from one another a wide degree of behaviour that might be distressing and seem deviant. Communalism means that the unit's functioning should be characterized by tight-knit inter-communicative and intimate sets of relationships. Finally, reality confrontation means that patients should be continuously presented with interpretations of their behaviour as it is seen by most others.

Rapoport points out that the three fundamental propositions, and the themes which underlay them, are used in the Unit without qualification, or overall integration. This baldness results in several problematic aspects of the ideology: problems of limits; problems of qualifications; problems of hierarchization of themes; problems of resolving treatment-rehabilitation dilemmas.

The first three problems are self-evident: first, there are limits to extreme democracy or permissiveness, for example, set by the environmental context of the unit (the NHS, the local village); second, and more specifically, implicit qualifications surround, for example, communalism, where free communications are encouraged in groups rather than between individuals; third, some situations come under the jurisdiction of two themes simultaneously, such as dominant behaviour, which if tolerated permissively may be undemocratic.

The fourth problem refers to Rapoport's view that the unit unrealistically blurs the distinction between treatment and rehabilitation (chapter 1, *passim*). He argues that rehabilitation goals demand that the hospital should approach a replica of outside life. In contrast to this, treatment goals require that the patient, as a casualty of social process in the world outside, may need different conditions in which to recover. Blurring of this distinction is considered misleading. Indeed, Rapoport states that this 'problem . . . is one toward the solution of which this entire book is directed' (p. 71).

This documentation of the ideology of the unit, and in particular of the ideology in relation to the ongoing practice of the unit, contrasts remarkably with Maxwell Jones's writing. Rapoport crystallizes neatly the underlying ideas, and systematically relates them to activities which face community members. This throws up a multitude of problems surrounding the implementation of the ideology. These problems are experienced by staff and residents alike as disjunctions between reality and the ideal. Each must find resolutions as he or she can, particularly in the first months of working.

## CRITICISMS OF THE RAPOPORT STUDY

Since being published this book has furnished many practitioners with a concise guide to Maxwell Jones's therapeutic community ideology. But the larger part of the discussion concerning the problems of implementing the ideology has been less well attended. This may be due to selective perception on the part of the reader. There is no doubt that it is also due to the fact that Rapoport did not bring out coherently how the unit remained integrated in the face of these problems. He stresses the individual and isolated nature of (staff) members' *ad hoc* resolutions. This seems to have been the result of failing to identify social processes independent of the ideology — a point, ironically, that Rapoport actually wished to make. This perspective perhaps resulted from his training in anthropology in which the traditional subject matter exhibits a much closer congruence between ideology and social structure than is common in western societies. Sociological writing on organizations, however, has pointed out that:

organisations have latent as well as manifest structure . . . . But it is commonly assumed that there is a dominant, modal pattern of role-performance corresponding to the structural requirements. It is well known, however, that this is simplistic. Many forces both from the organisation and the person interact to produce performance. (Levinson, 1969:69).

Also Rose Laub Coser (1969) in criticizing Goffman's concept of 'role-distance', says:

with 'role distance' Goffman confirms a recent trend in sociology which asserts the actor's creativity in predefined situations. . . . Role distance enables a person to tolerate contradictory normative expectations (sociological ambivalence) . . . refusal to live up to role requirements leads to better role performance. . . . in this sense 'role distance' is an essential part of role relationships (p. 318 ff.)

It seems then that organizations, even flexible therapeutic communities, will have informal aspects to their social system which will consist in part of individuals' responses to 'sociological ambivalence' in patterned ways. In other words, individuals will 'take distance from' expectations conferred on them as a normal part of role relationships. These informal adjustments are also surrounded by normative patterns, which Rapoport misses when he asserts the individual nature of reactions to ideological implementation. The effects of this informal system as a powerful third source of expectations, along with the formal ideology and the NHS environment, will be shown to have influenced the long-term development of the unit later in this chapter.

In subsequent discussion of the 'system of social roles' in the unit, Rapoport (1960, chapter 5) once again manifests a considerable sophistication in analysis when compared with Jones's exposition. He meets well the criticisms voiced by Gross (1958) about the neglect by early theorists of role conflict and its resolution:

Little research has been done on the degree of role consensus and role conflict resolution . . . consensus amongst those defining the role is certainly problematic. Role conflict not only stems from simultaneously occupying two positions, but also from conflicting expectations attached to a single position. (Introduction)

Levinson (1969) also notes: 'If a close fit is assumed between behaviour, disposition and societal prescription . . . this assumption restricts our understanding of organisational dynamics and change' (p. 299).

However, Rapoport restricts the influence upon actual role performance to the two formal prescriptions (unit ideology, and NHS environment) as mediated through the individual (see figure 4.1).

*Figure 4.1* Determinants of staff roles (1)

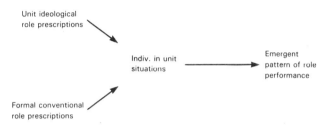

*Source*: Rapoport, 1960:105

But the informal social system already suggested in the resolution of problems in implementing the unit ideology also operates to pattern the ways in which roles are performed. Thus figure 4.1 should be modified (figure 4.2).

*Figure 4.2* Determinants of staff roles (2)

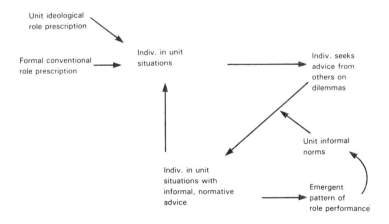

107

The additional elements are alluded to by Rapoport in the body of his text without being brought clearly into the analysis:

> A problem for the new doctor from early on in his absorption into the Unit is that of assimilating ideal-real discrepancies that he observes. . . . When a novice enters the unit he can learn relatively easily what the ideal system is . . . . On the other hand, mastery of the informal system, according to which the qualifications are provided for the ideal precepts, and acceptable tested solutions to the typical dilemmas are worked out, takes more time. (pp. 114–15)

Furthermore, these additional elements make a feedback loop in the patterning of roles which incorporates a greater sense of individual creativity and an informal social system, suggested both by the theoretical literature and indeed by Rapoport's own description.

This consideration of the individual's influence on the system, through the development of informal processes, has significant consequences for the long-term development of such a unit which will be examined below.

In chapter 7 Rapoport reports a lengthy analysis of the effects of the unit on the patients. As with his discussion of the ideology and the social structure, this section is relatively sophisticated, but marred by some serious flaws. The major one is the measurement of 'improvement' used. The concept of improvement is well known to be multidimensional (Bergin and Lambert, 1978). Many factors contribute to clinical judgement in a process which is far from clearly understood. Rapoport himself notes consistent differences between doctors' judgements and patient characteristics, yet proceeds to use these judgements. Moreover, when following up ex-patients he then substitutes the first set of judges for a second (sociologist and social worker). This change upsets any possibility of controlling for judgement bias.

The weakness of Rapoport's (and others) attempts to evaluate the effect of the therapeutic community as a treatment technique will be discussed later in presenting the data from such an attempted evaluation of therapeutic communities in Australia (chapter 5). The consequences of the absence of demonstrable effects, in terms of the professional acceptability of therapeutic communities, are frequently displayed in journal articles hostile to therapeutic community work.

Several further aspects of the unit not brought out clearly in Rapoport's book need to be mentioned here. The first is the role of

Maxwell Jones as leader. Rapoport throws little more light on this matter than Jones did in his earlier book. In the latter case this is understandable, but one can only surmise that relations between research director and medical director made this difficult in the former case. More recently Rapoport (1970) has written:

Maxwell Jones, in the Belmont days, was the archetypal charismatic innovator. His enthusiasm was infectious — not only to staff but to patients as well. He was one of those reformist enthusiasts whose work, when reviewed by a WHO expert committee, was praised but queried in terms of 'how much was the method and how much was the man?' All utopian reformers think and act to some extent ideologically, using faith and conviction in the absence of demonstrated scientific principles. Maxwell Jones is of this ilk. (p. 407)

A second problematic aspect of Rapoport's book is the focus on the unit itself to the relative exclusion of boundary problems. These not only affect staff and patients who enter and leave, but more importantly they concern the relations of outside bodies to the unit. Little mention is made of administrative relations to the parent organization (Belmont Hospital); and some excellent work by Irving Rosow (1957) on the reactions of the psychiatric world to the unit is scarcely mentioned.

A third problem in Rapoport's study was the tacit 'no-conflict' assumption; the idea of resolving conflicts by working them through in a group (or, for example, the idea that Stanton and Schwartz's (1954) 'hidden staff disagreements' can disappear by unmasking them) misses the existence of real conflicts of interest which are not soluble. Thus the interest of NHS administrators in smooth efficiency, or doctors in medical careers, or young working-class people in instant material success, may all be outside the scope of action of a therapeutic community. The best that can be achieved is some measure of compromise which does not solve the conflict but merely supresses it.

This situation throws up a fourth difficulty surrounding the exercise of social control. Rapoport underestimates the importance of social control. This point is substantially confirmed in data presented below which demonstrate that the therapeutic community at Henderson Hospital mainly relies on two types of activity — small psychotherapy groups for treatment, and the community meeting for social control. In the former, a senior staff member is clearly in charge; but in the latter, peer group participation predominates. However it is the latter which is experienced as controlling, precisely through the encouragement of pseudo-democracy. It is clear then that despite its radical position in psychiatry, the therapeutic community shares the conservative position of psychiatry in general, in that it attempts to control and change people. Whether the original ideology set out to be more than this is uncertain. Morrice (1972) has argued that over the years expectations of the therapeutic community have become idealized myths. Yet it may be that reality has, rather, dictated a revision of those ideals.

A final problem, again connected with boundaries, is the relationship of therapeutic community practice to professionalism — the *sine qua non* of medical, and increasingly of paramedical and social, work. The patient is treated as a whole person, and doctor, psychologist, nurse, social worker and social therapist can work without splitting up their subject matter. But the therapeutic community also suffers the consequence of team-work, that professional workers lose their treasured autonomy. In reality an uneasy negotiation continues for jurisdiction in one area or another ('finding your role'), which as argued later has made therapeutic community practice too threatening for many practitioners to embrace.

A close consideration of Jones's and Rapoport's books has revealed many aspects of the therapeutic community. Equally significant are those aspects which are not brought out: sociological understanding in the former, and a glossing over of the vital informal side of the unit in the latter. Some of these aspects, vital to an understanding of the development of the therapeutic community, are now explored in detail with data from the Belmont unit, for the 1970s. This was the point at which the unit (since 1960 a hospital) had settled into a stable state.

## THE HENDERSON HOSPITAL IN THE 1970s

The Henderson Hospital began life as the Belmont Industrial Neurosis Unit in 1947 with Maxwell Jones as director. It was located in a wing of Belmont Hospital, a typically Victorian structure erected in Belmont village near Sutton, Surrey, in 1843 as a workhouse. The unit had accommodation for 100 in four wards when it opened. By the early 1970s patient numbers averaged forty, making available additional space for activity rooms.

Of those forty patients, about one third were usually female. The age range was from 17 to the early 30s, with a heavy concentration between 19 and 25. Diagnosis varied amongst: psychopath, sociopath, character or personality disorder, and some sorts of neurosis. Patients with organic brain damage were usually rejected on the grounds that they would not participate fully in the very active community life of the hospital. Similarly patients of high IQ were favoured (the average is 110) for their verbal ability which is an important resource for the treatment process.

At that time the number of patients admitted annually had been steadily declining, and then stabilized: a 43 per cent reduction in admissions between 1965 and 1973. This was not due to a substantial increase in the average length of stay, which had actually declined slightly from seventeen weeks in 1954 (Rosow, 1955) to fourteen weeks in 1971–2. The total number of staff was thirty-three of whom several worked part-time. This total includes four psychiatrists, two social workers, twelve nurses, eight social therapists, three secretaries, and one each of probation officer, disablement resettlement officer, chaplain, and cleaner. Administration was shared with Belmont Hospital.

Some aspects of staff structure and relations, staff/patient and patient relations, ideology, culture, etc. had changed little since the descriptions given by Jones and Rapoport, discussed above. These aspects of the therapeutic community have been mentioned. Here, interest is in what changes may have occurred. Rosow (1955) has described how the Henderson was very much an experimental unit in the early 1950s. Referrals were largely made in support of the experiment, so that the unit might have patients to treat, and so that the rest of psychiatry could try out this new facility. Twenty years later it was to be expected that the unit could no longer claim to be experimental, and therefore referrals would be made for the pragmatic reason that the unit could deal with the particular patient, rather than as an experiment or trial. In this sense the Henderson was becoming a part of 'normal' psychiatry. If this was so, then one would expect changes within the hospital to reflect this.

In order to measure changes within the unit, some of Rapoport's (1960) study was replicated to compare values and activities over an eighteen-year period. Rapoport identified four ideological themes which together constituted a rather vague ideal culture and its constituent values. The themes, 'permissiveness', 'communalism', 'democracy', and 'reality confrontation ', were combined subsequently into a Likert-type attitude scale. This 'values questionnaire' attempted to measure a single dimension: from traditional treatment values to therapeutic community values. Fourteen statements were included in the scale (see table 4.1) and the respondent asked to strongly agree, partly agree, disagree or strongly disagree with each one. Every statement was either definitely pro therapeutic community values, or pro traditional treatment values. Each response was scored 0, 1, 2, 3 according to how near it accorded with therapeutic community values, higher scores being closer to those values.

*Table 4.1* Statements used in the values questionnaire by Rapoport

---

1. Psychiatric hospitals should provide a change from ordinary life, with emphasis placed on rest, comfort and escape from stress and strain.
(2.) Patients should take a good deal of the responsibility for treating other patients.
3. A restful night is very important for treatment and should be assured, if necessary, by giving sedatives.
4. Hospitals should be organised according to a regular set of rules that cover most situations so that each person can know what is expected.
(5.) If a patient is very abusive or destructive in hospital, it is better to try to discuss it with him than to discipline him.
6. Many things a patient thinks while in hospital are nobody's business but his own, and he shouldn't have to talk about them.
7. It is important in the running of a hospital that orders should be obeyed promptly and without question.
8. While a patient is in hospital, he should try to forget about his outside problems as much as possible.
(9.) Patients should help to decide how their fellow patients should be treated.
10. Every effort should be made to keep patients from feeling tense or anxious while in hospital.
(11.) If everyone in hospital freely expressed his thoughts and feelings to everyone else, it would help the running of the hospital.
(12.) If it were possible, staff and patients should share all facilities and activities in common — cafeterias, workshops, socials, meetings, etc.
13. Psychiatry is for the treatment of sick people and belongs in hospitals and doctors' offices, not in homes, schools and outside communities.
(14.) Everything patients say and do while in hospital should be used for treatment and not only what happens when doctors are around.

---

Note: ( ) = pro therapeutic community values

This scale was administered to all staff and to groups of new patients on admission in 1955 by Rapoport and again in 1973 by the present writer. Further measures were taken in 1977 to check on the stability of the 1973 results. The general object of this was to find out: (a) the staff values, which were the views of the 'culture-carriers' in the hospital; and (b) the values of patients coming into the hospital. A comparison of (a) over time, (b) over time, and the difference between (a) and (b) over time was carried out to estimate changes in the hospital culture, changes in new patients' values and the interaction between these two.

This scale is a measure of the values of the staff group; a second measure was used to evaluate the activities that are actually pursued within the hospital. The second measure should show the extent to which the ideal (a high score on the values questionnaire) is reached in practice. This does not involve measuring the 'improvement rate' but rather what specific aspects of the hospital activity are felt to be most helpful to those in it, both patients and staff.

As Wing has noted (1972) the therapeutic community, like psychotherapy, is difficult to evaluate. Each is designed to promote inter-personal interaction and allow for its exploration with a view to modifying behaviour where appropriate in order to enhance the quality of ongoing interactions. The patient is largely able to appreciate for himself the good or bad effects of treatments, although his views may well differ from those of the staff. Rapoport's second measure therefore was the simple one of asking all staff and patients which three groups of the many which go to make up the day's activities they considered most and least helpful, in order of preference. A first choice was scored 3, a second 2, and a third 1. This measure throws light on the internal differences in the hospital between staff and patient evaluations of the treatment process. To the extent that the results have changed between 1955, 1973 and 1977, indications about long-term trends in the hospital organization can be noted.

## Values questionnaire: results (1973)

In figures 4.3 and 4.4 can be seen the percentage of cases from the values questionnaire which fall into one of six score intervals. The distribution of values for both staff and new patients has moved up the scale between 1955 and 1973. The staff mean score has moved from 26.7 to 30.7, and the new patients' from 19.9 to 25.4. Hence the difference in mean value scores between the staff and new patients remains, though slightly reduced.

This shift in values over time could be attributed to several causes: changes within the structure of the staff group, such as to show an apparent overall shift; a change in staff/new patient values within the hospital; or a change in general social values. The first possible cause does not appear to have had a substantial effect. A reduction in the number of auxiliary staff (a low scoring group) and social therapists (a high scoring group), and an increase in the number of nurses (a

*Figure 4.3* Treatment values of staff

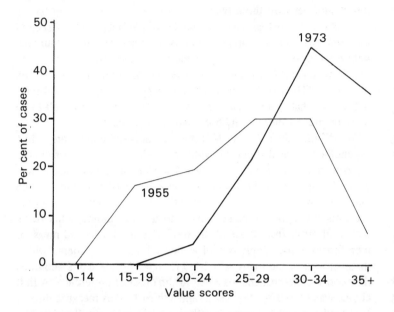

*Figure 4.4* Treatment values of new patients

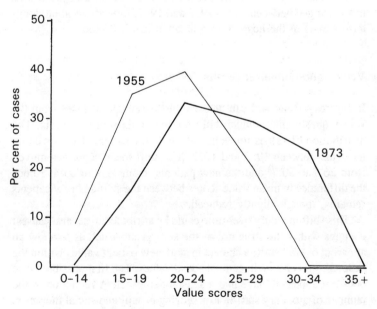

medium scoring group) suggests little systematic change of value distribution in any one direction.

A change in staff/new patient values within the hospital was clear. New patients were selected more carefully for motivation and insight, and this was likely to bias the value scores of those accepted, for these characteristics were associated with the therapeutic community view of active treatment. New staff also were selected for their interest in this way of working, and with the general growth in the application of social scientific views in psychiatry, more appropriate potential staff members were available. A change in general social values had no doubt also occurred since the 1950s. However, this was not necessarily in the direction of therapeutic community ideology. New organic techniques had, rather, encouraged a public image of modern psychiatry as decidedly medical (Jones, 1972a).

## Group ranking: results (1973)

Since the treatment values of both staff and patients had moved closer to the ideals of the therapeutic community, one might suppose that practice (as reflected in judgements about the helpfulness of various groups) would have similarly been nearer the ideal. However, the second measure revealed a significant change. Rather than coming to favour all groups (i.e. all aspects of the patient's waking life) in the daily programme, the staff seem to have emphasized one or two groups as fundamental (in particular more formalized group psychotherapy), while relegating the rest to a marginal place. A similar process had occurred amongst the patient group. Furthermore differences between staff and patient evaluations had increased rather than decreased, despite the common move in values towards the ideal, revealed by the values questionnaire.

The proliferation of numerous administrative and leisure groups since 1955 made the comparison of least helpful groups impossible, since this resulted in a very diffuse spread of choices. Although this increase in the use of 'rehabilitative' groups might have indicated an increased involvement in rehabilitation (a central aim of therapeutic community practice), both patients and staff concurred in their choice in 1973 of treatment oriented groups as the five most helpful groups.

Figures 4.5 and 4.6 summarize the distribution of scores for each group, by staff and patients in 1955 and 1973. In 1955 the top five groups chosen by the staff were the same as those chosen in 1973. Moreover the proportion of total scores accounted for by this top five

*Figure 4.5* Staff evaluation of most helpful groups

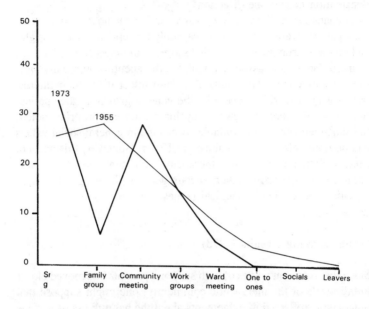

*Figure 4.6* Patient evaluation of most helpful groups

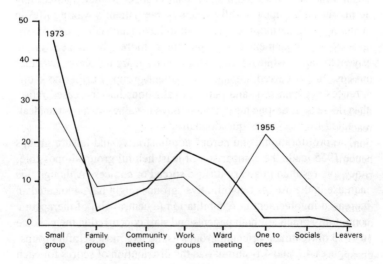

(out of a total of eight) was 94 per cent in 1955, and 81.6 per cent in 1973. However, this apparent consistency and uniformity appears less marked if the change in rank orders is considered. An application of the Spearman rank correlation test shows no significant association between the 1955 and 1973 top five group rankings.

Ranking by the patients had also changed considerably since 1955. In fact in 1973 they placed two groups in the top five which were not there in 1955. This change brought the patient choice into agreement with staff about the top five groups. However, within that top five, there were considerable disagreements between staff and patients about ranking which can be uncovered by a closer look at the position of the key groups.

Differences in score between patients and staff, and changes between 1955 and 1973, should be treated with caution for a number of reasons. The knowledge and participation of staff and patients varies, and the meaning of the group may have changed over time. For example the family group was far less popular in 1973 for staff, partly because families were less often brought into contact with the new types of patients, partly because research in 1955 stimulated an interest in families, but also because the hospital had become increasingly a specialist service for psychiatry, and thus one stage removed from direct family contact.

In 1955, individual interviews with doctors were valued very highly by the patients (21 per cent) but not all in 1973 because the culture of the hospital allowed no room for them. However, it seems that their function had been largely taken over by the small group (which is doctor-led), since the drop in proportion of responses for individual therapy (20 per cent) was matched by a similar rise for the small group (17 per cent). This dramatic swing in evaluation away from individual therapy indicates the success with which the hospital culture had reached an ideal of group therapy acceptable to the patient population. However, this type of interpretive psychotherapy had now become outstandingly important for both staff (32 per cent of responses) and patients (44 per cent of responses).

For staff it seems that the small group (for therapy) and the community meeting (for social control) had become the mainstays of the hospital, in comparison with a more even spread of scores in 1955. Although patients concurred in this evaluation of the small group, they had moved further away from the staff evaluation of the community meeting. They experienced it largely as a controlling device. Information was shared about anti-social activities which were interpreted not only as malfunctional for the individual, but more importantly as malfunctional for the community. This 'public information', available to the whole community, was of course often uncomfortable for the individuals concerned, but was vital in maintaining a common definition of reality.

## The 1977 results

Both of these measures were repeated in 1977 to check that the substantial changes expected, and found, between 1955 and 1973 had stabilized. The distribution of staff scores on the values questionnaire was much the same in 1977 as in 1973. The theoretical limits are between 0 and 42 (the higher the score, the more therapeutic community values expressed). The average scores in 1955, 1973 and 1977 were 26.7, 30.7 and 30.7. It was not possible to collect results from a series of new patients as before, but the existing patient group's average score was 29.8 in 1977 — broadly in line with the staff group, and consistent with the trend in new patient averages of 19.9 and 25.4 in 1955 and 1973.

In contrast to this consistently high score on therapeutic community values, there were again in 1977 some interesting and provocative changes in the evaluation of groups by staff and patients. The 1973 findings showed that the staff and patients emphasized one or two groups as fundamental and that differences between staff and patient evaluations had increased, despite the common move in values toward the ideal. This trend was in general continued, although differences between staff and patient evaluations declined in 1977. The staff demonstrated quite clearly by 1977 that they agreed almost unanimously on the small psychotherapy group and the community group as the essential groups: no other groups except the work group came in the first three choices of any staff member. Within the patient evaluations, the low score of the community group in 1973 was largely reversed, although it still provided the greatest point of disagreement with the staff. Overall, the distribution of patient and staff scores was broadly similar.

The 1977 data confirm the trends detected in 1973: that staff depend heavily on the small group for therapy, and the community meeting for social control; and that patients increasingly concur with this arrangement. Other groups are unanimously judged to be of less importance. This is counter to the philosophy of a 'twenty-four-hour' programme, where 'everything is treatment', which the staff and patients espoused in the values questionnaire. This gap between ideals and reality, between culture and structure, tentatively explored through the 1973 data, was now confirmed more firmly with the 1977 data.

## Interpreting the results

The main points which arise out of the results are that despite the successful selection and socialization of staff (and, to a limited extent, new patients) into ideal treatment values, the actual evaluation of the treatment programme indicates that staff depend heavily on; (a) small group psychotherapy for treatment; and (b) the community meeting to maintain social control. Furthermore, patients similarly evaluate the psychotherapy group (almost as highly as all the other groups put together), seeing it as the main source of treatment, while evaluating the community meeting at a lower level.

Thus, staff and patients agree on the desirability of psychotherapy, and by implication the situation whereby 'treaters' (the skilled doctors in the small psychotherapy group) are essential to the group, which is 'being treated'. This element of the 'sick role' is an aspect which the early therapeutic community movement sought to eradicate, emphasizing rather the creative and active side of the patient (Main, 1946). Evidence of its reappearance in Henderson Hospital, even in a limited way, illustrates the sort of pressures placed on such an institution: both staff and patients can find such an arrangement seductive; and exterior pressures towards skilled treatment and containment in an established hospital, no longer sheltering under the category of 'experiment', invite subversion of the ideology.

The holistic nature of the therapeutic community makes the evaluation of such individual aspects of the programme difficult, however. It is claimed that there are emergent properties which are attributable to the whole programme, and not merely to the sum of its parts. To examine each part without reference to the whole would be to commit the reductionist fallacy of failing to consider the interactive effects of several attributes working together. For example, to a certain extent the psychotherapy group is the most helpful group only in the context of the rest of the programme, which both provides material for psychotherapy and provides opportunities for patients to try out new behaviour stimulated through insights developed in psychotherapy. However, if this were the case, one would expect a more equal distribution of scores for the other groups. The emphasis on the psychotherapy group remains a clear indication of which activities are favoured within the hospital.

119

As we have already noted, Rapoport discussed at length the problem for staff of operationalizing ideological themes in practice. It might be supposed that this problem would have resulted in the movement of the ideology and practice of staff closer together over these fifteen years. It appears that this has not happened. Indeed the reverse is in evidence. This divergence betwen 'values' and 'practice' indicates two possible processes at work. First, the divergence of ideology and practice may be a methodological phenomenon. It is known, for example, that attitudes expressed towards whole categories (in this case psychiatric hospitals) do not always apply to each individual case within the category (i.e. Henderson Hospital) (Fishbein, 1971). However, in this case, informal observation suggests that the staff and resident groups would express *more extreme* values about Henderson Hospital in particular thus tending to increase the gap between values and practice rather than reduce it. Second, the gap may be real. This may be understood by reference to several possible models, suggested by the literature:

1 *Idealization*. Morrice (1972) has suggested that therapeutic community values have become exaggerated over time, for example through the uncritical acceptance of slogans such as 'everything is treatment'. Limits and qualifications are forgotten, and principles such as democratization are transmuted into sacred myths. A variant of this argument is to be found in Festinger's (1956) study of a 'doomsday' prophecy cult in the USA, where he found that the 'cognitive dissonance' generated by the failure of the prophecy resulted not in the dissolution of the cult, but rather a renewed vigour in proselytizing beliefs. Hence, we might suggest that the failure of research to demonstrate the efficacy of therapeutic community principles leads to a closer adherence to ideals, and, therefore, higher scores on the Henderson values questionnaire.

2 *Experience*. Jones (1976) and Whiteley (1979) have noted the common observation that the therapeutic community operates with principles more basically discovered in group psychotherapy and organization development. The complex interaction between the personality and its social environment, and hence the mutual influence of the one by the other, is well documented. The therapeutic community's strength was the promotion of these ideas in psychiatry, and more recently in other groups dedicated to personal growth. Therefore, to maintain momentum and develop their work, therapeutic practitioners are extending the theoretical limits of their principles further;

120

for example, greater democracy or more extreme confrontation.

3 *Theoretical contradictions*. Even while recording the now famous themes of democracy, permissiveness, communalism, and confrontation, Rapoport (1960) acknowledged their obvious contradictory implications. Where should limits be set? Which dictate is superior to which? Are not treatment and rehabilitation ('growth' and 'adjustment') different? Subsequent critics have pursued the discovery of these difficulties (Morrice, 1979; Zeitlyn, 1967), in a process common to almost all scientific progress (Kuhn, 1962): the construction of a theoretical ideal (paradigm), within which contradictions (anomalies) are steadily accumulated, until a new theory must be constructed to explain the contradictions (paradigmatic revolution). We may be witnessing, therefore, a contest between the old therapeutic community paradigm and its accumulated anomalies. Those who support the original paradigm may cling more tightly, as revealed in the Henderson values questionnaire, while more recent formulations develop. This tension may also affect practice (see model 6).

4 *Attitudes — behaviour discrepancy*. The gap between what people say they do (or will do) and what they actually do has been a source of puzzlement for social psychologists. However, Fishbein (1967, 1971) has recently arrived at a celebrated solution. He argued that the difference between attitudes expressed (for example, xenophobia) and actual behaviour (racial discrimination), noted frequently in the literature, could be explained by informal norms which surround and constrain everyday behaviour. 'Behavioural intention' leading to actual behaviour emerges from both enduring attitudes, and more immediate norms:

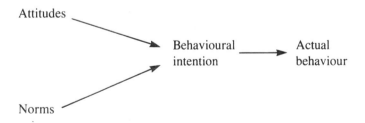

These day-to-day norms have been explored in descriptive accounts of therapeutic communities but not yet categorized systematically. For example, while 'role-blurring' and 'multiple leadership' might be endorsed as part of therapeutic community ideals, in fact staff members

121

observed at Henderson Hospital were quite competitive in demonstrating specifically psychotherapeutic/interpretive skill in the pursuit of stable leadership status. The source of such counter-ideal norms may come from the personalities of staff (see model 5), or the difficulties of community work (see model 6) or more generally the environment.

5 *Informal social life.* From the study of formal organizations (Roethlisberger and Dickson, 1939), it has been recognized that all such social institutions have an 'under-life', unacknowledged and without a formal 'map', which participants must discover for themselves. It has been one of the central tenets of the therapeutic community that such behaviour be brought into the official 'public arena' of the community meeting for analysis in the pursuit of treatment. However, even in the most ideal 'twenty-four-hour' treatment environment, community members will have plenty of time to develop alternative 'coping' mechanisms and views (see Mahony, 1979); staff may live in a hostel, or meet socially, and patients can relax when 'off-stage'. Indeed, the change of patient evaluation of groups at Henderson, measured in 1977, towards the staff evaluation, may be closely connected with the new building that Henderson moved into. Patients now have individual rooms, which tend to preclude the germination of such a rich 'alternative' culture as the open wards of the old hospital. This under-life is connected closely with the individual needs of community members. For example, Menzies (1960) has argued that many social forms are constructed so that the individual can manage anxiety. And indeed the therapeutic community often deliberately fosters such constructions (permissiveness) so that the way an individual or group manages its anxiety can be explored. But to the extent that such processes escape public acknowledgement, the implementation of ideals may be undermined.

6 *Practical contradictions.* Members of the community, in addition to spontaneously creating social life, described above, also try to manage or reconcile inherent conflicts in the ideals to be followed (see model 3). How much democracy? How much permissiveness? What kind of interpretation? Sharp (1975) has described in detail the way staff members have used 'managerial' concepts to mediate between contradictory demands, trying to maintain the status quo. Perrow (1965) has also discussed the contradictory pressures of the therapeutic community's social structure, goals and 'technology', which do not fit together. The problem is that of balancing a commitment to a set of ideals on the one hand with certain emergent realities

of social life such as social control or authority on the other (Kanter, 1972; Punch, 1977); for example, management anxieties over the growth of democracy. Often such difficulties are managed on behalf of members by charismatic leadership, which unfortunately only delays the day when such charisma has to be 'routinized' (Weber, 1947). Leaders do not last for ever, and the attempts of their followers to resolve internal contradictions often results in instability, leading either to the ultimate demise of the community, or to its fundamental transformation.

7 *Administrative disapproval.* For the Henderson, and many other communities, this means the National Health Service. As Kennard (1979) points out, this effect depends on the permeability of boundaries. A therapeutic community which has independent hospital status is in a relatively strong position to resist direct pressures, although the Henderson has recently been severely tested. The Paddington Day Hospital has had several such interventions, which have now resulted in radical transformation of both ideals and practice, and the removal of the consultant psychiatrist in charge (Baron, 1985). For a ward within a hospital, such pressures are more difficult to resist and it is correspondingly more dependent on a protective leader.

8 *Neighbourhood disapproval.* Pressure from the local community can be as difficult for independent or social services' hostels as a hostile administration (Dear and Taylor, 1982). Indeed, it is more difficult to sit down and explain theoretical ideas to a neighbourhood than to a sceptical committee. Sharp's (1975) study of such a hostel led him to reject the 'interactionist' perspective whereby the ideals and practice of the hostel developed solely from the 'logic-in-use' of the members. This common assumption by 'sociologists of deviance', he argued, ignores the very real pressures on such a community from the environment, which distort social processes inside the community. He particularly dwelt on the issue of social control, necessary to maintain a 'quiet' community but which subverted ideals of permissiveness and confrontation.

9 *Professional careers.* It is commonly observed that the professionally trained doctor or nurse experiences acute role conflict in his early days in a therapeutic community. Indeed, Rapoport (1960) described the 'emergent pattern of role performance' of such an individual as a result of two pressures: therapeutic community ideology and conventional 'role prescriptions'. As was argued earlier, this model is far too mechanical. Rather, the individual (professional or

123

not) has to remould his expectations with the help of informal advice and cues from other staff and patient members. But this informal culture (see models 4, 5 and 6) not only serves to change the individual, but also enables the individual to undermine the community's ideals and practice. For example, doctors tend to take up leadership positions, running psychotherapy groups, and so on. This process encourages fantasies of dependence in patients, and aspirations for psychotherapeutic skill in medical staff who might be better used in more community–oriented activity. These difficulties, of course, are much fewer in non-medical settings, although the steady development of a professional self-image amongst social workers may bode ill for the future. For example, a new certificate in therapeutic community practice, approved by the Royal College of Nursing, began in 1986.

10 *Legal obligations*. Many therapeutic communities have patient-members on probation. This symbolizes most forcefully the function of social control required of therapeutic communities, whether part of the health or social services. Here we can see the conflict beween 'social adjustment' and 'self actualisation' (Sharp, 1975) brought into sharp relief. It may be (and heard in more than one therapeutic community) that for a person to become a better (i.e. more successful) criminal would be a fully successful 'goal-attainment' (Kiresuck, 1976). However, most therapeutic community leaders faced with such a real-life problem would modify both their ideals and practice to avoid conflict with a wider social obligation for control. Just as progressive schools were constrained by being *in loco parentis* from any excesses which might be construed as damaging their pupils (Punch, 1977), those communities acting 'in place of prison' or even within the prison system (Morris and Morris, 1963; Parker, 1971; Briggs, 1972), have to be suitably gymnastic to maintain a balance between their radical and conservative activities.

Thus, activities at Henderson Hospital occur in a tension between general values on the one hand, and specific normative prescriptions on the other. This tension may not be felt as much if values and norms are applied in different areas with little overlap. For example, a common model used by the psychiatrists is that in which community-living aspects of the hospital provide material for psychotherapy, which is subsequently worked through in small groups. Thus psychotherapy within a community setting is seen as a balanced approach between the general values of sociotherapy and a normative commitment to specialist psychotherapy. However, other staff (particularly nurses and social therapists) cannot so easily resolve these two aspects of working. Just as the psychiatrist values psychotherapy highly and sees him/herself as the main source of skill in this area, other staff also come to value psychotherapy in comparison with working in the community setting. But the psychiatrist can also value community-living because it provides material for psychotherapy and it does not occupy the major part of available working time. Other staff, on the contrary, spend much of their time in the community-living area while coveting psychotherapeutic work. Thus, although they work in an area theoretically central to the therapeutic community, they perceive it as of little real worth to the staff group, and hence undervalue their own work.

The consequence of this situation can take one of three forms. Staff members can fail to perceive this conflict, and become confused; or they can successfully perceive it and work with it, realizing the limits of their ability to be psychotherapists, and come to value work in the community-living area; or finally they can perceive it, but feel increasingly dissatisfied, and react by withdrawing at work, becoming cynical and finally leaving.

This disjunction between values and practice results in recurring tension within the staff group. This may or may not be detrimental to the work of the community depending on the individuals involved, but certainly affects the daily round of activities. In so far as normative beliefs have become centred on psychotherapeutic interpretation, therapeutic activities in the Henderson have moved in a similar direction (to be seen in the group ranking results), away from the ideal contained in staff values. Thus the hospital has adapted internally to its modern role of 'normal' psychiatric activity, with the attendant phenomena of status competition amid stability and skilled psychotherapy.

## PATTERNS OF REFERRAL

In this section, further comparative data are considered for the years 1953-5 and 1970-2. In order to find out how the Henderson fits in to the wider spectrum of psychiatry, an analysis of referral activity is undertaken and the major determinants of this patterning are outlined. The development of therapeutic communities analysed in previous chapters, and the concept of the Henderson as increasingly part of 'normal' psychiatry, gives rise to certain expectations about the external position of the hospital. Rosow's study of referrals in

1955 provides a useful set of data which can be compared with patterns in 1970–2. The change in patterns would clearly be expected in certain ways. We can expect that there would be:

1   A change in the referral pattern from a highly skewed 'experimental' distribution to a more diffuse and general pattern.
2   A drop in the proportion of referrals from 'advanced' (i.e. teaching) hospitals, and highly active individual doctors.
3   As the knowledge about the Henderson as a treatment centre spreads, the characteristics of referral sources should affect the referral rate more clearly. This will relate to the number of opportunities psychiatrists have to refer, rather than to whether they have knowledge of the new technique, as happened in 1955.
4   Greater selectivity in choosing patients, as the hospital comes to know which types respond best to the treatment techniques developed.

The concept of referral can be difficult to define precisely for analytical purposes. In 1955, Rosow defined a referral as

any application for a prospective patient's admission to the Unit. Such application may be formal (as in direct requests for admittance) or informal (as in enquiries about the suitability for treatment of a person whose history is often 'enclosed' or summarised). The application may come from various people (panel doctor, social workers, probation officer etc.), but typically comes from a psychiatrist who has seen the patient. (p. 1)

Furthermore, there may be a discrepancy between the official and the actual referrer of two kinds: 1) the formal application for admission is made by a person with principal responsibility for the case while the recommendation for treatment in the hospital is made by somebody else, such as junior doctor; or 2) the formal application is made by one person acting on behalf of another. The hospital staff, through their extensive experience, expressed confidence that this 'official–actual' discrepancy was small, and that where it occurred the 'formal' referrer invariably acknowledged the 'actual' referrer's suggestion. In these cases, the actual referrer was recorded.

The sample used was 100 per cent of referrals made to the Henderson Hospital during 1970, 1971 and 1972. This data were initially classified by: date; the response of the hospital to the referral (refusal, selection, admission, etc.); referring institution; and referring individual. From these basic categories further analysis continued according to the characteristics of each initial category (such as geographical location, type of institution, activity of individuals, etc.). Only first referrals were considered (re-admissions constituted less than 5 per cent of all referrals for both samples), and lack of information reduced the total sample by no more than 1 per cent in each case.

In 1953–5, 36 per cent of prospective patients were not admitted, by 1970–2 this had become 59 per cent despite the fact that average total referrals per annum had declined from 378 to 286. This confirms that there was greater selectivity in choosing patients. Of the 59 per cent not admitted, roughly one half were refused, and roughly one half cancelled either before the hospital made a decision, or after they had been accepted for admission — a similar proportion to that for 1953–5. Of course, given that almost twice the proportion of referrals were not admitted, and that the total number of annual referrals had declined by 25 per cent, the average number of patients admitted per annum had declined by 50 per cent (from 241 to 117). This number is not accounted for by any substantial change in the length of stay of the patient population, but a decline in the average size of that population (from around 80 in 1953–5 to 40 in 1970–2). The reasons for this decline are complex, for even though staff argued that the smaller average size was the most suitable, a restriction of patients admitted is likely to discourage referral agents, and lead to a reduction in referrals received in the long term, thus giving less choice for selection, and indeed resulting in a declining patient population if selectiveness remains the same. As was noted above, there was a steady decline in annual patient admissions in the eight years up to 1972. This may have been a result of a 'natural process' by which the community reached its most comfortable size. However, referrers may have choosen to look to other treatment possibilities if admission was difficult to obtain, and the effect of this, combined with the rapid growth in hostel accommodation elsewhere and the use of group therapy techniques in other organizations, may have been a more realistic explanation of the declining population.

## Institutional factors in referral

In the 1950s and the 1970s, the vast majority of referrals came from hospitals, a significant proportion of which were the London teaching hospitals. This was particularly noticeable in the 1950s, probably because new experimental techniques would be known earlier to such 'leading' hospitals. An immediately apparent fact from these referrals is that many hospitals refer a few cases each, and a few hospitals refer many cases. This is a distortion from the 'normal' situation where all hospitals refer more or less according to the patients passing through their hands. Such distortion may be caused by teaching-hospital 'leadership' effect, accessibility to the unit, whether the hospital is psychiatric or general, or the practice of individual doctors. That the distortion exists can be seen by constructing a Lorenz curve in which the cumulative percentage of hospitals is plotted against the cumulative percentage of referrals. If all the hospitals referred an equal number of referrals, the 'curve' would be a straight line rising from the point of origin at 45°. To the extent that they are not referring equal numbers, the curve is distorted away from the 45° line.

This distortion can be measured by means of the Gini coefficient of concentration (or the concentration ratio). The coefficient merely measures what proportion of the total area under the 45° line lies between that line and the Lorenz curve, defined by the formula:

$$G \text{ (Gini coefficient)} = 1 - \sum_{r=1}^{n} (x_r - x_{(r-1)}) (Y_r + Y_{(r-1)}).$$

The coefficient varies form 0 to 1, and the larger it is the more distorted is the referral pattern away from an equal distribution of referrals from each hospital.

The curve for 1970–2 was nearer to the 45° line than the curve for 1953–5, both for London and provincial hospitals. This confirms the expectation that the referral pattern would be less distorted. The Gini coefficient tells us precisely what the change in distortion is: 0.62 (1953–5) to 0.46 (1970–2) for the London hospitals, and 0.54 (1953–5) to 0.47 (1970–2) for the provincial hospitals. Thus the London hospitals moved from the most distorted referral pattern in 1953–5 to the least distorted in 1970–2. Indeed, the change in distortion was about twice as much for London hospitals (0.16) as for provincial hospitals (0.07). This change is further illustrated when we see that the percentage of hospitals referring more than 2 patients had gone *up* since 1953–5 (from 50 per cent to 60 per cent for London, 20 per cent to 27 per cent for the provinces), while the percentage referring ten or more had gone *down* (68 per cent to 37 per cent for London, 41 per cent to 28 per cent for the provinces). Thus there was a higher proportion of hospitals referring a moderate rate of 2 to 10 referrals in 1970–2.

One of the reasons for this is that most teaching hospitals are in London. These hospitals are more likely to take up a new idea early on and try it (in this case by making referrals) — thus distorting the pattern for 1953–5. Through the influence of these hospitals other London hospitals are likely to know of the unit more uniformly by 1970–2 than more distant, provincial hospitals, thus leading to a greater reduction in distortion in 1970–2 in London. A more detailed look indicates that the change in referral rate was dramatic. The average teaching hospital referral rate dropped from 20 (1953–5) to 7.7 (1970–2). In 1953–5 the teaching hospitals referred three-quarters as many referrals as the remaining London hospitals, and 38 per cent of all medical referrals in the London district. In 1970–2, these hospitals referred only one-quarter as many as the remaining London hospitals and only 18 per cent of all medical referrals in the London district.

Despite the more even spread of the referral pattern, and the decline in leadership effect of the teaching hospitals, the same high percentage of referrals came from London in 1970–2 (79 per cent) as in 1953–5. Obviously, since this ratio of referrals between London and the provinces reverses the overall population ratio, some intervening factors were in operation. The decline in teaching-hospital leadership effect eliminates one factor. Other possibilities are that there were more potential referring agencies *per capita* in London, or that there was a tendency for potential patients to drift to London. A more probable cause is the fact that the unit is reasonably accessible to most of London. This has become increasingly important since 1960, as from that date all potential patients had to come to the unit to attend a pre-admission selection group which discourages referrals from any distance. A separate factor is the responsibility of the unit since it became a hospital in 1960 to its regional hospital board to take patients from within their area, and only to take those from outside who are deemed of special interest. In fact this responsiblity does not have a large effect, since the staff are able to interpret their position liberally, although they sometimes used the restricted catchment area as an excuse to refuse undesirable patients from further away.

Overall, there does seem a greater rate of referral per institution for London than in 1953–5 which illustrates this tendency: the referral rate per hospital was 4.0 in 1953–5 and 4.9 in 1970–2, whereas it only changed from 2.6 to 2.7 for the provinces. That accessibility was not an exclusive influence is illustrated by the high rate of referral from St Luke's, Huddersfield (12 in 3 years). However, this activity was due entirely to one doctor. Indeed analysis of the characteristics of individual doctors, presented below, is as important as the analysis of institutional variables such as teaching/non-teaching, psychiatric/non-psychiatric, and size.

The next factor looked at is that of the size of the hospital. This would seem to be an obvious choice, for it is to be expected that a larger hospital will refer more often, since it has a greater chance of diagnosing suitable patients. However, this is not necessarily true, for some hospitals are more in the centre of new ideas and developments, and some have more active doctors. It is interesting that Rosow found in 1953–5 no relationship between hospital size and referral rate when he had controlled for the effect of teaching hospitals and doctors' activity. Since knowledge about the Henderson was still spreading in 1953–5 it must be assumed that many hospitals, although diagnosing plenty of suitable patients, did not know of the Henderson well enough to think of making referrals. Hence any effect of hospital size would be overshadowed by the delay in the spread of knowledge.

Nearly twenty years later, it could be expected that knowledge would have spread more completely, and hence the effect of hospital size, if there was one, would show. Moreover, the two 'contaminating' factors of teaching hospitals and active individuals should have less effect. The leadership effect of teaching hospitals was reduced as was indicated above; and there were fewer very active doctors referring, for whereas 34 per cent of medical referrals were from doctors referring ten or more patients in 1953–5, this proportion was only 11 per cent in 1970–2. In view of these changes one would expect any effect of size of the hospital on referral rate to show when *all* hospitals are considered as well as when teaching hospitals, and those with highly active individuals, are left out. This is indeed the case. Controlling for the contaminating factors, less than 50 per cent of large hospitals referred less than twice. This proportion was considerably more than 50 per cent for medium and small hospitals. Correspondingly, a higher proportion of hospitals referred three or more times amongst the larger hospitals.

A third institutional variable, as important as that of size, and teaching/non-teaching, is the specialization of the hospital. In this case psychiatric hospitals will be broadly compared to non-psychiatric hospitals. In 1953–5 28 per cent of medical referrals came from psychiatric centres. In 1970–2 this figure was 54 per cent, or almost twice the proportion. In 1953–5 there were fifty-seven psychiatric hospitals out of a total of 186 referring hospitals. In 1970–2 there were seventy-five out of a total of 140. It seems then that not only were more psychiatric hospitals referring, but that they had become the dominant category. This change may reflect two things: the change in focus of the unit onto young personality disorders (away from a general cateogry 'in need of social rehabilitation') which were more likely to be referred from a psychiatric centre; and the possibly greater preference of psychiatric hospitals for the Henderson treatment compared with non-psychiatric hospitals.

## Individual factors in referral

So far some of the institutional variables involved in referral have been considered. Doctors, too, varied in referral activity — some referring often, and most only occasionally.

For instance, Dr X was a highly active referrer, with thirteen referrals in 1970–2, but only two of those thirteen referrals were admitted as patients. As far as the unit was concerned, the other eleven referrals were of no use. Dr Y on the other hand referred ten people of whom eight were admitted during the same period. Since the Henderson is interested only in the patients it admits, Dr Y may be considered to have referred four times as many suitable patients as Dr X, even though his total referrals were less. The reasons for these diffcrences can only be explored in further research, but it may be that these two doctors refer for different reasons. Dr X could be suspected of 'dumping' unsuitable patients, whereas Dr Y appears only to refer people with a good chance of admission. The whole question of whether the Henderson was referred to more positively (because it offers special treatment) or negatively (because patients with personality disorders are a nuisance in general psychiatric hospitals, or prisons, etc.) is very interesting. Rosow collected information in 1957 on this subject which was followed up in 1975. For instance, in the group of doctors referring at a moderate rate in the 1950s, 56 per cent admitted to a willingness to dump difficult patients. This is perhaps expected, for a new unit willing to take traditionally difficult patients could solve problems for a harassed psychiatrist. In the 1970s, with a greater spread of knowledge about the Henderson, less dumping would be expected and a more positive referral pattern should be found. The small survey of referring doctors carried out in 1975 confirmed this expectation: only 24 per cent admitted to dumping difficult patients through referral to the Henderson (Manning, 1977).

The pattern of individual referrers can be represented by a Lorenz curve, as for the hospital referral pattern. The sample for 1970–2 was, as expected, less distorted than that for 1953–5. The Gini coefficient moved from 0.52 to 0.37, which is equivalent to the move in the coefficient for the London hospitals. In fact 0.37 is lower than any of the hospital Gini coefficients.

The largest category of referring doctors was of those working within psychiatric hospitals, who constituted 62 per cent of all referring doctors. If this category is divided geographically between those working in the London area and those working in the provinces, the distribution of referrals was somewhat different. For those working in London, $G = 0.39$, whereas for those working in the provinces, $G = 0.58$. This shows that the referral pattern of provincial hospital doctors was still quite distorted. It may be that 'provincial psychiatric hospital doctors' is the category which takes longest to assimilate newer techniques into its repertoire of everyday alternatives for patient referral.

That there was a more equal referral pattern was useful for the Henderson for in 1953–5 the hospital depended on fewer, and thus more vital, referral links. However, although knowledge about the therapeutic community treatment method had spread, fewer hospitals and fewer doctors referred in 1970–2 compared with 1953–5. Although it can be argued that the Henderson came to specialize in a specific type of patient, and thus received fewer referrals, this should mean fewer referrals *per hospital* rather than fewer hospitals referring altogether. What caused this decline?

Rosow analysed the marked differential referral activity of doctors in 1953–5 by establishing four categories of doctors: the 'casuals', the 'actives', the 'stars' and the 'supers'. These corresponded to an average annual referral rate of less than one, one to two, two or three, three or more. There was a reduction in the proportion of more active doctors, with supers and stars referring 50 per cent of the cases in 1953–5, but only 19 per cent in 1970–2.

The mobility of doctors with high referral rates had also declined since the 1950s: 'supers' serving an average of 2.46 institutions in 1953–5, 1.50 in 1970–2. Evidently supers had become less mobile. If one assumes that high mobility is the active coverage of several hospitals simultaneously, it seems the Henderson no longer got many referrals from these very mobile doctors. The latter may be the dynamic ones in the forefront of psychiatry who favoured the Henderson when community therapy first appeared, but no longer did so. Or pehaps these mobile doctors worked in understaffed areas which were no longer suffering from such shortage, and hence these doctors were generally less mobile.

Another likely reason for the decline in 'super' referrals, stemming from the general spread of knowledge about the Henderson, was the growth in the awareness of social relations and the use of groups in other agencies. From this point of view the function of the Henderson as a generator of knowledge and an inspiration to new outlooks may have resulted in more people being helped indirectly despite the falling numbers referred to and treated in the unit itself. The decline in 'supers' making referrals did not lead to an increasing heterogeneity in the patients referred, as Rosow feared, for at the same time more and more 'casuals' are getting better informed as to the appropriate patients to refer.

Finally, Rosow also looked specifically at Belmont Hospital as a referral agency for the Henderson (which was then the Belmont Social Rehabilitation Unit) and reported that it was by far the most active referrer (125 cases during 1953–5). This provides good evidence for characterizing the Henderson as being very much in an experimental stage at that time, with interested personnel referring large numbers of patients to get the unit off the ground. Even by the end of that research period (1955) the referral rate was dropping off from Belmont Hospital, indicating that support for the experimental unit was being withdrawn in favour of referrals being attracted independently from outside.

## Summary of referrals data

Earlier in this chapter, four expectations were set out about the changed place of the Henderson Hospital in the wider social system in which it is embedded. These were explored with data comparing referrals in 1953–5 and 1970–2. In all cases, the data supported the expectations:

1 Change in referral pattern from 'experimental' to general.
2 Fewer referrals from 'advanced' hospitals, and active individuals.
3 Institutional factors should take effect as knowledge of the Henderson spreads more uniformly.
4 Greater selectivity in choosing patients.

Overall, this chapter does indicate that the Henderson Hospital had become part of 'normal psychiatry'. Furthermore this recognition of 'normality' by the wider psychiatric world, was complemented by internal specialization and selection by the hospital in order to be maximally effective rather than experimental. Finally, there are indications that the hospital began to experience competition for referrals from other therapeutic communities which had drawn on its knowledge, and were now able to offer equivalent treatment facilities for patients and the equivalent style of work for interested staff.

# 5

# The therapeutic community in Australia

In this chapter, a number of themes will be taken up. The problems of conducting evaluative research on the therapeutic community will be reviewed. This will be followed by the presentation of some research results gathered through a design specifically set up to overcome these research problems. Since this particular piece of research was carried out in communities in non-medical community settings, but which nevertheless draw their inspiration from the 'democratic' strand of therapeutic community work, this is also an opportunity to review an area where these ideas have greatly prospered in recent years, in comparison with their relative marginalization within mainstream psychiatry. It is with an account of these communities that the chapter begins.

## THE THERAPEUTIC COMMUNITY IN THE COMMUNITY

In chapter 1 it was argued that the therapeutic community developed in part as a reaction to practices originating in the nineteenth century. During the nineteenth century, mentally disordered people in industrial societies were likely to be detained in public asylums. In the early part of the century the policy was based on the assumption that the strains and stresses of an increasingly urban and industrial way of life precipitated mental breakdown. However in subsequent decades the rural retreat which such asylums provided metamorphosed into overcrowded human warehouses for a variety of cases distinguished less by a particular medical disorder, than by a common failure to survive in a world of wage labour and factory discipline. The gap which such overcrowding generated between principle and practice stimulated a stream of criticism from the 1870s onwards, suggesting not merely that medical treatments were ineffective but that the effects of asylum life on inmates might be as, if not more, damaging than life outside.

While the therapeutic community offered radical change within the old asylums, the 'literature of protest' (Jones, 1975:290) culminated in the mid-twentieth century in a new policy for mentally disordered people, namely community care. To be fair this policy change has also been linked with new medical developments such as drug therapy and 'social' psychiatry, and with changing mechanisms of social control and economic priorities (Scull, 1977). Initial enthusiasm for this approach, in principle, peaked in the USA and UK in the 1960s, and somewhat later in other countries, for example the late 1970s in Italy and Australia. However in practice, despite declining bed numbers in the old asylums, little in the way of new community services appeared, resulting in a dispersal of such cases rather than their care: to prisons, board and lodging houses, or for some the final ignominy of street life in the full sense of the term.

However, relative neglect by state agencies has in recent years been offset by growing efforts within the voluntary social services sector to develop community services for this group of clients in two ways: not only to replace the residential function of the old asylums, but to develop new technologies to enhance the potential functioning of mentally disordered people drawing on social psychiatric innovations. And this effort has in turn now drawn an official if belated response by some governments in the 1980s to develop a working partnership with the voluntary sector in order to match the emptying of mental hospitals with the development of community services. One such voluntary sector effort, the Richmond Fellowship, and its relationship to government policy is examined in this chapter. The Richmond Fellowship itself should be related to three significant contexts: community care, the voluntary sector, and the use of therapeutic community principles.

## Community care

This term is used to cover a wide variety of policies and activities. A common distinction is to separate care by, for and in the community (Walker, 1982). Care by the community means care in everyday settings by ordinary, lay individuals. Overwhelmingly these carers are kin, and mostly female kin, rather than more general community members such as friends and neighbours. Care for the community has been used to identify policies which aid or hinder the capacity for such care by the community. However by far the most general use of the term community care is in the third sense of care in the community. This normally comprises statutory or voluntary provision of non-institutional services such as day centres, small-scale residential provision and domestic support.

Recent work has identified the burden that care by the community places on women in particular, and the extent to which care in the community can and should relieve this burden through the better financing and planning of community services (Finch and Groves, 1983). Indeed there is clearly a critical boundary between these two forms of community care, since informal carers find themselves having to expand or contract their efforts to meet those needs not covered by local community services. A second critical boundary, more commonly the subject of debate, divides community care from residential care of a more institutional kind such as the traditional mental hospital. And it is the movement across this boundary which has been the dominant theme in mental health policy in recent years. Governments have been more enthusiastic about crossing this latter boundary than worrying about what happens on the other side of it, particularly the extent to which clients have overshot and landed on the other side of both boundaries, with no support of any kind.

If there is a case for holding clients somewhere between institutional care, and care by the community, as recent policy pronouncements in Britain (Social Services Committee, 1985) and Australia (Richmond Inquiry, 1983) suggest, the question arises as to the nature of this community provision. Good community residential care has been advocated as both a relief to informal carers (Finch, 1984), and as a positive alternative to the vicissitudes of institutional life. Yet this begs the question of what good community residential care entails. While there has been an explosion of literature in recent years about residential care, and the planning of such services (see for example the Tavistock Residential Social Work series), there are still few coherent philosophies which provide a clear guide to practice. One of these, the therapeutic community, has been adopted by the Richmond Fellowship.

## The voluntary sector

The voluntary sector is an essential complement to state social services. It, like the term community care, is used to mean a variety of services, from small neighbourhood associations of unpaid volunteers to highly professional national organizations with many paid staff and substantial funds. While this sector can be differentiated from private welfare organizations by the criterion of the profit motive, there is a great deal of overlap with state activities in so far as many such organizations depend heavily on state finance, and may be quite closely regulated by statutory requirements. Indeed, particularly in countries like the USA and Australia they are explicitly used by government departments as quasi-state agencies. We can indicate something of the size and variation of the voluntary sector by comparing some general data for the USA, UK and Australia (table 5.1). While the figures available cannot be precise due to the difficulty of identifying the boundaries of the voluntary sector, it is clear both that the voluntary sector effort is substantial, and moreover that it is particularly important in the context of the relatively residual welfare states of the USA and Australia. Allowing for the small population of Australia, its voluntary sector is comparatively the most important in terms of numbers of organizations, income, volunteers and paid staff.

*Table 5.1* The voluntary sector in USA, UK and Australia: some general data

|  | Approx. population (millions) | Voluntary organizations (thousands) | Income (millions) | Unpaid volunteers (millions) | Paid staff (thousands) |
|---|---|---|---|---|---|
| USA | 230 | National welfare associations 37 | $48,000 | 37 | — |
|  |  | Voluntary associations 6,000 |  |  |  |
| UK | 55 | Registered charities 133 | £1,000 | 5 | 15–20 |
|  |  | Voluntary organizations 200 |  |  |  |
| Australia | 15 | Non-governmental welfare organizations 26–49 | $5,000 | 0.5–1.7 | 660–800 |

*Sources*: USA: Kramer (1981); UK: Hinton & Hyde (1982), Wolfenden (1978); Australia: Graycar (1984)

Although the voluntary sector is, along with state social services, an object of public concern about quality, the key issue involves the vexed question of costs and finance. The Wolfenden Committee (1978)

study of British voluntary organizations confirmed the widespread assumption that voluntary organizations can be cheaper *pro-rata* than statutory services. Further research in this area clearly indicated this cost advantage, but found that it was almost entirely a result of 'greater commitment that a voluntary organisation can in some circumstances elicit from its staff, and their consequent willingness to work harder and/or for less money' (Hatch and Mocroft, 1979:404). For many voluntary organizations including the Richmond Fellowship there is considerable tension in the practical job of accomplishing sufficient commitment in staff/volunteers to offset the relatively reduced financial rewards available. Indeed the recently celebrated problem of staff burnout (Cherniss, 1980) in human service agencies indicates one unpleasant side effect of what Coser (1974) has characterized as 'greedy' institutions.

It is unlikely therefore that such income deficiencies are designed, and we might more reasonably look to three factors particularly associated with the USA and Australia which exacerbate this situation. First, the opportunity for voluntary organizations to raise further income from voluntary donations or fundraising is limited by the relative inelasticity of supply of such funds and keen competition over their distribution. Second, the capricious and slender nature of government funding to the voluntary sector. Third, the federal structure of government leads to demarcation disputes between different departments, such that many organizations find themselves falling between the priorities of central and state level finance. In Australia, for example, funds for community care of the mentally ill can come from social security (central government) and/or health services (state government), with no clear co-ordination between these levels. The significance of precarious funding for the Richmond Fellowship is discussed below.

### The Richmond Fellowship therapeutic communities

This voluntary organization was established by Elly Jansen as a result of her own attempt to give shelter to ex-mental patients as a social work student in 1959. Since then it has grown into a large international organization running more than seventy halfway houses in the UK, USA, Australia, New Zealand, Austria and other countries. It has thus made a major voluntary-sector contribution to the provision of community care for the mentally ill. An account of its work can be found in Jansen (1980).

Each house is organized in an autonomous manner within the general principles of therapeutic community work. In England staff move between houses as their expertise and experience develop, and many have been involved in the establishment of houses in other countries, operating as 'culture carriers'.

Jansen records that in the early days there was no clear idea of how each house should work, her intent being the more practical one of providing some kind of community residential facility in the spirit of the 1959 Mental Health Act, which stressed the idea of community care. She recalls two general problems. The first was that of gaining legitimacy from her most likely source of funding under the 1959 Act, the local authorities. This is a common and ironic problem for therapeutic communities which both reject (at least in part) 'conventional' society, yet necessarily require external support. The second problem was that of formulating a *modus vivendi* for the internal affairs of the house. Beginning with an ideal of a staffless, totally egalitarian community, she quickly came to see herself as having different motives to those of ex-psychiatric patients. She recalls that she recognized that she was a provider for others' needs, that she had 'final responsibility', and that she 'had to exercise leadership'. Within months, members of the house had come to agree on their common task as promoting interpersonal understanding, good relationships, social and work skills, so that members worked 'towards the eventual independence of each member and his reintegration into society' (Jansen, 1980:381).

At some point during the 1960s, weekly group meetings were begun, although even as late as 1967 Jansen acknowledges that staff were ambivalent about such ideas, deferring to more professionally trained social workers in the areas of residents' emotional and relationship difficulties. Not until the 1970s did the Richmond Fellowship fully embrace therapeutic community principles, although Jansen is careful to repeat that she has drawn on a variety of sources for ideas, in an explicitly eclectic mixture. Indeed her account is notable in this respect, for it devotes a great part of its analysis to an exercise in comparative distancing from other well-known innovations in the field, such as 'concept' houses for drug abusers, and existential experiments like Laing's Kingsley Hall.

In common with other practitioners' accounts (such as Jones's work discussed in chapter 4), Jansen describes her work in terms of thematic description and prescription. Experience, principles and events are mixed into an account in which certain practices are said to 'have a place' or be 'required' (p. 34), others are 'offered' or are 'found necessary' (p. 33). On the whole, psychological and psychiatric ideas predominate, not merely in what is probably her most explicit statement that 'The Richmond Fellowship, whilst eclectic in approach, bases its view of individual development mainly on Freudian and post-Freudian theory' (p. 26); but also in the scattered use of ideas from Maxwell Jones (1952), Rapoport (1960), Bion (1961), Schwartz (1957), Guindon (1959), and Laing (1967).

With respect to the therapeutic community, Jansen draws heavily on the Maxwell Jones and Tom Main tradition discussed in chapter 1, and in particular on the four famous ideological themes identified by Rapoport. In terms of the tension which Rapoport identified between treatment and rehabilitation, however, Jansen's model lays clear stress on the latter, for although personal change in individual residents is desired, this is clearly and continuously related to the readjustment of residents to independence in the wider society. This is most noticeable with respect to the Richmond Fellowship's house rule that residents should find work, or purposeful activity, outside the house during the day.

It seems, then, that the Richmond Fellowship is running a set of houses which look relatively familiar within the tradition already outlined in earlier chapters. Perhaps the most notable difference is not so much within the houses, but outside them. It is most unusual for a whole set (seventy or more) of communities to be set up in this way, given the experience of previous therapeutic communities as precarious survivors, heavily dependent on individual charismatic leadership. The Richmond Fellowship is an interesting example of the successful institutionalization and routinization of such innovatory charisma. This has been achieved through the development of a 'college' in which staff can be trained, and by moving staff between houses to provide some kind of career, and the refreshment of new environments to counteract staff 'burnout'. However, it is interesting to note that the kind of organization problems which inevitably arise in such an enterprise, over resource allocation, power distribution, and so on, are emphatically not handled in the democratic style apparently endorsed by Jansen at the beginning in 1959, and supposedly one of the key elements of therapeutic community practice. Rather, Jansen has chosen to adopt a model of central control, justified by the use of some imagery adopted from Kleinian object-relations theory:

Staff members have a tendency to abdicate responsibility, to lose sight of financial realities, and to become antagonistic about restrictions in spending. The problems with which the staff in the houses have to cope are often such that they in turn wish to act out, and attach their feelings to inappropriate issues, especially in relation to the parent body. This then appears to be a depriving object, withholding material and emotional food and failing to protect staff. . . . In estranging the parent body (i.e. the very people who are most needed to give support), alternative support is looked for, at times in the form of the psychiatric consultant or the local house committee, who are invited to support the house director and if possible are split off. Because of their proximity to the house and their desire to assist, or at times take over, the psychiatrist or the committee can easily collude, unwittingly supporting irrational demands, and increase the tension. (pp. 384–5)

While this may be an adequate account of the emotions generated in such conflict, Jansen does not acknowledge the point made in research arising out of the Wolfenden Committee (1978) report on the British voluntary sector (mentioned earlier in this chapter), and also clearly evident in the Australian data, that as employers, the voluntary sector including the Richmond Fellowship relies on paying low wages to young enthusiastic staff.

A further doubt about the adequacy of Jansen's organizational account arises ironically in connection with the interface between her own organization, and government policies and finance. Nowhere in a lengthy introduction of seventy pages to the third part of her book does she apply object-relations theory to her own strident demands for 'material and emotional food' (i.e. money) from her own 'depriving object' (i.e. the government). No doubt a government concerned with containing public expenditure would regard her own requests for the money necessary for adequate community care as an 'irrational demand', but she doesn't see it this way!

Jansen's commitment to pragmatic rehabilitation for individual residents, and her exercise of central control, however necessary in the real world of late twentieth-century industrial society, raise questions about the Richmond Fellowship's use of the therapeutic community as developed in the Jones/Rapoport tradition. These questions can best be explored (as was the case for the Belmont unit), by turning away from the practitioner's own account to more sociologically informed studies.

## SOME SOCIOLOGICAL ACCOUNTS OF THE RICHMOND FELLOWSHIP

In this section three independent pieces of sociological work carried out on Richmond Fellowship houses will be used to construct a more critical account of the Fellowship's work. The first is Sharp's (1975) study in detail of what was considered at the time to be the leading house, both as an ideal model of the therapeutic community in action, and as a training setting for new staff. Sharp's approach is reminiscent of Rapoport's (1960) study of Belmont, in the sense of an extended participant observation of the community in action, from which a general anthropological description of the ideology, social structure, and changing rhythms of the community is built up. Indeed Sharp makes explicit use of Rapoport's study in many places, particularly his observations about ideological themes and contradictions, sub-grouping and oscillations in tension in the community, and the underlying tension between treatment and rehabilitation.

However, in many respects Sharp's approach is quite distinct. He provides in greater detail than Rapoport an analysis of the conversational exchanges involved in the staff's day-to-day work, and an analysis of the way that individual residents react to the 'assault on self' that being in a therapeutic community entails. In terms of the latter he gives a great deal of emphasis to the residents' experience, drawing on some of Goffman's ideas (discussed in chapter 1) about mental patients' reactions to mental hospital life, and in particular tracing the way that three sub-groups, the 'dissidents', the 'conformists', and the 'elite', formed as collective resident responses to the demands of community life.

Despite Sharp's commitment to a residents' perspective in his study, he reserves his strongest contribution for a discussion of staff practices. The original therapeutic community problem was identified by Rapoport as the tension between treatment and rehabilitation, which he suggested could not fruitfully be merged; this is taken by Sharp as a research topic: how are they fused, and what do staff have to do to maintain the fusion? In Sharp's terminology, how do staff ensure that residents both 'self-actualise' and 'self-adjust', or how do staff provide both care and control?

Sharp suggests that typically in his community, care and control are fused in the process of reality construction, whereby staff build 'case-pictures' of residents and community processes in psychodynamic terms. Borrowing Berger and Luckmann's (1967) discussion of the way in which any consistent symbolic universe of

143

meaning is created, Sharp suggests that staff work up a definition of the situation in which individuals (especially newcomers) and events are transformed into psychodynamic terms, while alternative interpretations are either rejected as bad, or more extremely 'nihilated' as illegitimate conceptions. When successful, this strategy leads to control because residents agree to perceive the world from the staff's point of view. Troublesome events or individuals can then be analysed in terms of individual pathology. From this point of view, the much celebrated democracy of therapeutic communities is of a distinctly patronizing kind — residents can exercise power as long as they do it in ways congruent with the staff's ideology.

The fragility of this system in therapeutic communities is legion, resulting in periodic tensions and crises. Indeed such oscillations are seen as part of the rich life experience that residents are offered. However, such crises threaten to expose the care-control fusion. In a subsequent article Sharp (1977) focuses on the way the resident sub-groups generated a crisis which threatened to undermine the legitimacy of the staff ideology. He notes that when this happens the control part of the care-control fusion comes to the fore, which he traces in the use of managerial concepts in staff language, and the reversal of their previous judgements about the nature of individuals and sub-groups:

> What appeared to be of particular significance at this time, from the research angle, was the staff's utilisation of managerial concepts. . . . While managerial concepts could, and did, change in the case-pictures of certain individuals, whatever the 'state of the organisation', there occurred here a fairly large scale reversal in their usage. Thus, members of the hitherto 'lively', 'contributive', and 'constructive' elite sub-group were now perceived of as 'destructively acting-out', 'manipulative', 'irresponsible' and 'shitty'. The conformists, on the other hand, became 'mature', 'responsible', and were 'not in need of norms'. (p. 238)

For Sharp, then, social control is the bedrock upon which the Richmond Fellowship therapeutic community is built. Any pretensions of democracy, and the caring, self-actualizing elements of staff work, depend crucially on burying social control, ideally inside each resident or between residents, as self or community control:

> Staff as carers, are carriers of an egalitarian ideology. At the same

time, however, they act as agents of control, as functionaries in an agency with adjustive ends, whose concern is with the resocialisation of members for a non-egalitarian society which is geared to the efficient functioning of individuals in the work-force and reproductive systems. (p. 240)

This conclusion has been contested recently by Bloor (1986) on the basis of a comparative study of two Richmond Fellowship houses, as part of a wider comparative ethnography of therapeutic communities. This second piece of sociological work on the Richmond Fellowship was carried out about ten years later than Sharp's, but used a similar approach (participant observation) and theoretical line (Berger and Luckmann, 1967; Schutz, 1964). Bloor locates the issue of social control in a wider recent literature on the effects of general health care as control, and argues that the therapeutic community may be seen as a test case, since it espouses as a central idea the democratic empowerment of the patient. If health care, free of social control, is to be found anywhere, it should be found here.

Bloor suggests that therapeutic communities provide not merely a different treatment, but a new social world, a new way of seeing social life, and a new felt social identity. This process, which he terms 'reality construction' (Bloor and Fonkert, 1982), involves imbibing a series of particular accounts of community social structure, of therapy, and of residents' difficulties, for, he argues:

A crucial aspect of the new subjective reality of the therapeutic community is the vocabulary of its expression. Indeed, the newly learned vocabulary of motives, feeling states, and descriptions *constitutes* that subjective reality, since only thought is conceptual, that is verbal. (Bloor, 1988:72, typescript)

Such reality construction, Bloor claims however, is not to be understood as merely social control although of course it can be, and perhaps often is. He disagrees with Sharp, for whom the staff's work is entirely suffused with social control, by giving examples of occasions in which the staff either deliberately abstained from interventions in troublesome events (e.g. when a resident takes an overdose — other residents are left to cope with the emergency), or feigned certain kinds of reaction (e.g. being over-authoritarian) in order, as he puts it, to 'orchestrate' certain kinds of resident actions

145

(e.g. helping suicidal members, or coping with authority). Bloor senses that this could be construed as a rather weak case on two grounds: that orchestration is merely delayed social control — tolerable as long as residents exhibit the 'right kind' of autonomy; and that in a crisis orchestration may be rapidly suspended. However, he argues that any demonstration of the absence of social control is sufficient to make the case for separating care and control in principle.

It seems, nevertheless, that this is a very weak case. Orchestration is patently little more than deferred control, in the same way that Sharp observed that 'constructive' behaviour in the residents he studied could earn considerable autonomy. Moreover, it is surely crucial that orchestration is only defined by Bloor in terms of the absence of social control. It is an entirely parasitical concept through which no different class of actions or functions is elucidated.

The most notable contribution of the part of Bloor's study which is devoted to the Richmond Fellowship, then, is how similar, ten years on, on his own admission, are the processes he observes to those in Sharp's book. The Fellowship had clearly established by the early 1970s a stable and reproducible regime, just as we noted in chapter 4 that the Henderson had done.

The third sociological study of the Richmond Fellowship also examines the issues of control, ideology, and personal change, but in a comparative study of 'intentional communities' (Shenker, 1986). Shenker sets out to examine what the conditions are which make for the successful survival of networks of communities, comparing the Hutterities, Kibbutzim and the Richmond Fellowship. His approach is functionalist, in the sense that the objectivity and structure of the communities are taken to be the reality he analyses, independent of particular actors' views. He therefore is concerned with the problem of order in a social system, which must accommodate the realities of both external system inputs, and the satisfactory management of the internal life of social individuals in the communities. This is a very different theoretical project to the ethnography of Sharp and Bloor, both of whom explicitly adopt a phenomenological approach to social reality in which an individual's perceptions (especially a low status individual) are privileged as the key to the social reality under study. In this sense Shenker's study is sociologically old-fashioned.

However, Shenker's approach highlights familiar issues. In his terms, a successful community has to resolve the problem of providing individual members with a satisfactory source of identity not merely in material terms, but crucially via an effective ideology which sustains commitment and deals with externally generated change and with internal developments, non-conformity and social control. Sharp's study highlighted the staff's crucial position in this process, whereby these system requirements (in Shenker's terminology) were combined in the act of staff interpretive interventions. Control was a continuous requirement. Bloor's objection that control can be deferred on occasions, nevertheless adopts Sharp's working presumption that continuous control is necessary. Shenker's approach however is more thorough, in the sense that he begins with the question of how much control is necessary for any social individual.

Displaying a slightly disorienting eclecticism, Shenker begins with a consideration of identity and alienation as essential bases for considering the way in which communities can create and sustain satisfactory conditions for the social life of individuals, and the role of ideology in this process. His answer is that individuals will remain committed to a community to the extent that they positively value the way of life, and general aims of a community, and that they thereby obviate the need for social control. While newcomers will inevitably provoke greater or lesser control activities from the established community, Shenker implies that routinized community membership will necessarily be largely self-policing in a successful community. Hence the common expression in therapeutic communities about residents 'getting into the group', or 'getting into the community'. The issue then is not as Bloor suggests that of whether staff can momentarily relinquish control in favour of orchestration, but that of bringing new residents to the point at which they voluntarily choose to base their identities on the prevailing community ideology ('gaining insight', in psychodynamic terminology):

> Ultimately (in terms of his life in the community) he will, if he has achieved such awareness and the basic 'tools' of maintaining it, have made this necessary breakthrough. It is this breakthrough that the community aims at. (p. 100)

Once this situation develops, Shenker argues, minor rule-breaking is not only not a threat to community life, but has the positive function of both allowing individual self-assertion and demarcating the position of such rules. In other words detailed control, in the sense of Foucault's 'medical gaze', implied in Sharp's formulation, is simply unnecessary.

We can now return to Rapoport's original problem of the balance between treatment and rehabilitation, which Jansen herself seemed to have resolved in favour of the latter, and which Sharp suggested makes social control the central dynamic in Richmond Fellowship communities. Shenker's analysis provides a basis for accepting the early Belmont slogan that 'all treatment is rehabilitation'. For Shenker, living in society, as living in a community, entails compromise and balance. The individual 'self-actualizes' through society, not in isolation. Sharp's contention that the Richmond Fellowship is readjusting individuals for an inegalitarian society assumes that somehow individuals could in principle exist outside of society. Shenker's position makes this both a theoretical and empirical impossibility.

## EVALUATING THE SUCCESS OF THE RICHMOND FELLOWSHIP

Shenker's starting point, the successful survival of communities, raises the issue of success for therapeutic community work. In chapter 6 we will argue that therapeutic communities have been fairly hostile to evaluative research, as a consequence of which their ideas have not been as influential as they might otherwise have been. Part of the difficulty has been that traditional research designs do not fit therapeutic community activities very well. Evaluative research has been traditionally associated with the medical field. Similar work within psychology and criminology has also been developed, but often with the use of medical models, or modification of them. The experimental drug-trial epitomizes this approach to evaluation. However a growing body of literature in the late 1960s and 1970s has taken issue with many aspects of this model, as evidence accumulates to show its inadequacy when used to look at complex behavioural phenomena. This literature has appeared mainly in the fields of criminology, psychotherapy, and to a lesser extent social action programmes.

Much of the discussion revolves around the fact that previously accepted models and methods of research have not resulted in the answers sought in relation to the effect of a wide variety of change-induction techniques. This result has directed the discussion into two areas: (a) Is the question being asked in the right way, and indeed is it answerable at all? and (b) If the question is appropriate, what ways can the techniques be improved in seeking the answer? These two questions reveal contrasting approaches within this general area, and by means of a consideration of these, some problems of relevance to evaluating therapeutic communities can be tackled.

148

Perhaps one of the most general concerns has been the question of the relationship between outcome studies and studies of process. Much previous work can be classified as either one or the other. But Wilkins (1964), Clarke and Sinclair (1973), Clarke and Cornish (1972), Paul (1967), Bergin (1978) and Bottoms and McClintock (1973) have all pointed out that this opposition of outcome and process studies is misguided. Clarke and Cornish argued strongly against 'spot the winner' studies, but found that on considering the processes that might affect outcome they were unable to isolate any clear causal factors. The dilemma is that unless the change-inducing techniques can be described in sufficient detail to reproduce them, then the knowledge that some unknown thing is effective is not very useful. On the other hand taking 'flight into process' (Zubin, 1964) will not answer the question of whether this technique works or not in the hands of a sample of therapists. Thus, Paul argues for a balance between process studies and a complementary assessment of outcome if real evaluation is to be achieved.

The dichotomy between outcome and process studies has arisen through the problem of the way in which questions of evaluation are posed. Wilkins, Clarke and Sinclair, Paul and Bergin have stressed very forcibly that the single question 'Does X work?' is meaningless, unless divided into a series of smaller, more specific questions which can be looked at in turn. Paul restates the question as: '*What* treatment, by *whom,* is the most effective for *this* individual with *that* specific problem, under *which* set of circumstances?' (p. 111). Similarly, Bergin argues for specific interventions for specific problems with specific outcomes. Thus what may be improvement for one patient (relief from depression) may not be for another. In the same way, Wilkins prefers a step by step 'panzer' strategy to a 'mass attack'; and Clarke and Sinclair argue that for studying ongoing systems, small-scale studies are needed, focused on particular aspects, instead of 'monolithic' projects of the form 'Does treatment X work better than treatment Y?' They advise the avoidance of more formal evaluative designs.

As a first step to evaluation, we can look at research in similar fields for ideas. Psychotherapy and criminology have flourishing traditions of evaluative research. The former has developed a whole battery of intra-psychic and behavioural measures of outcome over the years. The latter has advanced the technique for predictive analysis, and struggled with the problem of institutional evaluation. These fields have tended to use psychology on the one hand, and sociology on the other. Neither has integrated these disciplines adequately but rather the current practice of sociologists is to standardise by matching persons on psychological factors, and of psychologists to standardise by matching on sociological factors, and thus to try to avoid considering explanations of their observations which derive from the other's field of theory. (Wilkins, 1964:282).

The therapeutic community falls between these two fields. Situated in the field of psychiatry, it uses both psychological and sociological ideas. Its psychotherapy is connected with institutional processes in common more with penal measures (such as approved schools, or borstals), than classic psychotherapy. On the other hand it assumes more explicitly than such penal measures that the individual manifests some definitive pathological state which, if corrected, will lead to behavioural change. However, criminologists and psychotherapists would agree with Kurt Lewin that behaviour is a function of both personality and social environment. Indeed the split between one dealing with personality disorders, and the other dealing with environmental disorders (such as subcultural, or ecological theories), is rapidly giving way to the view on both sides that physical–social life environments interact with social–personal characteristics to produce behaviour (Paul, 1967), and that pre-institutional behaviour and problems, attitudes and behaviour in the institution, and post-institutional conduct interact together and with the varying environment in complex ways (Bottoms and McClintock, 1973). This means that, for example, follow-up should ideally entail a detailed study of the environment in which the subject is living, for this will affect the schizophrenic's chances of relapse (Leff, 1973), or the probationer's outcome (Davies, 1969).

In both these fields, both experimental and non-experimental designs have been used. However not all experimental designs work out, as Clarke and Cornish (1972) found to their cost. Despite perfect conditions for randomization between a therapeutic community and a traditional house in an approved school, they found that the effects could have been explained by several factors other than the orientation to therapy. They argue that the controlled trial in institutional research is therefore not feasible. However, what they have done is to mistakenly consider a whole approach (the therapeutic community) as a single variable. This is the real reason for their failure. A radical approach is not a unitary dimension, and hence 'spot the winner' research explains little. Thus Bergin (1978) showed, for example, how evidence now points to the fact that an increase in the variance, rather than the mean, of outcome scores is more common in psychotherapy, since some patients get very much better but some also get worse.

Comparing whole institutions, then, is not very helpful when they are multi-dimensional. Rather each constituent dimension must be considered, and then experimental methods would be more useful. Until this degree of precision is possible, non-experimental designs can be used. In this case, systematic manipulation of independent variables is often not feasible. The only possibility is to exploit natural variations in the subject matter. Hence instead of experimentally comparing just two institutions, it is necessary to look at several and use their natural differences to explore relationships. Such a 'cross-institutional design' (Clarke and Sinclair, 1973; Rossi, 1978) may involve the use of prediction methods to standardize the relative risks distributed in the populations of each institution, so that differences between predicted and observed outcomes will indicate the relative effectiveness of different institutions. Needless to say, such a design requires complementary process anlysis to explain the possible causes of differential effectiveness.

Experimental designs are thus only appropriate when a single dimension can be isolated and manipulated. To the extent that multi–dimensional studies are undertaken (as with the therapeutic community), a cross-institutional approach, together with a breaking down of the complexity of each case, must be used. Bergin (1978) dismisses the 'Bugaboo of complexity' whereby a process is claimed to be violated if reduced to its component parts, by pointing out that any understanding requires simplification, and then re-combination (as in the workings of a computer, for example).

Guttentag (1971) and Rossi (1979) note that this kind of evaluation research is qualitatively different from basic research: the subject matter is predefined; control over variables is small; a programme rather than a variable is studied; judgements of worthwhileness are involved; it is assumed that treatment effects overcome the cumulative effects of other variables; the relationship between inputs and effects is predefined; and inputs and outputs are fixed. In short, the researcher must accept the goals of the institution as the evaluative guide. These goals, derived from both stated and covert aims, will lead to the relevant criteria. For the therapeutic community, these goals are manifold, and hence alternative criteria are available. For example it seems that staff dissatisfaction may be higher in the permissive atmosphere of a therapeutic community. There is also some agreement that therapeutic communities are exhausting for their leaders

151

and indeed have resulted in the breakdown of those in such positions. Should such criteria be used to evaluate such an institution? To the extent that a method is relatively new and one is trying to establish its validity, criteria most relevant will be those which set the method in a favourable light compared with other established techniques. Whether increased therapeutic gains are made at the expense of staff well-being and whether these two should be balanced are very different questions. The first may be fairly answered with research. The second depends on more political considerations.

Moreover the ranking of aims may well vary over time. As we have seen, in the early 1950s Henderson Hospital was best known as an experimental therapeutic community. This goal was of sufficient importance to justify the existence of the unit, whether great therapeutic gains were made or not. With the passage of time, the spread of new organizational concepts, and changing trends within the mental health services, the goal of experiment recedes in importance while the need to prove that the hospital does produce therapeutic gains, and for types of patients not adequately dealt with elsewhere, becomes a more urgent objective.

Suchman (1967) has differentiated five areas in which evaluative data can be collected: effort, performance, adequacy, efficiency, profit. Obviously a combination of the aims of the research, and the programme, determine which areas are examined. In general, studies have concerned themselves with the last factor of profit — is the outcome (or therapeutic gain) being attained. Therapeutic communities would certainly vary on these five areas. Many make considerable efforts, but the level of performance varies widely. Moreover the adequacy is also variable. For example, Henderson Hospital deals with a narrow range of patients, and is thus inadequate as a general source of treatment. Other units are more open. Finally efficiency is often directly balanced against profit in the therapeutic community. A popular image is that where there is disorganization and inefficiency then sociotherapy can happen, but where there is quiet efficiency in a well-run unit, the organizational goals have taken precedence over therapeutic goals and there will be little therapeutic profit, and may even be loss (e.g. institutional neurosis (Barton, 1959)).

However, to the extent that outcome is an essential goal to evaluate, appropriate criteria are hotly disputed. Bergin (1978) presents a useful list of outcome criteria available to psychotherapy. Generally measures may be divided into internal (intrapsychic) or external (behavioural). The latter are easier to measure (and favoured by criminologists), though relative importance is debatable. Paul (1967), for example, argues that ultimately we are interested in changing behaviour — the way a person relates to the social environment — and that it is here that a therapeutic success or failure should be decided. Truax and Carkuff (1967), however, point out that the initial level of behavioural disturbance is generally negatively related to outcome, while the initial level of inner disturbance is generally positively related to outcome. This would seem to militate against the treatment of behavioural disturbance. On the other hand Brooks (1972) argued passionately against the idea of 'adjustment' as a primary objective; it is merely a beneficial, though unintended, pay-off from helping delinquent boys to: develop their potential; become better organized persons; find an authentic self; mature; gain insight; experience self-actualization; and so on.

In a sense this debate is between those who look on the creative side of the human personality as a potential for growth, and those who are more concerned with adjusting unacceptable (both to the patient and his environment) behaviour. In fact many studies combine both aspects; however, this combination is often rather a blanket coverage of all possible indices. Clarke and Sinclair (1972) have therefore argued that intermediate criteria should be used so that outcome may be measured longitudinally during the career of the subject, rather than at one point of time, such as is usually done in follow-up studies. They mention two possible criteria which would give an indication of a subject's progress before it became swamped with post-treatment influences: absconding (drop out from voluntary therapeutic communities); and 'treatment potential' — a measure of popularity amongst both peers and staff, related to outcome.

It seems then that studies of the *careers* of patients from pre-treatment, through treatment, to post-treatment, with sustained attention at each stage, may be essential to a better understanding of the place of treatment and the chance of effectiveness in such a career where other influences will be working before and after treatment.

The choice between experimental and non-experimental designs often involves the practicalities of comparative methodologies. In the Clarke and Cornish (1972) study the opportunity for randomization of input was available though not of input of staff, which Fairweather (1964) had achieved — this may be crucial in the light of Clarke and Cornish's finding that staff group variables may have been more powerful than treatment orientation effects.

When this is not the case, comparison requires some method of controlling for differential inputs to the treatment situation. Wilkins (1964) severely criticizes *ex post facto* matching, for without randomization any statistical inference is impossible. He prefers, in this situation of looking for a control group for an ongoing unalterable experimental group, to use prediction or regression matching. Here the multiple correlation between independent (usually pre-treatment) and dependent variables (outcome criteria) enable the two groups to be matched by their regression weights. In other words the pre-treatment distribution of risks of success or failure may be matched up, or differences compensated for. Then the relation of actual outcome to predicted outcome can indicate the differential effectiveness of various treatments. Unfortunately, correlation between pre-treatment variables and outcome can never be high because the intermediate effects of the actual treatment experience, and the post-treatment environment will have considerable power (Simon, 1971). Copas and Whiteley (1975) have successfully applied this method to Henderson Hospital.

The derivation of prediction analysis has been comprehensively covered by Simon. A crucial problem is to build the prediction equation for a specified population. It is impossible to transfer an equation built for one population (e.g. in treatment in a particular unit) and use it for another. It may be that if the populations are similar the equation may be transferred, but in that case it is essential that it be re-validated on the new population. If this proves successful, then the equation may be used to match the two populations.

A further problem is obtaining sufficient information from the pre-treatment situation to devise a prediction of any useful power. This has in general been more problematic in the penal services than in psychiatry, where case notes contain more elaborate descriptions of the patients' background. Whereas it might be thought that intra-psychic factors would be more relevant in this latter situation it is interesting that Ullman (1967) found marital status the best predictor of his 'early release criterion' of success. It is important that in general the prediction formula should include variables that affect the selection procedure in an ongoing system. If this is not the case the actual distribution of risk in a population may, for example, be better than shown by prediction, since in effect the selection procedure is acting as an undetected prediction device by choosing suitable cases which will do well subsequently. At Henderson Hospital, for example, where a selection committee of staff and patients votes for or against each applicant, the score obtained by counting positive votes can add strength to a prediction of the outcome of that applicant.

Whether one can randomize or not, comparison on many more than one variable (as in the case of therapeutic communites) would seem to require a rapidly increasing sample size for comparison. Path analysis offers a solution to this problem which is illustrated with the Australian data below, but the measuring device has to be easily applied and reliable, and from some perspectives would therefore seem rather coarse.

In the light of the above discussion, it can be seen that therapeutic communities present particular characteristics with respect to research methodology:

1 They are multi-dimensional, and research is often designed to investigate single dimensions.
2 They combine efforts at both intra-psychic and behavioural change.
3 Up to now most studies have been descriptions and analysis of process, rather than outcome.
4 They have multiple goals, of which outcome is but one; these goals have changed and will continue to change.

These factors militate strongly against comparing, for example, the therapeutic community with the traditional institution, in a single-shot study. A more productive approach should be at four levels:

(a)  Comparing a number of therapeutic communities, in order to use natural variations to suggest relationships between constituent variables (such as size, staff training, leadership, environmental context, organizational arrangements, length of stay, etc.).
(b)  Studying individual aspects which go to make up the therapeutic community; in other words attempting to dissect the constituent parts to see how they work together, which are more effective, and why. For example, it would be valuable to know how far the context of '24-hour' treatment is important for small group psychotherapy, or to what extent 'role-blurring' results in status competition amongst staff.
(c)  Studying natural fluctuations within the community over time to ascertain relationships between, for example, levels of tension and the age distribution of patients, as Hall (1973) has done.
(d)  Attempting to delineate more clearly the individual requirements of each patient, or at least of types of patient, so that on the one hand treatment can be more closely matched to needs, and also that 'improvement' may be more clearly defined for each case or category. Hood and Sparks (1970) argue for more of this basic typological research, in order to show empirically the relations, for example, between inter-personal maturity

155

and role career, or self image and rated 'amenability'.

This approach will inevitably be messy, and will not appear to follow the single-shot orthodox experimental design. The overwhelming weight of opinion, however, rejects such classicism.

## THE AUSTRALIAN STUDY

The Richmond Fellowship operated eleven half-way houses in Australia in 1983. Some of these had been in existence for ten years, but several were just starting up. This project set out to evaluate the Richmond Fellowship effort in Australia for three reasons; first, that there had been no systematic review of operations, and that sufficient time had elapsed for the longer-established houses to settle down into a regular programme; second, that as we have indicated, new efforts to develop community care for the mentally ill were being encouraged; third, that most of the income for the houses was from government sources, both as direct grants to cover running costs, and via the clients' payment of fees out of individual social security entitlements, and the Commonwealth Department of Health was prepared to fund a study which would indicate whether this money was being well spent. The project therefore aimed at

an evaluation of the operation of the Richmond Fellowship (of Australia) half-way houses for the mentally ill in two parts: (i) philosophy, practices and costs of each houses; (ii) effectiveness of each house as judged by clients, staff, reviewers, and local policy criteria. (project application)

Traditional randomized control trials could not be used for two reasons: first, the practical impossibility of controlling the allocation of clients to different programmes; second, the desirability of studying natural variatons between houses in the field to ascertain those aspects within programmes related to successful outcome, rather than merely which programme overall works best.

A further consideration necessary for ascertaining effective factors within programmes was the disaggregation of different units of analysis termed (from systems theory) 'levels of resolution': the individual, small group, community group, local policy environment, and so on (Lees and Millard, 1979). Thus the design adopted was the measurement of natural variations between Richmond Fellowship houses of individual staff and resident characteristics, their experiences in different groups in the programme, and the general social climate and resources within each house. These were then related to measures of the change in functioning of individual residents. In addition data were collected for each house about the local policy environment, referral agents and costs, although not all this data will be reported here. Set out in terms of levels of resolution, the measures taken are indicated in table 5.2, some of which were used in the previous chapter on the Henderson. The measures were all pilot-tested in England before data collection.

*Table 5.2* Levels of resolution and the measures used

| Level | Measures |
|---|---|
| Local policy environment | 1. Postal questionnaire to state govt. health departments |
| Referral agents | 2. Postal questionnaire to all major referral agents |
| Houses | 3. Multiphasic environmental assessment procedure (includes architectural, policy, staff and resident resources, and the internal social atmosphere) |
| | 4. Programme timetable |
| | 5. Costs |
| Groups | 6. Rank ordering of groups |
| Staff | 7. Social history questionnaire |
| | 8. Opinions (about treatment) survey |
| Residents | 9. Social history questionnaire |
| | 10. Opinions (about treatment) survey |
| | 11. Kelly grid |
| | 12. General health questionnaire |
| | 13. Outcome questionnaire (levels of psychological and interpersonal functioning) |

Out of the eleven possible houses in the sample, the two which specialized in adolescents were rejected since their particular clientele and thus specialized programmes were incommensurate with the other houses. Three further houses were rejected from the sample since they were not fully operational. Consequently six houses were studied, the first being used simultaneously as a second pilot for testing the measures used in the Australian field. The houses contained twenty-seven staff and eighty-two residents altogether, of whom twenty-one and fifty-nine were located and interviewed, in July–September 1983.

In order to create some continuity with the previous chapter, and to establish the general aims and practices of Richmond Fellowship work, some general data on the staff and members across all six houses will be presented initially.

## Values questionnaire

The staff score on this measure of commitment to therapeutic community values was 30.6, almost identical to the Henderson staff score in 1977 of 30.7. The residents' average score here was 23.5, which is markedly lower than the Henderson residents' score of 29.8 in 1977. This gap between staff and resident values in the houses may well be the cause of Sharp's analysis of staff interventions as social control, since clearly Richmond Fellowship residents, in the Australian houses at least, had not fully imbibed therapeutic community values.

## Group ranking

Staff and resident judgements here are set out in table 5.3. As with the Henderson data, the small group and community meeting are highly valued by staff; and, again, the residents also highly value the small group, but not the community meeting. This pattern of staff and resident agreement over small groups, and disagreement over the community meeting, is striking in its similarity to the Henderson data.

Table 5.3 Staff and resident rank ordering of helpful groups (Ranked 1st scores 3 points; 2nd scores 2 points; 3rd scores 1 point)

| Staff | |
|---|---|
| Small group | 31 |
| Community meeting | 30 |
| Outings | 17 |
| Work group | 16 |
| One-to-ones | 13 |
| Residents | |
| Small group | 53 |
| Community meeting | 20 |
| Outings | 20 |
| Work group | 65 |
| One-to-ones | 40 |

## House atmosphere scale

This in essence was a simple adaptation of Moos's Community Oriented Programmes Environment Scale (COPES). The scale gives scores on ten dimensions gathered from 100 questions about the house, each dimension ranging from 0 to 10. This scale has been used by Moos in a variety of institutional and community settings. The results for staff and residents are set out in figures 5.1 and 5.2: comparative scores for a large sample of similar community programmes in the USA and UK are supplied for comparison (Moos *et al.* 1974). While it is difficult to give a simple summary of this scale, Moos groups the ten dimensions into three domains of 'relationships', 'programme', and 'system maintenance'. It can be seen that the staff judgements compare well with American and British staff, particularly on their treatment-programme scores. While one might expect their involvement score to be higher, their use of therapeutic community principles is clearly reflected in their higher scores on spontaneity, anger and aggression, and programme clarity, and their lower score on order and organization. Residents' judgements about the house atmosphere indicate, like the staff judgements, that the houses tend to score higher than the British and American programmes. The pattern, as for the staff, is also as expected from therapeutic community principles: noticeably higher on spontaneity, personal problem orientation, anger and aggression, and programme clarity, but lower on order and organization. No similar data were collected for the Henderson.

## Multi-phasic Environmental Assessment Procedure (MEAP)

This measure, also devised by Moos (1980), focuses on the resources contained within a house in terms of four areas: physical/architectural resources; policy/programme resources; resident/staff resources; and a general rating scale covering physical attractiveness, environmental diversity, and resident and staff functioning. MEAP also includes the house atmosphere scale already reported for staff and residents.

The MEAP package records considerable detail about a house for each of the four resource areas. Since the package was developed to cover community facilities for old people, a few of the items related to physical disability were omitted for this project. The scoring method is to allocate points for items on the various dimensions, and calculate the percentage of a theoretical maximum that each house scores.

159

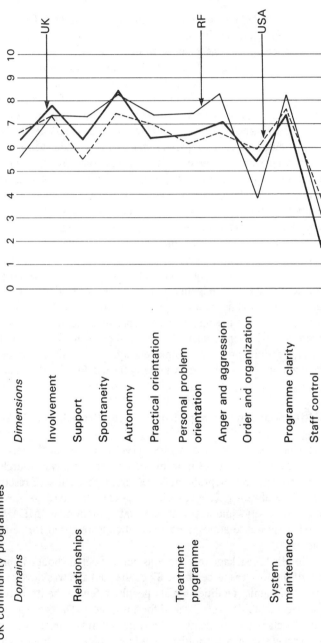

*Figure 5.1* Staff scores on the house atmosphere scale for the Richmond Fellowship of Australia, compared with USA and UK community programmes

Figure 5.2 Resident scores on the house atmosphere scale, compared with USA and UK

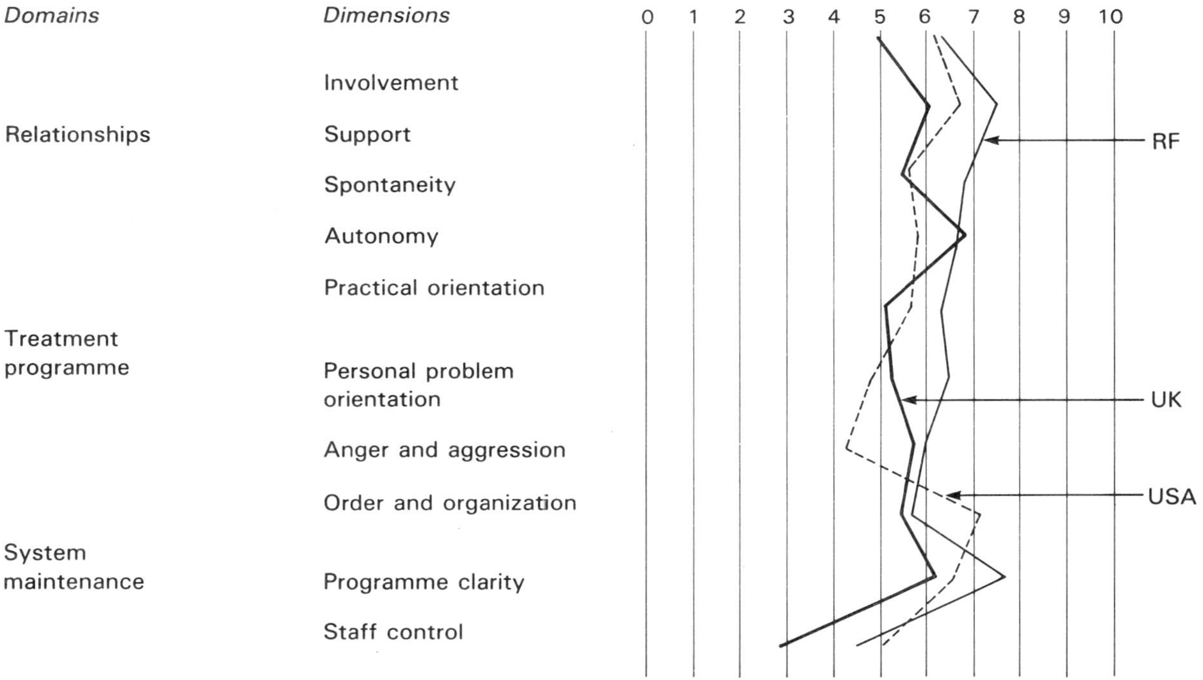

Table 5.4 MEAP subscales, summary scores (%) × house

| | Number of items in each dimension | min | max | average |
|---|---|---|---|---|
| *Part A. Physical and Architectural Resources Dimensions (PARD)* | | | | |
| 1. Physical amenities | 31 | 48 | 74 | 59 |
| 2. Social-recreational aids | 26 | 52 | 72 | 63 |
| 3. Prosthetic aids | 31 | 25 | 63 | 54 |
| 4. Orientational aids | 15 | 13 | 33 | 20 |
| 5. Safety features | 20 | 21 | 53 | 41 |
| 6. Architectural choice | 13 | 25 | 55 | 41 |
| 7. Space availability | 13 | 50 | 99 | 84 |
| 8. Staff facilities | 11 | 18 | 36 | 32 |
| 9. Community accessibility | 20 | 53 | 95 | 82 |
| *Part B. Policy and Program Resources Dimensions (PPRD)* | | | | |
| 1. Selectivity | 10 | 40 | 50 | 45 |
| 2. Expectations for resident functioning | 10 | 1 | 99 | 31 |
| 3. Tolerance for deviance | 18 | 44 | 78 | 54 |
| 4. Policy clarity | 10 | 25 | 75 | 49 |
| 5. Policy choice | 20 | 50 | 90 | 70 |
| 6. Resident control | 29 | 48 | 75 | 68 |
| 7. Provision for privacy | 10 | 40 | 50 | 43 |
| 8. Availability of health services | 8 | 13 | 50 | 31 |
| 9. Availability of daily living assistance | 15 | 53 | 87 | 70 |
| 10. Availability of social-recreational activities | 13 | 27 | 46 | 39 |

|  | Number of items in each dimension | min | max | average |
|---|---|---|---|---|
| **Part C. Resident and Staff Resources Dimensions (RSRD)** | | | | |
| 1. Staff variety | 14 | 14 | 57 | 36 |
| 2. Resident social resources | 5 | 31 | 51 | 42 |
| 3. Resident heterogeneity | 10 | 30 | 60 | 40 |
| 4. Resident functional abilities | 15 | 70 | 95 | 87 |
| 5. Resident activity level | 13 | 37 | 63 | 49 |
| 6. Resident integration in the community | 14 | 17 | 90 | 58 |
| 7. Utilization of health service | 8 | 13 | 99 | 47 |
| 8. Utilization of daily living assistance | 15 | 42 | 80 | 63 |
| 9. Utilization of social-recreational activities | 13 | 50 | 91 | 68 |
| | | | | |
| **Part D. Rating Scale Dimensions (RSD)** | | | | |
| 1. Physical attractiveness | 11 | 65 | 87 | 77 |
| 2. Environmental diversity | 5 | 53 | 84 | 62 |
| 3. Resident functioning | 5 | 67 | 93 | 81 |
| 4. Staff functioning | 5 | 60 | 93 | 77 |

Note: The average score is weighted by the number of residents in each house.

Table 5.4 gives summary scores for the thirty-two individual dimensions. Points to note about the MEAP scores are first that the weighted average used for table 5.4 helps to indicate the average experience of these resources per resident and second that the wide range of scores on some dimensions, particularly dimension B2, is produced by the deletion of a proportion of the constituent items because they focus on physical disabilities.

Dimensions on which the houses averaged high scores include space availability, community accessibility, policy choice, resident control, daily living assistance, resident functional lability, recreational activities, and three of the four general rating scales. Dimensions with low average scores are orientational aids, staff facilities, expectations about residents' functioning, availability of health services and staff variety. While some of these relate to the nature of the houses used, others relate to the therapeutic community principles adopted. The pattern of high and low scores is very much as expected for the Richmond Fellowship in terms of the kind of houses it buys, and the kind of programme it uses.

It is clear from these initial measures that the Australian houses exhibit both in theory and practice a commitment to therapeutic community work. However, the main point of the research design is to use natural variations between houses to establish what factors are associated with 'improvement' in residents. However, the measurement of 'improvement' is not straightforward. As we pointed out earlier this might range from rehospitalization or reconviction, through to a highly sensitive clinical profile of intrapsychic change. For this project, therefore, improvement was measured through a specially devised and piloted outcome questionnaire, which was filled in for each resident according to their own judgement, and according to a staff member's judgement about that resident. It requested that the resident be located on a score between 0 and 10 according to how *appropriately* they were functioning on five separate dimensions, both at the time of admission, and at the time of interview: cognitive, emotional, behavioural, interpersonal interactions, and work/task orientated activities. The first three dimensions were designed to measure psychic functioning, and the fourth and fifth dimensions were designed to measure social functioning. Table 5.5 indicates the average scores for residents on the five dimensions estimated by themselves and by the staff, for the time of admission and the time of interview. The change in scores over time is indicated, and the difference between resident and staff estimates of change. This general indication of change must be interpreted with extreme caution, since individual changes from very large or very small scores will be adversely affected by the statistical effect of regression towards the mean discussed in detail in the following section. This table also indicates the general agreement between staff and residents on outcome judgements.

## Analysis of outcome

In addition to the descriptive statistics given so far, we are also vitally interested in establishing which of these factors can be related to the successful improvement of residents — their 'outcome'. Commonsense would suggest that we can subtract the admission score from the interview score to obtain an estimate of each resident's improvement. Indeed we have presented such data in table 5.5. However, this can be a misleading measure because of the statistical phenomenon of regression towards the mean. This merely means that in any normally distributed set of social data there is a strong tendency for any particular case, with a score greatly at variance with the mean of the whole sample, to change its score, when measured on a second occasion, towards the mean. In this project, for example, those residents with a very low or very high score on admission will tend to score higher or lower, respectively, when measured at interview, whether or not the whole sample has tended to improve.

*Table 5.5* Resident scores on the resident outcome questionnaire: a summary

| | Staff estimate | | | Resident estimate | | | $(I-A)$ Residents $-(I-A)$ Staff |
|---|---|---|---|---|---|---|---|
| | A | I | I-A | A | I | I-A | |
| Cognitive | 4.9 | 6.9 | 2.0 | 5.6 | 7.4 | 1.8 | -.2 |
| Emotional | 3.8 | 5.7 | 1.9 | 3.8 | 6.6 | 2.8 | .9 |
| Behavioural | 4.6 | 6.2 | 1.6 | 4.8 | 7.3 | 2.5 | .9 |
| Interpersonal | 4.0 | 6.0 | 2.0 | 4.5 | 7.1 | 2.6 | .6 |
| Work/task | 4.4 | 6.6 | 2.2 | 3.8 | 6.5 | 2.7 | .5 |
| Total | 21.7 | 31.4 | 9.7 | 22.5 | 34.9 | 12.4 | 2.7 |

Note: $A$ = admission; $I$ = interview

Despite considerable debate in the statistical literature on methods to deal with this problem (Lord, 1963; Nunnally, 1975; Bebbington, 1978, nd; Youngman, 1979), the most common practical solution is to use the first score to predict the second score by constructing a linear equation using least-squares regression. The slope of the line obtained is then used to adjust the first score before calculating the change in score for each case. This has the effect of reducing low admission scores less than high admission scores, and hence cluster those scores nearer the mean before the change for each case is calculated.

The result of this adjustment for resident judgements is given by the regression of scores at interview $(I)$ on scores at admission $(A)$:

$$I = 30.6 + 0.204A.$$

Thus all these admission scores are multiplied by 0.204 before outcome is calculated. The result for staff judgements is:

$$I = 23.24 + 0.397A.$$

Thus all these admission scores are multiplied by 0.397 before outcome is calculated.

The next problem is to build a model of the way in which the factors we have already reported at different levels of resolution can be combined to predict the adjusted outcome that we observe in different residents. A traditional method is to see which factors are highly correlated with outcome, and to report the strengths of these correlations. This would normally be done through the construction of a single linear equation which best predicts the outcomes observed.

However, this gives us only a limited view for the following reasons. First, a single equation merely gives each factor correlated with outcome, in the context of all the other correlated factors; but we don't know how those factors affect each other. For example the strength of these correlations will depend on the order in which they are entered into the equation, unless they are all completely unrelated to each other. Second, such a single equation cannot tell us, therefore, how much of the total variance in the outcome explained by the equation is attributable to each factor uniquely, and how much is attributable to particular combinations of factors.

We will proceed therefore to use path analysis (Macdonald, 1977; Namboodiri *et al.*, 1975) to build a model consisting of several simultaneous equations, which is fully recursive (i.e. self-contained except for incidental error terms, and in which causality between each factor is uni-directional), grouping some sets of variables such as the residents' social background into 'block' variables in a method suggested by James Coleman (1975). We will then be able to establish the causal links between factors affecting outcome. Finally we will disaggregate the contribution each factor makes uniquely to the total variance explained, and the contribution that sets of factors make jointly to the explained variance (Mood, 1971).

In order to build such a causal model, it is necessary to begin with a theoretically derived structure which is tested against the existing data and then refined in the light of the data. The success of the model in explaining outcome tells us how successful our theoretical choices have been. The simplest method of devising such a structure is to theorize the temporal ordering of significant factors. For the Richmond Fellowship houses we shall begin with the proposition that the following sequence of factors affect outcome:

1 Residents' social background is a prior influence on . . .
2 Residents' level of functioning at intake, which is a prior influence on . . .
3 The Richmond Fellowship house of the resident, which is a prior influence on . . .
4 The resources available in that house, which are a prior influence on . . .
5 The perceptions of the resident about the house, which are a prior influence on . . .
6 The 'treatment' experiences of the resident in the house, which are a prior influence on . . .
7 The outcome of the resident.

In addition we will assume that all prior factors may influence subsequent factors anywhere in the sequence. If we draw a single headed arrow to indicate the direction of such influences, we get a set of such 'causal paths' leading to outcome, illustrated in figure 5.3. Renaming factors 1–7, $X_{1-7}$, we can write down the equations for this causal model, as in figure 5.3.

Factors 2, 3 and 7 are single variables and can be used without further preparation. The rest of the factors however consist of a variety of variables. These will be combined into 'block' or composite variables made up from a weighted combination of the most important variables in that general factor. First we must choose the relevant variables for each block, and then decide how to weight them. Choosing potentially relevant variables is a theoretical decision in the same way that choosing the relevant factors is. We shall consider the following for each block:

Figure 5.3 Theoretically derived model of causal influences on outcome, with its equations

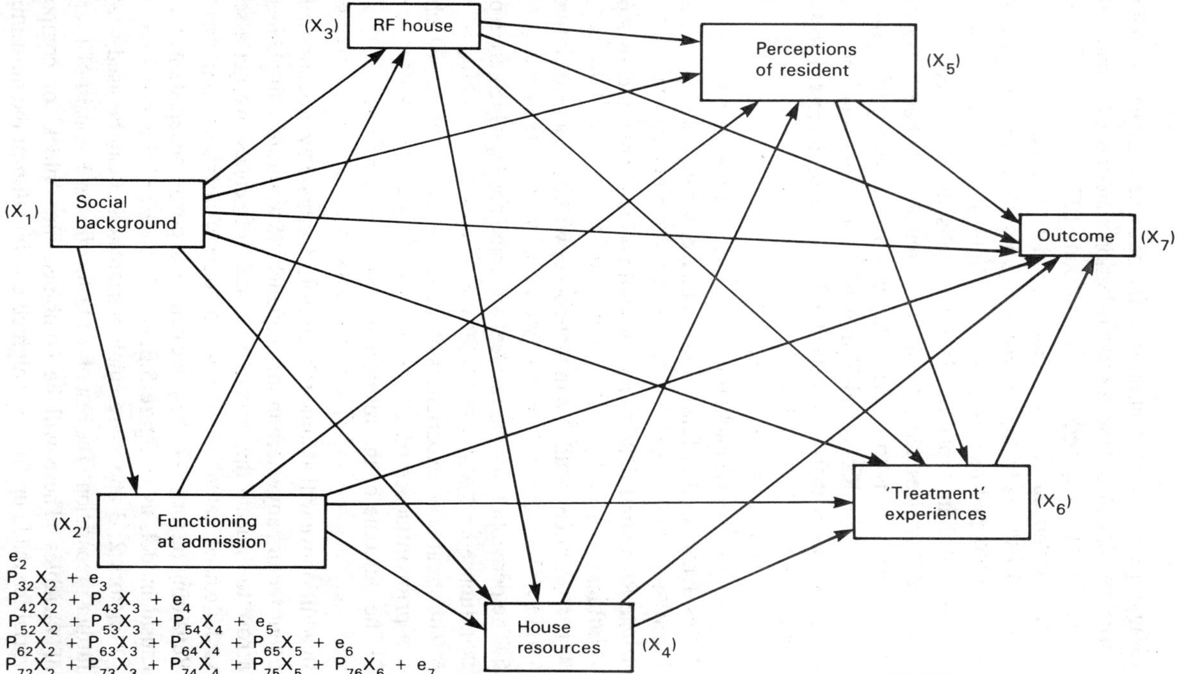

Equation number

(A) $X_2 = P_{21}X_1 + e_2$

(B) $X_3 = P_{31}X_1 + P_{32}X_2 + e_3$

(C) $X_4 = P_{41}X_1 + P_{42}X_2 + P_{43}X_3 + e_4$

(D) $X_5 = P_{51}X_1 + P_{52}X_2 + P_{53}X_3 + P_{54}X_4 + e_5$

(E) $X_6 = P_{61}X_1 + P_{62}X_2 + P_{63}X_3 + P_{64}X_4 + P_{65}X_5 + e_6$

(F) $X_7 = P_{71}X_1 + P_{72}X_2 + P_{73}X_3 + P_{74}X_4 + P_{75}X_5 + P_{76}X_6 + e_7$

where P = path coefficient = standardized regression coefficient, or 'Beta' coefficient and    e = residual path = $\sqrt{1 - R^2}$ for each equation

1 Residents' social background:
   All the variables recorded in the residents' social background questionnaire.
4 House resources:
   All the variables recorded in MEAP, other than the house atmosphere scale.
5 Perceptions of residents about the house:
   House atmosphere dimensions and opinions (about treatment) scale.
6 'Treatment' experiences of residents:
   Rank ordering of groups as helpful; staff and resident judgements as to the helpfulness of the Richmond Fellowship house on the five outcome dimensions; length of stay; weekly time in formal groups.

For each of these blocks of variables a linear equation was estimated, using least-squares regression, of their prediction of outcome. Those variables significantly able to predict outcome were then weighed by their regression coefficients and added to form the composite block variable. An alternative method suggested by Reis (1982), using factor analysis, tries to identify the underlying or 'latent' structure which integrates the variables in each block. This was not attempted with this data.

At this point we must remember that we have two distinct measures of outcome, since the outcome judgements were made separately about each resident by both that resident and the staff. From this point onwards, then, we are constructing two parallel models — one based on staff outcome judgements, and one based on the resident's own outcome judgements. This gives us a very useful way of double-checking the validity of our findings ('triangulation' in social research terminology).

Using these two outcome measures to sort out the relevant variables for each block, we derive two sets of seven factors with which to build our two parallel models, as follows (variables which do not appear, are not significantly related to outcome):

*For (staff) outcome scores*

*Block 1* $(X_1)$ = resident social background variables related to adjusted outcome
= $0.72 \times$ A112 + $4.40 \times$ A136A + $3.24 \times$ A9B − $2.58 \times$ A94A − $2.03 \times$ A42A + $2.65 \times$ A27A

A112 = longest spell, in months, held by a resident in a job
A136A = diagnosis
A9B = religion
A94A = whether a resident has experienced a loss/death in the family
A42A = father's occupation
A27A = accommodation prior to entering Richmond Fellowship house

*Block 2* ($X_2$) = aggregate functioning level at admission (simple variable)

*Block 3* ($X_3$) = which Richmond Fellowship house a resident is in (using dummy variables)
= $5.18 \times A3E + 6.88 \times A3B + 3.86 \times A3D + 4.89 \times A3A$
A3E = House no. 5
A3B = House no. 2
A3D = House no. 4
A3A = House no. 1

*Block 4* ($X_4$) = house resources (aggregated into the 4 MEAP areas)
= $- 0.44 \times RSRD$
RSRD = resident and staff resources dimensions

*Block 5* ($X_5$) = perceptions of residents
= $- 1.6 \times A206 + 0.78 \times A204$
A206 = resident house atmosphere dimension of 'staff control'
A204 = resident house atmosphere dimension of 'order and organization'

*Block 6* ($X_6$) = 'treatment' experiences
= $1.83 \times A188 + 3.25 \times A167 + 1.05 \times A146C + 1.02 \times A149C$
A188 = resident judgement as to whether Richmond Fellowship had helped functional change
A167 = staff judgement as to whether Richmond Fellowship had helped functional change
A146C = rank order score for small group
A149C = rank order score for work group

*Block 7* ($X_7$) = adjusted (staff) outcome score

*For (resident) outcome scores*

| | | |
|---|---|---|
| *Block 1* ($X_1$) | = | resident social background variables related to adjusted outcome |
| | = | $- 11.21 \times$ A81A $+ 7.35 \times$ A113B $+ 0.09 \times$ A112 $-3.74 \times$ A9B $+ 4.65 \times$ A97A $+ 4.89 \times$ A75A $-0.71 \times$ A4 $+ 3.43 \times$ A55A $+ 9.75 \times$ A80A |
| A81A | = | resident's father having marital problems |
| A113B | = | resident's longest held job |
| A112 | = | longest time resident has held job |
| A98 | = | religion |
| A97A | = | whether psychiatric treatment as an adult |
| A75A | = | whether father has had psychiatric illness |
| A4 | = | resident's age |
| A55A | = | whether resident is the eldest child in his family |
| A80A | = | whether mother has had marital problems |
| *Block 2* ($X_2$) | = | aggregate functioning level at admission (simple variable) |
| *Block 3* ($X_3$) | = | which Richmond Fellowship house a resident is in (dummy variables) |
| | = | none — i.e. none relate significantly to adjusted outcome |
| *Block 4* ($X_4$) | = | house resources (aggregated into the 4 MEAP areas) |
| | = | $- 0.03 \times$ RSRD |
| RSRD | = | resident and staff resources dimensions |
| *Block 5* ($X_5$) | = | perceptions of residents |
| | = | $0.62 \times$ A198 $+ 1.29 \times$ A200 |
| A198 | = | resident house atmosphere dimension of 'spontaneity' |
| A200 | = | resident house atmosphere dimension of 'autonomy' |
| *Block 6* ($X_6$) | = | 'treatment' experiences |
| | = | $3.49 \times$ A188 $-2.58 \times$ A153C $-2.87 \times$ A167 |
| A188 | = | resident judgements as to whether Richmond Fellowship had helped functional change |
| A153C | = | rank order score for sports recreation group |
| A167 | = | staff judgement as to whether Richmond Fellowship had helped functional change |
| *Block 7* ($X_7$) | = | adjusted (resident) outcome score |

Table 5.6 Simultaneous equations estimated for staff and resident judgement of outcome

| Equation number | $R^2$ | Sig. F |
|---|---|---|
| (Staff) outcome | | |
| (A) $X_2 = 0.14X_1 + 0.99e_2$ | .02 | .285 |
| (B) $X_3 = 0.22X_1 + 0.11X_2 + 0.97e_3$ | .07 | .144 |
| (C) $X_4 = 0.55X_1 - 0.76X_2 + 0.092X_3 + 0.39e_4$ | .85 | .000 |
| (D) $X_5 = -0.001X_1 + 0.15X_2 - 0.51X_3 + 0.78X_4 + 0.92e_5$ | .15 | .066 |
| (E) $X_6 = 0.11X_1 - 0.29X_2 + 0.23X_3 + 0.001X_4 + 0.22X_5 + 0.89e_6$ | .20 | .035 |
| (F) $X_7 = 0.39X_1 - 0.04X_2 + 0.49X_3 - 0.33X_4 + 0.19X_5 + 0.37X_6 + 0.70e_7$ | .50 | .000 |
| (Resident) outcome | $R^2$ | Sig. F |
| (A) $X_2 = 0.04X_1 + 1.0e_2$ | .00 | .742 |
| (B) [$X_3$ = missing] | | |
| (C) $X_4 = 0.25X_1 - 0.01X_2 + 0.96e_4$ | .06 | .158 |
| (D) $X_5 = 0.30X_1 + 0.09X_2 - 0.19X_4 + 0.94e_5$ | .11 | .092 |
| (E) $X_6 = 0.51X_1 + 0.11X_2 - 0.03X_4 - 0.01X_5 + 0.85e_6$ | .27 | .002 |
| (F) $X_7 = 0.59X_1 - 0.07X_2 + 0.06X_4 + 0.22X_5 + 0.16X_6 + 0.62e_7$ | .61 | .000 |

We are now in a position to estimate the set of equations in figure 5.3 twice (for staff and resident measures of outcome). We do this using least squares regression on the data from the project, which gives the results in table 5.6.

It is clear that some of the paths are very weak, and the next step is to eliminate those paths, and then recalculate the equations with those weak paths constrained to zero. There are two ways of deciding which paths to eliminate. One is to take an arbitrary decision on the lowest level to be accepted, and to eliminate all those paths below that level. The second and more precise method is to consider which of the partial correlations between the individual predictor variables, and the predicted variable, in each equation is less than an acceptable level of significance. Namboodiri *et al.* (1975) suggest the 10 per cent

*Table 5.7* Partial correlations in the models which *do not* attain 10% significance

| Equation number | Partial correlation | Significance level |
|---|---|---|
| *(Staff) outcome* | | |
| (A) | $r_{12}$ | 0.29 |
| (B) | $r_{23.1}$ | 0.42 |
| (C) | $r_{14.23}$ | 0.31 |
| | $^*r_{24.3}$ | 0.18 |
| (D) | $r_{15.234}$ | 0.94 |
| | $^*r_{25.34}$ | 0.25 |
| | $^*r_{35.4}$ | 0.18 |
| (E) | $r_{46.1235}$ | 0.98 |
| | $^*r_{16.235}$ | 0.40 |
| (F) | $r_{27.13456}$ | 0.69 |
| | $^*r_{47.1356}$ | 0.24 |
| | $^*r_{57.136}$ | 0.16 |
| *(Resident) outcome* | | |
| (A) | $r_{12}$ | 0.74 |
| (C) | $r_{24.1}$ | 0.94 |
| (D) | $r_{25.14}$ | 0.48 |
| | $^*r_{45.12}$ | 0.14 |
| (E) | $r_{56.124}$ | 0.93 |
| | $^*r_{46.125}$ | 0.80 |
| | $^*r_{26.15}$ | 0.34 |
| (F) | $r_{47.1256}$ | 0.53 |
| | $^*r_{27.156}$ | 0.44 |
| | $^*r_{67.15}$ | 0.15 |

Note: * = some other variable(s) already eliminated

*Figure 5.4* Estimated causal models of influences on (Staff) and (Resident) outcome

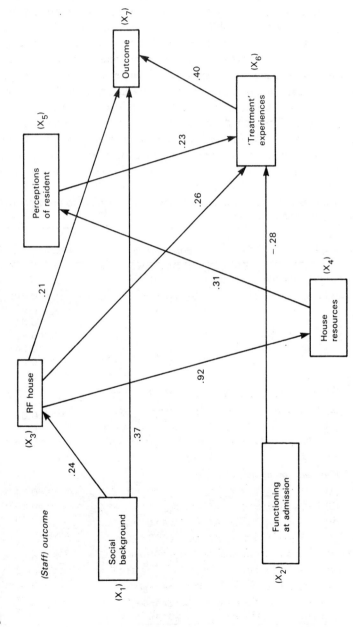

*(Staff) outcome*

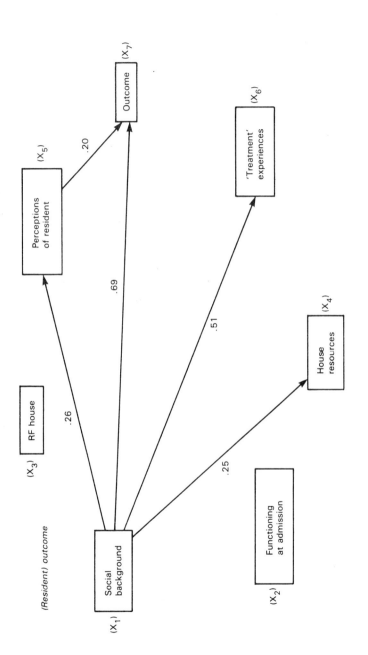

*(Resident) outcome*

level. It is necessary to drop the predictor variables from each equation one at a time since those partial correlations which may be insignificant in the full equation can attain significance when one other variable has been dropped (when for example the two variables themselves are inter-correlated). This necessitates continual re-estimation of each equation as the variables are dropped, and for this project such relative changes in significance do happen at each stage. (While this procedure sounds laborious, the 'Backward' regression procedure on SPSS[x] accomplishes this task ideally.) Table 5.7 lists the partial regressions which *do not* attain 10 per cent significance, and whose related paths are therefore dropped. The significance level quoted is that for the equation *from which the variable is dropped*, which may or may not be at the full equation stage. An * identifies those partial regressions for an equation in which another variable has already been eliminated.

We are now in a position to rewrite table 5.6 with those weak paths we have identified constrained to zero. This is presented in table 5.8. The paths here which are still included have sometimes changed from those in table 5.6, as a result of eliminating some variables from the equations. The equations in table 5.8 gives us a greatly modified causal model from that suggested in figure 5.3. Figure 5.4 presents the modified models for (staff) and (resident) outcomes.

We can use the models in figure 5.4 to calculate the direct and indirect effects of each block on resident outcome. The path

*Table 5.8* Simultaneous equations estimated for staff and resident judgements of outcome, with weak paths constrained to zero

| Equation number | $R^2$ | Sig. F |
|---|---|---|
| *(Staff) outcome* | | |
| (B) $X_3 = 0.24X_1 + 0.97e_3$ | .06 | .071 |
| (C) $X_4 = 0.92X_3 + 0.39e_4$ | .85 | .000 |
| (D) $X_5 = 0.31X_4 + 0.95e_5$ | .10 | .016 |
| (E) $X_6 = -0.28X_2 + 0.26X_3 + 0.23X_5 + 0.90e_6$ | .19 | .009 |
| (F) $X_7 = 0.37X_1 + 0.21X_3 + 0.40X_6 + 0.73e_7$ | .47 | .000 |
| | | |
| *(Resident) outcome* | | |
| (C) $X_4 = 0.25X_1 + 0.97e_4$ | .06 | .054 |
| (D) $X_5 = 0.26X_1 + 0.97e_5$ | .07 | .050 |
| (E) $X_6 = 0.51X_1 + 0.86e_6$ | .26 | .000 |
| (F) $X_7 = 0.69X_1 + 0.20X_5 + 0.65e_7$ | .58 | .000 |

coefficient from each block to outcome is added; where two or more paths are traced sequentially, their coefficients are multiplied to get the combined (indirect) effect (Macdonald, 1977; Namboodiri *et al*, 1975). The results of these calculations are given in table 5.9.

It is clear from figure 5.4 that outcome measured through resident judgements has produced a model in which social background is the only important factor, either directly or via its influence on residents' perceptions. Outcome measured through staff judgements produces a more complex model incorporating all of our posited factors either directly or indirectly. This cannot be interpreted as the staff wishing these factors to be important, since the outcome judgements were not made with these factors in mind. The most likely explanation is that residents were less discriminating in their judgements about their change in functioning, whereas staff members were more discriminating both about how each resident had changed, and how different those changes were on each of the five dimensions.

From table 5.9, we are able to note the extent to which factors operate relatively directly, or indirectly. For example, for (staff) outcome, most of the social background effect is direct, whereas the influence of the house is only partly direct, the remaining influence being via the house resources, perceptions, and treatment experiences of the resident. While it is tempting to speculate from figure 5.4 that those factors with big path coefficients are more important influences on outcome, and while this is indeed likely to be the case, it is not technically possible to conclude for example that a path coefficient of twice the size is twice as important (Macdonald, 1977). We must be careful what we mean by 'important' here. Technically the question must be couched in terms of how much of the variance is accounted for by different factors. Precisely because path analysis provides a more complex model than a single linear equation, in which we can apportion the variance between predictor variables, we must do some further calculations before being able to apportion variance in our causal model.

As a first step, we can use table 5.9 to suggest that while some of the individual paths in figure 5.4 are in themselves significant, they nevertheless in combination produce some fairly weak total effects between some factors, and the outcome score. We will therefore eliminate those factors with weak total effects. We cannot use the same test of significance that we used for eliminating individual paths (the significance of the associated partial correlation) as we are eliminating several paths at a time. However, we can check to see whether the removal of the ineffective factors significantly reduces the explanatory

*Table 5.9* The direct, indirect and total effects of each factor on outcome

---

*(Staff) outcome*

*Effects on outcome $(X_7)$*

| | | |
|---|---|---|
| *Direct* | Social background $(X_1)$ | $= .37$ |
| | Functioning at admission $(X_2)$ | $= 0$ |
| | RF house $(X_3)$ | $= .21$ |
| | House resources $(X_4)$ | $= 0$ |
| | Perceptions of resident $(X_5)$ | $= 0$ |
| | 'Treatment' experiences $(X_6)$ | $= .40$ |

| | | |
|---|---|---|
| *Indirect* | $X_1$ via $X_3$ | $= .24 \times .21 = .050$ |
| | $X_1$ via $X_3, X_4, X_5, X_6$ | $= .24 \times .92 \times .31 \times .23 \times .40 = .006$ |
| | $X_1$ via $X_3, X_6$ | $= .24 \times .26 \times .40 = .025$ |
| | Total $X_1$ indirect effect | $= .050 \times .006 \times .025$ |
| | — | $= .081$ |
| | $X_2$ via $X_6$ | $= -.28 \times .40 = -.110$ |
| | — | |
| | $X_3$ via $X_4, X_5, X_6$ | $= .92 \times .31 \times .23 \times .40 = .026$ |
| | $X_3$ via $X_6$ | $= .26 \times .40 = .104$ |
| | Total $X_3$ indirect effect | $= .026 \times .104 = .130$ |
| | — | |
| | $X_4$ via $X_5, X_6$ | $= .31 \times .23 \times .40 = .029$ |
| | — | |
| | $X_5$ via $X_6$ | $= .23 \times .40 = .092$ |
| | — | |

| | | |
|---|---|---|
| *Total* | $X_1$ | $= .37 + .081 = 0.451$ |
| | $X_2$ | $= -.110$ |
| | $X_3$ | $= .21 + .130 = .340$ |
| | $X_4$ | $= .029$ |
| | $X_5$ | $= .092$ |
| | $X_6$ | $= .40$ |

*(Resident) outcome*

*Effects on outcome $(X_1)$*

| | | |
|---|---|---|
| *Direct* | $X_1$ | $= .69$ |
| | $X_2$ | $= 0$ |
| | $X_3$ | $= 0$ |
| | $X_4$ | $= 0$ |
| | $X_5$ | $= .20$ |
| | $X_6$ | $= 0$ |

| | | |
|---|---|---|
| *Indirect* | $X_1$ via $X_5$ | $= .26 \times .20 = .052$ |

| | | |
|---|---|---|
| *Total* | $X_1$ | $= .69 + .052 = .742$ |
| | $X_2$ | $= 0$ |
| | $X_3$ | $= 0$ |
| | $X_4$ | $= 0$ |
| | $X_5$ | $= .20$ |
| | $X_6$ | $= 0$ |

---

power of the main equation in which all the factors are related to outcome, by conducting an 'F' test. For example, if we take equation (F) for (staff) outcome from table 5.6, and remove variables $X_2$, $X_4$ and $X_5$ on the grounds that the total effects of these factors (from table 5.9) are weak, we can check to see whether the reduced equation is significantly less powerful. If not, we can then use it as the basis for apportioning variance between the remaining effective factors. The 'F' test we will use (Macdonald, 1977) is as follows:

$$F = \frac{(RSS_R - RSS_U)/K}{(RSS_u/n-p-1)}$$

where
| | | |
|---|---|---|
| $RSS_u$ | = | residual sum of squares for our unrestricted equation |
| $RSS_R$ | = | residual sum of squares for our restricted model |
| K | = | number of factors removed |
| n | = | number of observations |
| p | = | number of predictor variables in the unrestricted equation |

For the above example, this gives $F = 1.19$, which is not significant. Repeating this exercise for (resident) outcome, and removing $X_2$, $X_4$ and $X_6$ (as indicated by table 5.9), we get $F = 1.04$, which is also not significant.

We can now use these restricted equations for apportioning the variance between the remaining effective factors. We will use a method suggested by Mood (1971). First of all the amount of variance in outcome explained by each individual factor, and each combination of factors, is estimated using new regression equations. For the staff and resident outcomes this requires 7 and 3 regression equations respectively, to provide all the combinations of factors and their associated explained variances. These results are set out in table 5.10.

However, these figures do not distinguish directly the unique and shared variance attributable to each factor but merely the total attributable to each factor. In order to disentangle the variance unique to each factor, and the variance shared between various combinations of factors, we must determine how much of the variance is explained when each factor or factor combination is added. For example, the (resident) outcome case is simple. The variance accounted for by $X_1$ and $X_5$ is 58.24 per cent. The unique variance attributable to $X_1$ is 58.24 per cent less that explained in total by $X_5$, i.e. 58.24 per cent − 14.01 per cent = 44.23 per cent. Similarly the unique variance

*Table 5.10* Total variance explained by different combinations of factors in restricted model equations

| | % variance explained $= R^2 \times 100$ |
|---|---|
| *(Staff) outcome* | |
| Regression of $X_7$ on $X_1$ | 22.98% |
| $X_3$ | 16.48% |
| $X_6$ | 26.23% |
| $X_1$ and $X_3$ | 32.04% |
| $X_1$ and $X_6$ | 43.13% |
| $X_3$ and $X_6$ | 34.02% |
| $X_1$, $X_3$, and $X_6$ | 47.04% |
| *(Resident) outcome* | |
| Regression of $X_7$ on $X_1$ | 54.58% |
| $X_5$ | 14.01% |
| $X_1$ and $X_5$ | 58.24% |

*Table 5.11* Unique and shared variance explained by different combinations of factors in restricted model equations

| | % variance explained $= (R^2 \times 100)$ | | |
|---|---|---|---|
| *(Resident) outcome $(X_7)$* | | | |
| | $X_1$ | $X_5$ | |
| Unique to $X_1$ | 44.23% | | |
| Unique to $X_5$ | | 3.66% | |
| Common to $X_1$ and $X_5$ | 10.35% | 10.35% | |
| Total | 54.58% | 14.01% | |
| *(Staff) outcome $(X_7)$* | | | |
| | $X_1$ | $X_3$ | $X_6$ |
| Unique to $X_1$ | 13.02% | | |
| Unique to $X_3$ | | 3.91% | |
| Unique to $X_6$ | | | 15.00% |
| Common to $X_1$ and $X_3$ | 3.88% | 3.88% | |
| Common to $X_1$ and $X_6$ | 2.54% | | 2.54% |
| Common to $X_3$ and $X_6$ | | 5.15% | 5.15% |
| Common to $X_1$, $X_3$ and $X_6$ | 3.54% | 3.54% | 3.54% |
| Total | 22.98% | 16.48% | 26.23% |

attributable to $X_5$ is 58.24 per cent $-$ 54.58 per cent $=$ 3.66 per cent. Finally the variance attributable in common to $X_1$ and $X_5$ is 58.24 per cent $-$ 44.23 per cent $-$ 3.66 per cent $=$ 10.35 per cent. These results, and the slightly more complex ones for (staff) outcome are set out in table 5.11. Reading down the columns of table 5.11 enables us to see how the variance attributable to each factor is divided between its unique and shared effects. Thus for example in looking at (staff) outcome, both social background $(X_1)$ and 'treatment' experiences $(X_6)$ have a powerful unique contribution to variance, whereas the Richmond Fellowship $(X_3)$ has little unique contribution, sharing most of its contribution with the other factors, particularly (as one might expect!) 'treatment' experiences.

We can now turn to a comparison of tables 5.9 and 5.11. It is clear that while the partitioning of the variance in table 5.11 follows the pattern of the size of the path coefficience in table 5.9 there are differences. In particular for (staff) outcome the examination of variance indicates that 'treatment' experiences $(X_6)$ are more important (indeed *the* most important factor) than the relative size of the path coefficients suggest in table 5.9, and second that the effect of Richmond Fellowship house $(X_3)$ is less direct than the path coefficients suggest, most of its effect being mediated via (i.e. shared with) other factors.

What can we conclude from this analysis of which factors affect the outcome of Richmond Fellowship residents in the study? As we have already suggested the staff and resident estimates of outcome produce two rather different models: for residents social background excludes the effects of all other factors except for the perceptions of the residents; for staff there is a more equal effect from social background, Richmond Fellowship house, and 'treatment' experiences, with perceptions of residents and (negatively) level of functioning at admission having effects small enough to be dropped from the model. We have suggested that there may well be a case for considering the resident outcome judgements to be less discriminating, and we therefore have doubt as to the usefulness of the model based on their estimates.

As we pointed out much earlier, when discussing different models of evaluation, we have rejected elsewhere the controlled trial model of evaluating the therapeutic community for practical, ethical and theoretical reasons. The alternative, the cross-institutional design, has been adopted here, combined with a technique of causal modelling which not only evaluates the contribution of 'in house' effects on outcome, but also enables us to build a causal structure of the way various factors affecting outcome relate together. This is a considerable advance over any previously published evaluations of therapeutic communities, such that this study has not only reported on the Richmond Fellowship in Australia specifically, but is a more general contribution to the field.

The most important finding comes from the (staff) outcome model, that the variance explained uniquely and jointly by residents' 'treatment' experiences is substantial, and the most sigificant factor. This is particularly so, since this model in total explains nearly 50 per cent of the total variance in outcome — a very good result indeed for this kind of social science data. Given that 'treatment' experiences and Richmond Fellowship house together account for 34 per cent of the explained variance, we are in a position to state unequivocally that the therapeutic community has a substantial effect on outcome, which is clearly more important than the contribution of social background. The relevance of this finding is in the criticism often made of therapeutic communities (and psychotherapy in general) that its effectiveness lies in a combination of spontaneous remission and a careful preselection of 'suitable' patients. The data from this study are quite clearly incompatible with such a model.

# 6

# Towards a sociology of the therapeutic community

In this final chapter, the material presented so far will be drawn together in a sociological account of the therapeutic community. The problem to be addressed is that of the way in which the original aspirations emerged, and their subsequent fate. Those aspirations were formulated in the 1940s, and continue to be presented, in terms of two distinct but closely interwoven themes. The first is the claim to have discovered a new treatment within scientific medicine. The second is the attempt to press for social change in the way in which the mentally ill are dealt with in the health and social services.

In the final section of chapter 2, four sociological accounts of the therapeutic community were noted, which were all stimulated by a desire to clarify the nature of therapeutic community practice. The first three focused respectively on the culture of the therapeutic community, its technology, and its power distribution; while the fourth account introduced the idea of the therapeutic community as a social movement for change. The last of these models will be given a fuller elaboration later in this chapter. The first three can be subsumed under a general model which takes as its central focus the claim to have discovered and elaborated a new therapeutic technique within psychiatric practice as a branch of scientific medicine.

## THE THERAPEUTIC COMMUNITY IN ITS OWN TERMS

From our knowledge of the origins of therapeutic community ideas (chapter 1) it is clear that powerful forces other than the rational application of knowledge to an area of human needs shaped developments. Even as a scientific development, the therapeutic community idea was profoundly shaped on the one hand by the general

183

expectations of social psychological work at the Tavistock Centre and on the other by the enthusiasm and charisma of a single man — Maxwell Jones. As such it illustrates well the social constraints on the scientific community identified by Merton (1968) as social control within the scientific community, and by Mulkay (1972) as the dependence of scientific ideas on personal careers through social exchange — in this case, Maxwell Jones.

In addition, the emergence of a therapeutic community movement (as opposed to a scientific development) opened the way still further to social influences. For example, it was the enthusiasm of Maxwell Jones rather than the science of the Tavistock Centre which really put therapeutic communities on the map in the 1950s in Britain and the US. The large-scale development of concept therapeutic communities for drug and alcohol users in the 1970s and 1980s spreading from the US to Europe and beyond extends this process even further. These new communities rely very strongly on zealous faith, commitment and a degree of anti-professionalism. As such they exhibit the classic style of a social/religious movement, not conducive to sober, scientific reflection (Glaser, 1977; Antze, 1979).

Therapeutic communities are not unusual in this respect. The helping professions such as psychiatry and social work, despite a ritual 'scientistic' veneer, have also been broadly shaped by non-scientific social influences. These professions have not developed their ideas as a rational response to research findings, but in response to the social distribution of power, and especially the ebb and flow of fashion (Ahmed and Plog, 1976; Baruch and Treacher, 1978; Halmos, 1965; Pearson, 1975; Rothman, 1971; Scull, 1977, 1979; Treacher and Baruch, 1981).

To look at the way that therapeutic community ideas developed, therefore, requires the use of a dynamic model which can incorporate the main processes of change which occurred in the growth, spread and application of those ideas from the early days of the late 1940s up to the present day. One of the most complete descriptions of the therapeutic community is contained in the substantial literature which has come out of the Henderson Hospital since it was first organized under Maxwell Jones (as the Belmont Social Rehabilitation Unit) — especially Rapoport's book (1960). This book might possibly be the place to look for a model which has been developed from first-hand contact with therapeutic communities. The criteria to be used for making this decision will here be largely informed by the writing of David Willer. In his book *Scientific Sociology* (1967) he rejects both Merton's (1968) 'middle range theory', and Mills's (1970) 'humanistic, imaginative study' as the proper approach to sociological research. He goes on to describe a new approach to organizing the method of research.

Briefly, Willer sets out a system of interacting parts which are : the model; the formal system derived from it; the operational system at which level relationships are tested, and where, if proved, validation may be found for propositions in the formal system. The model is a crucial element, for it is the place where ideas are formed and worked out, theories tentatively tried, and relationships culled. It cannot be proved or disproved but is the growing framework which may organize view-points and concepts into a cohering system. Consequently, models may be obtained from any source. Willer suggests three broad types: analogical, iconic, symbolic. Their sources are respectively: first, borrowed from other areas of thought (e.g. the 'biological' model of functionalism); second, from suggestive points in the data itself (e.g. ideal types, typologies or mere characterizations); and third, from suggestive relationships between the concepts themselves — i.e. the related concepts symbolize the set of phenomena. These are the sources for the model, but it is vital that such a model should contain both a 'rationale' and a 'mechanism'. The first merely means a basic point of view relating the phenomena. This gives rise to the second, which is the actual way the parts in the model are causally and meaningfully related — its structure. Different models may be differentiated by the nature of their mechanisms.

Since Maxwell Jones has tried more than any other person to formalize the ideas he has put into practice in his work, and since Rapoport has extensively studied Jones's methods, it would seem most useful to look directly at the characteristics of his therapeutic community to see how far it fulfils the conditions for a model laid down by Willer.

Although it is useful to try to isolate the mechanism in a model, and thereby discover the type and source, it presupposes that there is a mechanism. In order to establish this, we must look at some of the sources for the ideas in therapeutic community principles directly. The source, in fact, seems a mixture of analogic and iconic types. The therapeutic community is seen as a society, and in that way analogically related to the wider society itself. The social dimension of any situation, especially the resident's relationship to his peers and the staff, is held to be of significance. However, certain concepts are manifestly different from situations found in the wider society and have been developed specifically (i.e. iconically) within the community itself, for instance 'reality confrontation' and the 'community meeting'.

The question arises as to how this model of a therapeutic community can have two source-types, and consequently, two mechanisms. The answer to this is that the analogic source may be seen as a fundamental. The rationale is that a community is a small society of individuals (Caudill, 1958). The mechanism relating variables within it is that of the wider society. However, the model is limited and distorted from this fundamental pattern by several important factors: this society consists of a number of people who for various reasons are not able to function adequately in the wider society at the moment; it also consists of people employed to help the previous group to learn to function more adequately, and hopefully to return them to the outside society fully. This crucial therapeutic goal of better functioning may be seen as the mechanism underlying the iconic aspect of the model, which overlays the basic mechanism. The rationale of the iconic aspect is thus a belief in the efficacy of therapy.

We find here, then, a rigorous derivation of the fundamental conflict between 'rehabilitation' and 'treatment' highlighted by Rapoport (1960). The four crucial concepts in his model, communalism, permissiveness, democratization, and reality confrontation, are inter-related by the mechanisms of treatment and rehabilitation — the first three being sympathetic settings for the main work which is carried on by the fourth, reality confrontation. At least that is as it should be. However, Rapoport has argued that this very mechanism may unfortunately only result in rehabilitation within the unit itself. Also, communalism, permissiveness and democratization, though seen as ideally typical of a perfect society, do not exist in the outside world. This throws considerable doubt upon the fundamental rationale of trying to treat the community as a small society — it is in fact considerably different.

However, even if the model was applied only within the unit (i.e. as a closed system) and was completely iconic, Rapoport has still further damaging criticism — not of the internal consistency of the model itself, but of the fact that it appears to have left out several important factors by over simplification. They are: a hierarchical external administration; other treatment methods; previous experience of staff (and their own personal goals); the local social environment; the difference between staff and residents, and residents and residents, by age, sex, income, class, marital status, and types of problem. The explanation in Maxwell Jones's case seems to be that he was in the peculiar position of holding most of these factors constant: he was fairly autonomously in charge; he phased out other treatment; he used young untrained staff; and he maintained good relations with the local community. This does not invalidate his work in terms of being a model. However, it does imply that that model may only relate to a particular community at a particular time.

According to David Willer, the primary function of a model is to generate relationships. This is no doubt possible from Maxwell Jones's exposition, but only in terms of his particular unit. For instance, the cyclical fluctuation in terms of the application of the unit ideology by the staff, the consequent effect of reality confrontation, and so on reported by Rapoport was useful for identifying inter-relations. But such events may be totally different in another community, or not even happen at all (Manning, 1980). Attempts to generalize universal relationships by other writers have resulted in almost meaningless vagueness, or designed ambiguity in order to fit almost any situation. Zeitlyn (1967) has pointed out that therapeutic communities have been reported as encompassing whole hospitals as well as small intimate wards. Progressively administered (though traditional) mental hospitals, the holding of frequent meetings, freedom to talk to residents, or merely the acting out of neurotic behaviour of staff and residents which is dealt with by the psycho-therapeutic interpretation of unconscious drives, have all been claimed as therapeutic communities. Some are total conversions, and some merely 'approaches'. None of these descriptions are models with an internally consistent set of related concepts, a mechanism, a rationale, a generative capacity. And yet there is a feeling of common values running through them all — a reaction to authoritarian hospital administration, an increasingly wide concern with basic human rights, a conception of residents as merely people with problems, the recognition that personal breakdown could occur through social stress, and so on.

These more sociological factors did not take their place in Jones's model. Why not? As is often the case in social research, it appeared as though the ideas, concepts and values had arrived *de vacuo* in Jones's mind. However, it must be recognized that those ideas were the product of many inter-related factors such as those mentioned above, which operated on Maxwell Jones, his contemporaries, staff and residents alike. His model, then, must be inadequate to the extent that it fails to include these important influences for they may be a significant background against which his concepts (a concentration, perhaps, and extrapolation of social trends) are applied, and indeed may have the dominant effect on the recovery (or not) of his residents.

187

Maxwell Jones, many writers have noted, probably vastly underestimated two things. First, the influence of external social pressures and trends, and second, his own vital position in concentrating and channelling these forces.

When seen in this context, Jones's model appears very much a model of what he thought he was trying to do in an ideal sense. Rapoport's research unearthed a more real picture of what he saw as going on. However, he was still looking very much from within the system which appeared to be a fairly closed one. But such a model must be set in context. For instance, successful treatment and rehabilitation may be calculated in different ways. In terms of turnover, Jones's unit was remarkably successful. In terms of readmission, or rejection of difficult residents, it was not very successful.

The possibility remains, then, of constructing a more comprehensive model in which Jones's work and similar changes in hospitals and hostels up and down the country may be seen as products of more widespread influences, for instance, the influence of the medical profession on psychiatric practice. Therapeutic communities are much closer in origin, I propose, to changes in social values than to intellectual research, and a valid model cannot really be adequate on the level at which Maxwell Jones cast his explanation. The model which Jones and Rapoport have produced is thus inadequate. An alternative to using it is to look at other areas of sociological writing dealing with the spread of scientific ideas.

## THE THERAPEUTIC COMMUNITY AS SCIENTIFIC INNOVATION

There has been a growing literature on the way scientific ideas are produced in the scientific community (Mulkay, 1972, 1979; Brannigan, 1981). The first type represents the scientific method which is extolled by scientists themselves. Characteristics of this model suggest that the scientific community is impartial, objective, disinterested, original, and shares information openly. Such a model is not seriously upheld by those who have studied the area for it soon becomes apparent that scientists are not always objective or original and are commonly quite secretive about their current research. Furthermore, such an ideal is now being recognized as unreal by some scientists themselves (Medawar, 1969). In David Willer's terms, the rationale and mechanism of this model are seriously erroneous.

The second type of model is closely linked with Thomas Kuhn.

Kuhn (1962) presents a model of the growth of scientific ideas which assumes that scientists do not really support norms of open-mindedness. In fact, scientists maintain a strong consensus about standards for judging each other's work. These standards are embodied in a coherent viewpoint, called a paradigm, against which new ideas are measured. The consensus is maintained by excluding those who do not accept it from journals, research facilities and societies, and by a narrow system of education and socialization to maintain the correct viewpoint amongst younger research workers.

In this model, most research activity is 'normal science'. Minor problems are tackled within the current paradigm, but major issues and basic principles are taken for granted. However, as time goes on, an increasing number of anomalous findings accumulate which are not accounted for in the current paradigm. Eventually, the field enters a crisis stage, when new paradigms are proposed in the face of much resistance. Clear standards disappear until a new paradigm becomes generally acceptable to those who challenged the old one. The older generation resists, but as it retreats a new period of normal science sets in.

This model is very useful, for it recognizes the normative character of scientific knowledge, it explains radical innovations, and it ties in the process of education. From Willer's point of view, this model is quite successful. It contains a convincing rationale to explain the uneven development of scientific work — sometimes in periods of steady knowledge production, and sometimes briefer periods of intellectual crisis and reappraisal. It also contains a convincing mechanism: scientific work is controlled in fairly tight hierachies established around dominant approaches. These are subject to increasing strain as anomalous research findings accumulate until some scientists break out from their position and establish new dominant approaches with their attendant hierarchies of control.

However, Kuhn's model only applies to very pure sciences in which most research workers can agree on the basic paradigm. In what Kuhn calls pre-paradigmatic sciences, there is still disagreement over fundamental postulates. Psychiatry, psychology and sociology would all be included in this category. Mulkay (1972) has suggested that in these areas a third model is more appropriate. Social exchange, he suggests, operates in all disciplines whatever their stage of development, and is thus a more general model. Social exchange is a kind of market where information is exchanged for recognition, and recognition is exchanged for authority and research facilities. Such exchange is a more effective social control than socialization or

189

scientific authority. Hagstrom (1965) notes that such exchange is not recognized as such by scientists themselves, who prefer to consider that they are giving knowledge. That such gifts are in fact dependent on an acceptable exchange has been long recognized by anthropologists (Mauss, 1954), and Mulkay has shown that such exchange is actively sought after in expanding fields. Moreover, 'interesting' as opposed to 'mundane' knowledge is particularly valuable currency (Davis, 1970).

This clearly analogic model (i.e. based on a pseudo-market in knowledge) is again a strong one by Willer's criteria. Its rationale seems to explain well the competing paradigms which co-exist in social science, while its mechanism replaces the socialization and authoritative control of pure science, with the discipline of a pseudo-market place. It is particularly applicable to the growth of new ideas in social psychiatry. Here, as in other disciplines, new and especially 'interesting' developments confer status on the author. Moreover, psychiatry involves the application of new ideas by practitioners not engaged in research, and hence recognition can spread beyond the community of research workers to practitioners in the field. This wider audience for new ideas provides more widespread recognition for developments in psychiatry than for new work in one of the 'pure' sciences.

There is in addition a further incentive within psychiatry to develop new ideas. Psychiatry is part of medicine. Psychiatrists have to be trained in medical school, and qualified psychiatric nurses have to learn general nursing. In medicine, powerful techniques have been developed to prevent and treat disease, particularly with drugs and surgical skill. Practitioners of physical medicine can point with pride to the success with which many previously fatal diseases have been eradicated in the ninteenth and twentieth centuries. Psychiatrists and psychiatric nurses will thus have been socialized into expecting the gratification which results from the successful application of general medical techniques. But psychiatry is an area which has not had the spectacular success of physical medicine. Despite theoretical advances of great magnitude, and some successful treatments (for instance, individual and group psychotherapy, or the use of drugs), there is a great sense of dissatisfaction with the present state of knowledge. This mixture of clearly defined high-level goals and inadequate means results in a permanent state of 'anomie'. Merton (1968) has constructed a typology of modes of individual adaption to such disjunction between goals and means. Where goals are accepted, but the existing means for their attainment are inadequate and rejected, there is great incentive for innovation. In such a situation, a sacrosanct goal virtually consecrates the means. Hence such practices as 'ether-drip therapy', 'carbon dioxide inhalation therapy', 'brain surgery', 'electro-shock therapy', 'insulin coma therapy', etc. have all been consecrated by the sacrosanct goal of treating mental illness, even when the theoretical reasons for the effect of the treatment were not understood.

In this situation, where the attainment of culturally prescribed goals is not possible within existing social-structural means, psychiatrists are strongly motivated either to invent new treatments or to receive new methods with great enthusiasm, in the belief that each time they have a psychiatric panacea. Such pressure for innovation is an added factor to the 'normal' motivation of 'social exchange' of information for recognition mentioned earlier. This results in a pattern of innovation which is characteristic of psychiatry. Gralnick (1969) has made some pointed remarks about this:

Psychiatrists, as any human beings, will grasp for straws. With the introduction of insulin shock therapy, reports of 90% to 95% cures appeared, and we were carried away with enthusiasm. Thousands of papers were written on the subject, physiological explanations for its effectiveness were propounded. Yet, where is insulin therapy today? Who can report such cures now? That which was once heralded is hardly used today, only some decades since its introduction. Electro-shock treatment is not faring much differently. It is not uncommon to hear psychiatrists, who only recently waxed enthusiastic about this procedure, indicate equal enthusiasm about the tranquillizers. They are turning away from shock treatment. The explanations for its effectiveness are no longer meaningful, but those for the new drugs gain credence. How long before we witness the same thing occurring with the tranquillizers which are currently capturing the scene? In the light of what has happened with the others, it would not seem far-fetched to forecast the same doom for these drugs in psychiatry. (p. 90)

In psychiatry, then, innovation characteristically manifests itself as a widespread endorsement of a new technique, even though not thoroughly researched, and an almost equally rapid disaffection as more sober appraisal is undertaken. With respect to the growth and spread of therapeutic community techniques, similar structural conditions prevail. Despite claims that the therapeutic community is not merely another way of 'doing something to' the resident to make him 'better', and that it involves a radical reconception of the relationship between doctor and resident, nevertheless the course of therapeutic community developments has similarities to previous psychiatric innovations. When developed during the 1950s, the technique was claimed to be in many respects the missing dimension in psychiatric treatment which would revolutionize the mental health services. Such claims are associated with Maxwell Jones, amongst others: 'We believe that the application of some of the principles of sociology such as we have described would favourably alter the existing social structure of hospital communities with considerable benefit to the resident' (Jones, 1952).

Such views were developed as an alternative to the large traditional mental hospital. But, since the 1950s, there has been greater emphasis on community care and the passing of the traditional mental hospital. These changes in attitude, and the inevitable appraisal that follows an innovatory idea, have resulted in a more specific application of the therapeutic community to types of resident as a treatment method in its own right. The burning desire to find an alternative to the custodial mental hospital which added weight to the therapeutic community movement in the 1950s has lessened, though the rapid spread of the technique into other areas such as adolescent units, hostels, prisons, drug units, community schools, and so on, has resulted in a larger and equally zealous following in the 1970s and 1980s.

However, the essential conclusion to draw here is that the fortunes of this area of social psychiatry seem to be unrelated to any research process which has clarified the essential nature of the idea, or provided evidence of its effectiveness. Such an ideal for the rational development of medical science is increasingly challenged even for general medicine, and makes the relevance of research uncertain.

## The place of research

We can illustrate the difficulties of research within the therapeutic community as a medical scientific innovation by examining the way in which therapeutic communities have reacted to research activities. If we divide the history of therapeutic communities into three phases — innovation, wider support, and routine application — it seems that research activities underwent a greatly changed legitimacy at each stage.

First, innovation. As we have been arguing, there has been

considerable debate amongst sociologists and philosophers of science as to the nature of scientific innovation. Therapeutic communities illustrate well that the way in which an idea is born can affect its ultimate fate. In this case we find that the therapeutic community was 'invented' simultaneously in two different places, unknown to each other, during the Second World War in Britain. On the one hand it was invented by the Tavistock Clinic as a by-product of their investigations into group relations, personal selection, job placement, the promotion of health education and training, and even psychological warfare. In a sense it never 'stood out' as anything special in this collection of developments, and after the war became, in the hands of analytic Tavistock staff at the Cassel Hospital, subservient to Freudian analysis as the main therapeutic device. Tom Main led this development, becoming Director of the Cassel Hospital in 1946.

On the other hand Maxwell Jones, a research trained, clinically oriented psychiatrist, also hit on this new approach, but without the aid (or perhaps distractions) of a social scientific outlook. As a result he could concentrate on a method which his research training indicated worked most effectively without being side-tracked into generating other social psychological innovations. After the war Maxwell Jones did not slide back into a more trusted approach, but in an open-minded manner pressed ahead, and through not inconsiderable personal drive managed to push his idea through to stage two of our development structure, by getting wider institutional and, crucially, financial support at Belmont Hospital in 1947.

In this first phase of innovation, we can see that both inventions occurred in the early part of World War II, and had attracted wider support within five to six years. This period would seem to be a typical lapse of time after which, without support, such an innovation might well become forgotten. What were the roles of research and in particular the use of research as a political bargaining counter, at this time? It is clear from the literature (Bion, 1960; Kraupl-Taylor, 1958; Jones, 1952) that research activity was a vital source of information about the effectiveness of this method — the primary function of research; but it is also clear that research results were an important source of legitimation and status for both of these independent innovations — a secondary function of research. For example, on the Tavistock side, Bion's experimental intervention in Northfield Military Hospital, from which later ideas developed, was explicitly designed as research, and not as merely administrative change. More significantly both he and Tom Main published their findings at about this time, which increased support for their ideas. Maxwell Jones also used research techniques. Although he invented the therapeutic community intuitively, he soon attempted to establish its efficacy as he had been trained to do. And it is evident from his first book that the results of his work were important for gaining wider institutional support — first at Dartford Hospital in 1945–6, and subsequently at Belmont Hospital.

To summarize at this point: the movement from initial innovation to wider support, such as happened for the therapeutic community and might happen for any mental health innovation, is likely to take a standard length of time for this stage of development — about five years. And the most crucial factor in this development is the demonstration through research that the method is effective. Hence research activity enters into this development in a vital way, to provide evidence and status that the new method works. But of course wider support in this case merely means financial and other resources being available to continue the work in one or two places. What sort of processes govern the development from this point to widespread routinization and application? If this new method were a drug we would expect from studies of the diffusion of new drugs (Coleman, 1957) that a demonstration of effectiveness would almost automatically result in widespread usage, subject to resource limitations. But for the therapeutic community these resource and other qualifications are more significant — application of therapeutic community techniques is not widespread even after forty years.

At this point, then, we can spell out some of the factors which tend to limit the wider use of therapeutic community techniques, and the relevance of research to overcoming such limitations. First, therapeutic communities usually require above average resources per patient or resident. They require: more staff; higher quality staff; more space with suitable facilities for work activities and group meetings; and so on. This immediately provokes questions about what is gained for these additional resources — and inevitably research is demanded to prove that such resources produce better output.

Second, therapeutic communities, as many new innovations, are weak in the face of powerful established positions. Initially they overcame this problem through having highly dynamic leaders (and many still do). But this situation is unstable — leaders move on. The only way out is to gain status and therefore power by becoming professionally respectable; or to demonstrate in the language of the establishment (i.e. through research) that therapeutic communities deserve support because they are effective. Unfortunately becoming professionally respectable is as unsatisfactory a solution as charismatic leadership — either because it may distort the therapeutic process, or again because professionally acceptable personnel move on. A further alternative is of course to engage in collective action and fight a purely political battle for resources, as the Paddington Day Hospital did in London. But this is not possible unless the therapeutic community is established in an organization which has resources (like the National Health Service), and may well be a tactic from which even radical therapists will shrink. The result of these difficulties is that once again research is looked to as the way out and forward in the struggle for recognition.

Third, we can turn to the culture of the therapeutic community as a hindrance to wider acceptance. Rapoport's cultural themes of democracy, permissiveness, and communality in which confrontation can flourish, contrast markedly with those of the conventional professional community and thus have resulted in many professionals merely expressing sympathy with the ideas while politely declining to work in a therapeutic community. But if we look a little closer at the culture we find that self-examination and criticism are an essential ingredient. Indeed research was a central part of the early innovations — not just an activity grafted on to the side. And it is just this interest in research which can provide a cultural bridge to the more conventional professional establishment — who like it or not have an enormous influence over the distribution of resources, power and culture in this area of mental health.

In sum, there has been a much slower development from stage two (wider support) to stage three (widespread application), than from stages one to two. Moreover, research activity has played an important role in this differential rate of development. In the early stage it enabled the initial innovation to gain further support, but since then it has been less popular amongst therapeutic community practitioners — to their disadvantage, for each of the three areas of hindrance for expansion (resources, power and culture) could be helped through greater research activity.

To understand this relative decline in the use of research we must look not only at the internal development of therapeutic communities, but also their relations with the outside world — especially the psychiatric arena in which many of them are embedded. As far as the outside world is concerned the therapeutic community has come under increasing pressure to change from an experiment to a conventional treatment alternative — that is to say from 'innovation' to 'delivering the goods' in terms of patient treatment and improvement. This pressure is quite normal in that any new development is

195

given a certain amount of licence to begin with, but after a while, in order to continue in attracting interest, and funds, and in general to remain viable, the innovation has to provide in some way a technically applicable product. This involves insidious invitations to forsake pressures for wide change which the therapeutic community implied, and to come under the wing of conventional psychiatry, as yet another specific treatment alternative. However the point here is that experimental credit in a sense runs out, as we argued from the data on referrals to the Henderson in chapter 4.

Internally, the therapeutic community also developed away from research. Despite the early experimental approach, it was tempting after a number of years to feel that the major idea was worked out. There was a tendency to move therefore from asking 'what ideas can we use here?', to proselytizing a finished set of ideas to those who had not yet heard the message. There was thus a move from innovation itself to the spreading of that innovation, already accomplished.

These changes, internally and externally, can be recognized clearly in the appointment in the late 1950s of the team of research workers from outside the therapeutic community, to study the Henderson Hospital. This arrangement epitomizes on the one hand the split between experimental and applied therapy demanded by the outside world (i.e. the unit no longer does research, it does therapy and therefore outside research workers must come in to do research); and on the other hand the internal change from asking — 'How can we develop our ideas?', to asking — 'We have our ideas and method already, how can we improve the application and wider use of these ideas?'

However given these changes one may well ask whether, despite this split, research in such a climate has been useful? One answer is to look at the impact of that research team's work, culminating in Rapoport's book *Community as Doctor*. The current author and Rapoport examined this question in a study which identified some of the social processes surrounding the reception of the book (Manning and Rapoport, 1976). By looking at book reviews and questioning relevant individuals, we identified three major processes, and several more diffuse reactions.

The three major ones were rejection, implicit acceptance and reincorporation. These refer to Henderson Hospital's reactions. At first the book was rejected. Although this was partly due to the director, it is a common reaction to outside research reports. Implicit acceptance however, was occurring simultaneously amongst more junior staff members. Thus the second senior doctor used the book for the reason that its results were a useful way of tackling some of the problems of translating ideals into practice in the hospital. Significantly, it was not until the director changed that full reincorporation could happen amongst a staff group less clearly associated with the original research period. The rejection process seems to have been a defence against anticipated threatening criticism, amplified by the deep commitment of staff, compounded for new staff by the lack of personal contact with the research workers and therefore any confidence or support derived from this. Reincorporation on the other hand could only occur after a period of time had clearly elapsed so that the book took on a more academic and less personal relationship with the hospital.

The lesson from this could be that one has always to wait for five years or so before research findings can be accepted. But this would be patently absurd, for the vitality of research work is surely bound up with its rapid feed-back and use in developing further the practical work it has studied. There was however a more fundamental lesson, we argued. It is that the early splitting of the therapeutic community and research activity should be repaired. This split between practice and research activities, between systematic study from the outside, and haphazard reflection on the inside, was the chief source of hostility towards research workers.

We summed up this issue in five maxims:

1) The utilisation and diffusion of social research are sensitive to the effects of different, sometimes inter-related social processes.

2) The chances that there will be direct utilisation by subjects of an applied research study will be enhanced if the research formulation is collaboratively arrived at, and the research results are fed back interactively.

3) If, for any reason, collaborative formulation and interactive feedback are incompletely achieved, a defensive *rejection phenomenon* may be expected.

4) Overt rejection does not preclude covert acceptance of many aspects of the research, particularly if there are mediating individuals in the action groups.

5) Diffusion of the research on a broader basis may bring about a re-incorporation process within the action group at a later date, achieving a greater degree of ultimate utilisation. (Manning & Rapoport, 1976: 467)

To summarize, many therapeutic communities have abandoned the research orientation which was a central part of their early development, and as a consequence have had less influence within the mental-health field than they might have done, since research results appear to be one way of overcoming three important sources of hindrance to wider influence — shortage of resources, lack of power, and an unacceptable culture. The reason for abandoning research has been due both to external pressure to concentrate on providing a regular service, and to internal self-satisfaction that the basic idea had been sufficiently developed.

## THE THERAPEUTIC COMMUNITY AS A SOCIAL MOVEMENT

In this chapter we have so far argued three things. First, in its own terms the therapeutic community was inadequately conceptualized. Second, as a scientific innovation it was shaped by social contingencies at best irrelevant to, and at worst undermining, its scientific worth. Third, that research activities initially enhanced but subsequently hindered the spread of therapeutic community work. Perhaps, therefore, the therapeutic community could be better understood by abandoning any connection with ideas of scientific discovery and research, and by adopting a completely different model of it in terms of a social and political movement for change. The language of scientific innovation and research, from this point of view, can be reconceptualized as a part of therapeutic community ideology, rather than accepted at face value.

The sociology of social movements, like the sociology of science, has exhibited a theoretical progression in recent years such that there are now a number of competing models which can be used to examine the nature of the therapeutic community movement. The classic approach combined a psychological view of the reasons for individuals joining a social movement, with a life cycle model of the movement's organization which developed through charismatic leadership, and declined through routinization and goal-displacement.

The motivations identified for individual membership were derived from work on mass psychology concerned with the rise of fascism in the 1930s. For example Cantril (1941) suggested that a person's ego is particularly subject to 'suggestibility' in critical situations such as war-time when the social environment is rapidly changing. This idea was extended by King (1956) to include the experience of 'mass society' as particularly conducive to social movements. He argued that mass society exhibited cultural confusion, such that social norms were unstable and inconsistent. In order for individuals and sub-groups to get their voice heard in this socially heterogeneous context, they had to organize themselves, a process aided especially by the development of mass communications. Individual discontents, particularly the desire for consistent meaning, were thus exacerbated, the argument ran, by value conflicts, uncertainty over status, conflicting goals, and a consequent sense of personal inadequacy and uncertainty.

Smelser (1962) attempted to link this view of individual motivation to the wider social structure through the notion of structural strain. By this he meant for example the appearance of new knowledge, new social deprivations, changed norms or values, which 'demand readjustment in the social situation' (p. 290). Such a condition of strain, he suggested, gave rise to two kinds of generalized beliefs about the resolution of the strain: the creation of new norms such as new laws or social policies; or the creation of new values such as religious renewal, or communal or utopian social orders.

The growth and development of the democratic therapeutic community movement described in chapters 1 and 2 clearly fits this model. Long term dissatisfaction with the state of mental hospitals, and the growth of social science knowledge up to the 1940s provided the pre-conditions for structural strain which were exacerbated by wartime conditions: the rapid development of new knowledge, new social deprivations and particularly the widespread desire for more egalitarian social policies. Smelser also identifies accurately one of the major dilemmas in therapeutic community work in his description of belief systems as either norm-oriented or value-oriented. Therapeutic community writing has expressed a chronic uncertainty about whether to work with existing services towards 'better' social policies, or to withdraw from such co-operation to a more utopian and isolated life.

In considering the creation and development of concept and educational therapeutic communities, this model is even more appropriate. The phenomenal growth of concept communities across the world has essentially been fuelled by the chronic dissatisfaction felt by both clients and professionals with traditional methods of intervention in the addictions field. A similar though far less urgent concern is apparent in the longer history of communities set up for therapeutic education. In both cases the literature describing particular community developments frequently offers motivational accounts in terms of such dissatisfactions.

Since the early 1970s however, some social movement theorists have questioned such a psychological view of the origins of movements. Earlier, writers such as King (1956) had noted that while there are grievances and structural strains in all historical periods, only a few develop into social movements. This point has been taken up in the 'resource mobilization' model (McCarthy & Zald, 1977) to suggest that: 'Movements seldom develop except out of existing organised groups that already possess the resources necessary for providing selective inducements and exercising coercion over potential adherents' (Turner, 1981: 15). Thus the origin and development of a social movement are, it is argued, very little affected by the rise and fall of deprivation, or the extent of subjectively-felt grievances, or the spread of new beliefs and ideas. This model stresses, then, the central organization of inducements to and coercion of movement members rather than the spontaneous eruption of grievances.

This approach draws heavily on an economic conundrum first posited by Olson (1965). He argued that rational self interest could not possibly account for the combination of individuals into collective action since any subsequent benefits would be shared equally between activists and non-members. Since the contribution of any individual member would be insufficient to make a significant impact on total change, a rational individual would not pay the cost of activism, but passively enjoy any benefits as a 'free ride'. Consequently movements could not develop out of the interests of aggrieved individuals, and must necessarily therefore draw their economic, organizational and political resources from elsewhere.

To draw the contrast as clearly as possible, these two approaches to the motivation of movement membership stress respectively the creation of a movement out of the grievances of potential members on the one hand, and the recruitment of members to a new movement based on pre-existing resources and organization potential on the other. This latter view also suggests insights into the origin of therapeutic communities. In chapter 1 we saw how the democratic therapeutic community was spawned by general work at the Tavistock during the war, and by post-war problems of resettlement and unemployment. Both the key protagonists, Main and Jones, relied on the resources and support of the government departments of health and labour respectively. More importantly as respected members of the psychiatric profession they had direct access to sources of communication through journals, conferences and other professional networks. Educational therapeutic communities in a less intense manner have also developed through the professional and government resources available to the general field of education. By contrast, concept therapeutic communities have drawn on such sources of strength very little. Indeed in the early years, in the 1960s, these communities explicitly rejected such an idea, relying on a tightly organized self-help network to generate material resources and to communicate their ideas.

## Getting organized

Whatever the origins of a social movement, its growth and impact depend crucially on how it becomes organized. The classic view stressed two key features: the nature of the belief system or ideology which gave the movement its *raison d'être*; and the quality of leadership which expressed such beliefs and enabled the membership to come together psychologically and materially.

Smelser (1962) has argued most forcefully for a focus on the belief system as the defining characteristic of a social movement as against its classification in terms of members' psychological predispositions, or the patterns of communication and organization. As such, a social movement creates or alters the consciousness of members, their collective identity, and their sense of actual and potential social reality. Turner (1981) summarizes this in terms of 'reality construction': 'Altered ways of viewing both self and larger systems of social relationships are often more important products of social movements than any specific organisational or political accomplishments' (p. 6).

Bittner (1969) suggests that the nature of radical beliefs is distinct in two respects. First, it differs from ordinary social beliefs or commonsense in so far as the latter are made up of heterogeneous norms and values which are frequently inconsistent, and thus require practical wisdom born of social experience as to the selective relevance of social rules in any situation. This is the kind of practical consciousness we discussed in chapter 3 in connection with Gidden's work. Radical beliefs do not take such commonsense knowledge for granted, but subject it to radical re-appraisal. Second, Bittner suggests that radical beliefs, in order to undertake such re-appraisal, posit a unified and internally consistent interpretation of the social world. In this respect, radical beliefs share the same ground as the principles of scientific enquiry. However, radical beliefs forsake the moral neutrality of science in favour of some kind of 'salvation'. Bittner uses Max Weber's term, prophecy, to encompass this notion:

Prophecy always means, in the first place for the prophet himself,

201

and then for his helpmates: a unitary view of life won by taking a deliberately unified meaningful position to it. Life and the world, the social and the cosmic events, have for the prophet a decidedly systematic unity of meaning, and the conduct of them must, in order to bring salvation, be oriented toward it. (Weber, quoted in Bittner, 1969:296)

It is not difficult to see how these points relate to therapeutic communities. Democratic therapeutic community writers repeatedly refer back to two key statements of belief contained in Main's 1946 paper on the hospital as a therapeutic institution, and particularly Rapoport's 1960 formulation of the 'unit ideology', introduced in chapter 4. There he reported the three fundamental propositions that 'everything is treatment', 'all treatment is rehabilitation', and 'all patients should get the same treatment'; and identified the four cultural themes of democracy, permissiveness, communalism, and reality confrontation. These have now become enshrined through widespread repetition as the all-encompassing shibboleths of community life.

Turner's notion of 'reality construction' is particularly appropriate to therapeutic community work as documented in a recent book-length study of eight communities by Bloor *et al.* (1988) introduced in chapter 2. This study focuses explicitly on the nature of therapeutic community work as the reconstitution of reality:

A crucial aspect of the new subjective reality of the therapeutic community is the vocabulary of its expression. Indeed, the newly learned vocabulary of motives, feeling states, and descriptions *constitutes* that subjective reality since all thought is conceptual, that is, verbal. Reality construction in the therapeutic community involves imbibing (and possibly repeating) a series of accounts — accounts of the community social structure, accounts of the process of therapy, accounts of residents' difficulties, and so on. In the process of learning those accounts provided they are not opposed and contradicted by alternative accounts from other sources such as a resident counter-culture, then those accounts take on the appearance of objective fact — they become the reality of the situation they seek to describe. To resurrect a much-used trope, the new resident is like a stranger in a foreign land who at first struggles to master everyday phrases and labours to translate everything into his native tongue, but eventually that foreign language supplants the native tongue, becomes the language of thoughts and dreams, and translation is no longer necessary. (p. 72, pre-publication manuscript)


Even critics of therapeutic communities attest to their special beliefs in the dismissal of them as 'myths' (Morrice, 1972) and 'fantasies' (Zeitlyn, 1967). Indeed the maintenance of the unity of radical beliefs in the face of such criticism is a perennial problem from which therapeutic communities are not immune. Rawlings (1984) has argued that therapeutic community practitioners face three threats to their unity of beliefs: the uncertainty of evaluating therapeutic success; external criticism; and personal doubt and disillusion. She documents the way in which criticism can be discounted as ignorance or 'old news' while disillusion can be explained in terms of personal or group incompetence. Both strategies, also commonly observed in the social movements literature, are frequently used ironically to reaffirm the special and difficult nature of radical beliefs. However the problem of therapeutic evaluation has a special relevance to therapeutic communities as we noted at length earlier in this chapter. The common properties of scientific enquiry and radical beliefs, noted by Bittner as the rejection of commonsense, have resulted in both strengths and weaknesses for therapeutic community beliefs. On the one hand to the extent that evidence can be generated, which is scientifically acceptable, of the effectiveness of therapeutic community work (such as that attempted in chapter 5), therapeutic community beliefs can draw affirmation from a powerful form of modern legitimation. However, the absence of such confirmatory evidence may expose therapeutic communities to the extent that they claim to be scientific, to the loss of institutional funding and declining status. Ambivalence around this issue is nicely captured in De Leon's remarks quoted in chapter 2, page 37, on the use of research in concept communities.

The second key feature in the classical model of social movements was the crucial task of leadership in the maintenance and expression of beliefs, and the organization of the movement as the embodiment of those beliefs. This is typically portrayed in terms of the charisma of the leader, and the commitment of the members. The classical model leans heavily on Weber's typology of authority. He suggested that while stable authority systems might depend on either the traditionally or legally sanctioned distribution of power, at times of change and innovation, power and authority were exercised charismatically. Originally this model was drawn from Weber's study of religion. The religious leader was defined as inspired by divine or supernatural powers:

> The leader, in effect, heads a new social movement, and his
> followers and disciples are converts to a new cause. There is a
> sense of being 'called' to spread the new gospel, a sense of rejec-
> ting the past and heralding the future. (Blau, 1970:150)

However many writers have extended this model to encompass non-
religious affairs:

> scientific discovery, ethical promulgation, artistic creativity,
> political and organisational authority (authoritatem, auctor, author-
> ship) and in fact all forms of genius, in the original sense of the
> word as permeation by the 'spirit', are as much instances of the
> category of charismatic things as is religious prophecy. (Shils,
> 1965:80)

Although, as Parkin points out (1982:76-9), Weber did not
elaborate the ways in which charismatic and other types of authority
engineer popular compliance, it is clear that charisma, and the
inspiration it creates, is also importantly a quality residing in the relationship between leader and follower. Charisma cannot be exercised
in isolation. As we noted in chapter 2, Etzioni (1975) has suggested
that the other side of charisma is the positive moral commitment of
followers, which in the case of therapeutic communities helps to
explain the apparent paradox between a radically democratic structure and a morally authoritative staff group.

The nature of compliance in the classical view has been given an
influential formulation by Kanter (1972) based on an extensive study
of communes in nineteenth- and twentieth-century America, including
the original concept therapeutic community, Synanon. The primary
problem for a leader, she argues, is how to organize the group for
its successful survival, how to involve and satisfy its members, how
to get necessary work done, make decisions, and so on. She
summarizes this in terms of three problems: of commitment to the
group in terms of retaining members; of generating group cohesion;
and of establishing social control. Each of these is tackled in terms
of six paired processes, three of which involve detachment from the
past, and three of which correspondingly involve attachment to the
future: sacrifice of previously valued activities or things; investment
of time, effort or money; renunciation of family and previous
relationships; communion of shared work, regular meetings and

common culture; mortification of identity through mutual criticism, new rules and sanctions; and transcendence through ideology, charismatic leadership, mystery and tradition. This schema can be set out systematically as follows:

| Problem | Process of detachment | Process of attachment |
|---|---|---|
| Retaining membership | sacrifice | Investment |
| Group cohesion | renunciation | communion |
| Social control | mortification | transcendence |

Kanter's model expresses clearly the dominating totality of forms of collective life which Coser (1974) has aptly dubbed (and for obvious reasons) 'greedy institutions'. It also clarifies that the focus of the classical model is inside the social movement and its collective organization, and as such has been most effectively employed in the analysis of utopias (Goodwin and Taylor, 1982) religious groups (Lofland, 1985), and therapeutic communities (Manning, 1980), as well as communes.

With respect to the therapeutic community movement, charismatic leadership has most commonly been ascribed to Maxwell Jones, both in his early direction of the Belmont unit and in his subsequent career as proselytizer of therapeutic community principles in prisons, schools, hospitals:

> Maxwell Jones, in the Belmont days, was the archetypal charismatic innovator. His enthusiasm was infectious — not only to staff, but to patients as well. He was one of those reformist enthusiasts whose work, when reviewed by a World Health Organisation Expert Committee, was praised but queried in terms of 'how much was the method and how much was the man?'; All utopian reformers think and act to some extent ideologically, using faith and conviction in the absence of demonstrated scientific principles. Maxwell Jones is of this ilk. (Rapoport, 1970:407)

Now a self styled 'social ecologist', he has adopted the concept therapeutic community movement in a new burst of enthusiasm (De Leon and Zeigenfuss, 1986), trying to draw out as before the relevance of his early work for this most organizationally successful area of therapeutic community activity. However he continues to excite reverential interest amongst central British therapeutic community figures, who maintain close links with him and follow closely his shifts of interest in the USA. (Clark, 1987)

Concept and educational therapeutic communities also had early charismatic leaders, respectively Chuck Dederich and Homer Lane. Although these two individuals are no longer alive, their legendary charisma is still drawn on to inspire subsequent generations of workers.

In terms of compliance, therapeutic communities can be analysed differentially with respect to staff and clients, and again according to different historical periods in the movement. Using Etzioni's typology, presented in chapter 2, we can see that charismatic leadership ideally creates, at least for staff, a positive moral commitment to the community and its leader's exercise of normative power. However, as we noted in chapter 2, clients, at least initially, may not be committed in such a way to the community. This is particularly the case for concept communities. Indeed their special skill is in moving from the exercise of coercive power over an alienated addict, through remunerative power over a calculative addict (using the privilege system for 'payments'), to the creation of moral commitment in the ex-addict who can then be trusted to participate in a more democratic way in community life. A similar process of transition has been described by Whiteley (1972) as the movement from negative to positive transference in the emotional involvement of residents at the Henderson. Evidence for this can also be found in the study of residents' rank ordering of the helpfulness of groups at the Henderson (chapter 4), analysed by length of stay. Figure 6.1 shows how the community meeting, which in democratic therapeutic communities is the site for the exercise of community power over residents, suffers an initial decline in ranking followed by a rise, as residents stay longer.

For most communities, seeing residents through to this stage of positive moral commitment is seen as the key to effecting any lasting therapeutic range, and hence the problem of early leavers (or 'splittees' in American parlance) is a perennial concern.

Kanter's analysis of commitment suggests in more detail the processes which both staff and resident have to go through to attain this desired state. For example the addict newly arrived at a concept therapeutic community gives up drugs, and invests time and effort in the community; previous relationships in the addict world are renounced in favour of new relationships in the community; the old addict identity and life style are mortified in favour of a new ideology and self-concept. Staff are not immune from these processes. Since

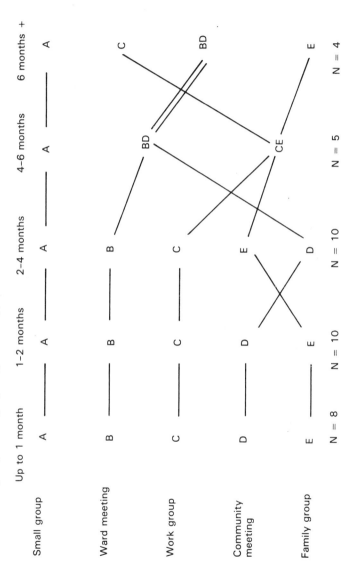

*Figure 6.1* Resident group ranking by length of stay, 1973

therapeutic communities are regarded as a radical break with traditional methods, psychiatrists and nurses in democratic communities sacrifice conventional career patterns and invest effort in new skills such as group work. Socially and professionally they tend to give up old contacts for a new social network both within their community, and within other therapeutic communities. Finally, for some, though not all, there is an experience of transcendence to a new identity.

While the classical model's emphasis on beliefs, leadership and commitment applies particularly to individual therapeutic communities, the resource mobilization model is more relevant to the therapeutic community movement writ large. Of course key members of the Association of Therapeutic Communities, for example, promulgate beliefs, cultivate charisma, and engineer commitment. But more mundane issues of recruitment, organization, and resources are prominent.

The resource mobilization model suggests that the origins and growth of a social movement owe much to the way in which the movement is organized, the resources available, and the target groups aimed for. Resources consist basically of money for advertising, meetings and publications, and labour for undertaking administration, public speaking, and writing. In addition, relevant expertise, public legitimacy, and the ability to reward potential and actual members are important.

The organization of these resources can be either through a traditional hierarchical bureaucracy, or a decentralized and segmented set of loosely affiliated groups. In general it is argued from this perspective that there is a trade off between these two structures. The former is task efficient and stable while the latter maximizes a sense of community and commitment. Whatever the mix, this model stresses the crucial role of the organizer, rather than the charismatic leader, in terms of resources and their effective organization. While one person may be both leader and organizer, many successful social movements rest on a division of labour between these two key people.

The crucial transactions for a social movement from this perspective are with its environment. Whereas the classic model focuses on the internal life of the movement — the psychological motivation of members and their commitment to charismatic leadership — the resource mobilization model emphasizes the external environment as the target for a movement, both to achieve social change and to raise the necessary resources. In terms of resources, the questions raised are about the conditions affecting the demand for and supply of social movement resources, and the costs and rewards for individuals and organizations of involvement in the movement. Some writers have drawn an extensive analogy with micro economics here, suggesting that there is a social movement 'industry' in which individual social movement organizations behave like individual firms (McCarthy & Zald, 1977).

In terms of the politics of social change, this external orientation focuses on the question of the range of possible actions the movement can take, the likely reactions (including suppression) from outside the movement, and the nature of various target groups of potential supporters, from activists, through sympathizers and the indifferent bystander, to opponents.

The resources available to individual communities and social movement organizations like the Association of Therapeutic Communities (ATC), the World Federation of Therapeutic Communities (WFTC) or the Planned Environment Therapy Trust (PETT), flow principally from governments either through the public employment of professional staff, or the right of clients to social security and to have their fees paid. For example, conferences, membership fees, and publications provide the ATC with money some of which comes direct from state employers and some from employees. Consequently it is crucial that therapeutic communities have sufficient expertise to run good conferences and publications in order to attract and reward membership, and that their work is seen as legitimate in the eyes of government departments. As was noted earlier in this chapter, the source of such legitimacy in the early years of the democratic communities was a kind of experimental credit, sustained in part by Maxwell Jones's charisma. After this ran out, in the 1960s, British therapeutic communities entered a phase of chronic legitimacy deficit, one consequence of which was the establishment of the ATC itself. However the resource really needed here is definitive proof of therapeutic effectiveness, which, as discussed in detail in chapter 5, and earlier in this chapter, has been difficult to obtain.

Legitimacy deficit is not however simply a matter of scientific demonstration. The resource mobilization model suggests that the kind of actions possible, and consequent reactions particularly of potential supporters, is also significant. For example, concept communities have grown rapidly and continuously around the world. Democratic communities on the other hand suffered declining interest in the 1960s and 1970s, now somewhat reversed. This difference is best explained in terms not of scientific proof or leadership inspiration, but of differential target populations: staff, clients, and administrators. Concept communities trained their own staff from ex-addicts, and provided a much needed service, however effective, in an area in which alternative services had singularly failed to work. Democratic communities however had to recruit and convert professional staff trained in a traditional, and potentially hostile, approach. They also had to compete in a rapidly changing service context, in which as we noted in chapter 2, a new emphasis developed on physical treatment, and subsequently on non-residential community based treatment. More recently, shortcomings of those physical treatments, and the continuing and indeed growing relevance of small community based residential facilities, have stimulated a revival of interest in therapeutic community work.

In addition to these externally generated demand elasticities, democratic communities have also had to contend, particularly in the 1970s, with periodic attempts at direct repression. Some well known British communities have been shut down. Others, including the Henderson, have only survived as a result of widespread political and academic lobbying in the face of closure proposals.

The organization of such resistance, and indeed of individual communities and the therapeutic community movement as a whole, has suffered particularly from the dilemma posed earlier of a trade off between task efficiency on the one hand and communal commitment on the other. Part of the irritation expressed by conventional psychiatry about therapeutic communities is the apparent celebration of disorganization, debate, and discussion as vehicles through which social and psychological dynamics can develop and be analysed. This can make communities difficult to deal with from the outside in terms of clear accountability and decision-making. Within communities concern for such 'realistic' issues as administrative clarity can lead to heated disagreement and splits between junior 'idealistic' staff and senior leaders. Task efficiency, it is felt, would destroy the very nature of the therapeutic community process. However gross task inefficiency could end up with the same result through closure. Most effective communities therefore have to operate with an uncomfortable compromise or cyclical oscillation between the two ideals.

The same problem has reappeared in the operation of the ATC. Originating as a forum for the exchange of ideas, its conference format settled down to a regular re-creation of large and small group 'experiences', familiar to many staff already. This was not at all conducive to the effective management of political advertising on behalf of therapeutic communities in general, nor academic or training activities. Neither was it very instructive for staff who worked in such groups during the year anyway. It has taken much of the ATC's fifteen-year history to slowly come to terms with the realities of organizing for effective action, and only in recent years have such activities as research, training, accreditation, publication, and charity incorporation been successfully undertaken. In terms of the resource mobilization model, J. Stuart Whiteley, director of the Henderson since the mid 1960s, has been the 'organization man' equivalent of Maxwell Jones, the charismatic leader of earlier years.

## Charisma routinized

The classical model is pessimistic about the survival of social movements. It draws on Weber's observations about the instability of charismatic authority:

> In its pure form charismatic authority has a character specifically foreign to every-day routine structures. The social relationships directly involved are strictly personal, based on the validity and practice of charismatic personal qualities. If this is not to remain a purely transitory phenomenon, but to take on the character of a permanent relationship forming a stable community of disciples or a band of followers or a party organisation or any sort of political or hierocratic organisation, it is necessary for the character of charismatic authority to become radically changed. Indeed, in its pure form charismatic authority may be said to exist only in the process of originating. It cannot remain stable, but becomes either traditionalised or rationalised, or a combination of both.
>
> (Weber, 1947)

This disintegration of charisma is said to give rise to three things (Zald and Ash, 1966): a primary interest in merely maintaining the organization of the movement; a transformation of goals in the direction of pragmatic, attainable and limited objectives; and the concentration of power in the hands of a stable leadership minority (called after Michels (1949) the 'iron law of oligarchy'). From this point of view, for example, revolutionaries, strikers, and religious sects metamorphose into governments, trade unions, and churches; radicalism changes to conservatism.

However, this use of Weber to argue that in some sense the essence of a movement is thereby eclipsed or bypassed in favour of a powerful conservatizing tendency is to present only part of his view. In addition Weber suggested that attempts are made, sometimes more or less successfully, to preserve charisma rather than dispense with it. Weber suggested that this might typically be done by organizing charismatic succession either through the family, i.e. by heredity, or through institutional means such as a leader's designation of his or her own successor, or through ritual or revelation.

While in general there is an assumed conflict between charisma and organization, since the two require radically different kinds of commitment from followers, Etzioni (1975) has suggested that charisma can be functional in organizations provided it is integrated satisfactorily. He suggests that organizations such as therapeutic communities can incorporate charisma in senior staff or leaders without destroying the bureaucratic requirements of the administrative environment through a division of labour between therapists and administrators. While of course there can still be conflict between these two, examples of which are legion in the therapeutic community literature, nevertheless the two can continue in day-to-day work in relative isolation, so that charismatic inspiration can flourish on the one side and bureaucratic efficiency on the other.

In an earlier paper (Manning, 1976) it was suggested that the therapeutic community movement exhibited many of the symptoms of movement stagnation suggested by the classical model. Routinization began as early as 1947 when Jones set up a unit within the National Health Service. This official recognition provided economic security for workers in the movement but required some evidence of success.

The Association of Therapeutic Communities also provided some evidence of the process of routinization. Although the character of the movement changed after 1960, particularly the spread of activity into wider fields, only in the 1970s did this growth and spread produce problems of co-ordination. Before, there had been few enough communities for all to maintain informal contacts. Subsequently there were too many for this arrangement to continue. King (1956) has noted that uncoordinated movements are unified through goals and doctrines. It is evident that as the therapeutic community idea spread, variegated interpretation led to differences in goals, and hence the need for official co-ordination to clarify and unify the movement.

The differentiation of goals is demonstrated by the heated discussion reported in the issue of the *Association of Therapeutic Communities Newsletter* of 20 February 1973. A small article is entitled: 'Is the Association of Therapeutic Communities an organisation designed to promote social change, or is it a group of professionals discussing a clinical process?'. In this article the problem of priority between political and therapeutic goals is discussed. It seems that the conferences organized by the association not only serve to co-ordinate local 'chapters' (therapeutic communities) but help to air differences of emphasis. Such differences crystallize around different leaders and, as Smelser (1962) points out, may lead to dis-unity in a movement.

Differentiation of goals may occur for a variety of reasons. In this example, the generalized goal of change is seen to have political implications. The goal of patient therapy may in the long term be served by this emphasis at the expense of short-term disruption. As well as this difference in time orientation, it may be that the stated goal of patient therapy has been challenged by the admission of an underlying goal of change within the psychiatric profession. This goal may generate other unintended goals such as pressure to remove more reactionary staff members who do not accept progressive ideas. Furthermore, goals vary from the point of view of the individual involved: the psychiatrist may join a therapeutic community with different goals in mind than the young social therapist. Thus a social movement will change depending on whether long- or short-term, stated or real, intended or unintended, or personal goals are voiced.

Moreover the goal (for instance real, intended, short-term) may be displaced or succeeded over time. Before 1960s the therapeutic community movement can be characterized as pursuing change within the small psychiatric unit, experimentation, and a small degree of proselytizing. After 1960, goals focused more on application to new areas, specialization to certain populations, wider proselytizing, and association with the values of the wider movement of social psychiatry. Within an individual therapeutic community, goals may also change. At the Belmont Social Rehabilitation Unit patients were initially the hardcore unemployed but interest soon changed to treating young people with personality disorders.

In addition to government support, and the slow concentration of goals on survival in the early days of the movement, recent developments suggest further routinization. The realities required by the task efficiency requirements of the resource mobilization model mentioned above, namely research, training, accreditation, publication, charity incorporation, and so on, are precisely the kind of pragmatic and organizational maintenance expedients that the classical model uses as evidence of routinization. The concentration of these activities in a small stable group of established therapeutic community leaders is in the sense used by Michels (1949) evidence of oligarchization predicted by his 'iron law'.

Nevertheless, charismatic inspiration still erupts from time to time in the ways Weber suggests, not least because as we suggested earlier leadership is a qualitative interplay between leaders and led. The messianic delusion brilliantly portrayed by Hobson (1979) as an ever present danger for zealous therapeutic leaders and dependent, paranoid members can, in its milder forms, lead to inspired efforts in individual communities to battle with hostile administrators for resources and to cope with difficult and demanding members.

However the 'shooting star' imagery of the classical model, predicting inevitable decline and burn up, can be subjected to severe criticism. Not only is it the case that not all social movements exhibit inevitable routinization, but that the original imagery of charisma may be overplayed. Banks (1972) argues that:

> Innovation, that is to say, does not win its own way. Some member of society must perceive its ultimate value and devote himself to its exploitation. Others, similarly, must see the value of the innovation to themselves, irrespective of the indifference or even the hostility, of the rest of the population. The two activities — invention and advocacy — may, to be sure, be performed by one and the same person, or two people in unison. They are, that is to say, forms of role behaviour rather than attributes of personality *per se*, and the reference to such a division of labour between roles draws attention to the social nature of the innovatory process as comprising a network of roles, all of which must be performed if innovation is to occur. (p. 38)

The simultaneous and original necessity of both innovation and advocacy leads Banks to suggest that:

> the analysis of creative social movements in terms of such a concept as 'bureaucratisation', especially where this is taken to imply some notion of 'the routinization of charisma', is . . . misleading . . . On the contrary, because enthusiasm is quickly dampened if an advocate is weighed down by the cares of earning a living . . . some attention must be paid by adopters to guaranteeing a regular source of income. . . . Paradoxically, social movements can continue to recruit champions the more they make room for the organisation men. (p. 38)

This point raises clearly the uncomfortable dilemma between processes internal to and external to a social movement: to reject the outside world may secure ideological purity at the expense of resources and support; to accommodate the world may secure resources and support at the expense of ideological purity. In either case, Niv (1980) suggests, decay will ensue either through stagnation or assimilation.

Zald and Ash (1966), however, reject the idea of inevitable decay. In an early statement of the resource mobilization model, they argue both that external processes are more important than the classical model allows and that these can be instrumental in both the continuance or decline of a movement, depending on circumstances. The key features of the external environment are, they suggest: the ebb and flow of public support for the movement; the success or failure in goal attainment; and opportunities for co-operation with other movements. Public support can make or break a movement irrespective of its organizational strength, just as complete success or failure would be likely to render a movement lifeless. Co-operation or even merger may result in growth if the movement gained overall control. There is, they argue, no simple natural history of a social movement.

For example Gillespie's (1983) study of tenants' organizations in the USA suggests that it is quite possible to adopt more conservative, limited, and pragmatic goals than before and discover that a movement is as a result more effective and successful than previously. Similarly, the famous study by Festinger *et al.* (1956) shows how the apparent failure of a religious movement's core predictions to take place resulted not in a decline but in a renewed growth of energetic proselytization.

This model then helps to explain the improved fortunes of the therapeutic community in the 1980s (Hinshelwood, 1981; Trauer, 1984): the ebbing of support in conventional psychiatry in favour of organic treatments in the 1960s and 1970s has turned round; there is a new constituency of potential and actual support in social service departments, and community care residential schemes; as a treatment model evidence slowly accumulates of its effectiveness and of its gradual acceptance in principle as a treatment method; the rapid spread of concept therapeutic communities has helped to sustain interest in the other two types as repositories of conceptual and practical resources. Twelve years on, it makes the conclusion of the 1976 paper quite prescient:

> It seems then that as a social movement the therapeutic community is nearing the end of its life. But, since we are discussing social rather than biological reality, this does not mean oblivions. Two

215

further options remain: the therapeutic community technique within conventional psychiatry remains respected by many, and indeed shorn of its proselytising image may become more acceptable to the psychiatric establishment; second both the technique and the movement may find and indeed have found growing support in non-psychiatric residential institutions. Thus the stream of visitors through Henderson Hospital shows no sign of slackening, but does now consist in large part of non-psychiatric personnel (social workers, probation officers, students and so on). (Manning, 1976:278)

## Crisis and survival

McAdam (1983) argues that the split between the classical model's focus on internal processes, and the resource mobilization model's focus on external processes leads both to miss the dynamic interplay between the two. Rather, he suggests, these should be combined through an examination of three factors: organizational strength, the structure of opportunities, and the response of other groups. While a significant negative change in any one of these may pose difficulties for a movement, and occasionally a stimulus to greater efforts, it would seem that negative change in more than one might spell the demise of a movement or some of its constituent organizations. This has happened for several well-known communities.

The collapse of therapeutic communities has rarely occurred as a result of the direct closure of a thriving enterprise. More often this has come when a community is in trouble internally — indeed such periods of internal disorganization seem particularly common to therapeutic communities and other psychiatric institutions. Studies of mental hospitals have frequently reported episodes of collective disturbance amongst patients on certain wards at certain times which appeared to be a function of the institution rather than individual pathology (Caudill, 1957; Kesey, 1973; Miller, 1957; Parker, 1956; Stanton and Schwartz, 1954; Strauss, 1964). Sometimes these outbreaks appeared to be the result of external pressures on the institution, sometimes a result of internal problems, and often a combination of both. The general pattern was clearly similar in the different settings, and can be characterized as follows:

1 Mutual withdrawal from interaction by staff and patients.
2 Breakdown in communications, classically portrayed by

216

Stanton and Schwartz's (1954) observation of the generation of 'pathological excitement' in patients as a result of 'hidden staff disagreements'.

3  Increase in tension evident through increased violence, rule-breaking and so on.

4  Partial disorganization of ward life, with messages forgotten or misinterpreted, decisions taken by default, greater absenteeism, and a general sense of imminent disaster.

5  Open collective disturbance amongst patients, often with one patient acting out particularly and, as Stanton and Schwartz (1954) put it, acting as the 'spark plug'.

At this point there is a clear sense that something 'has to be done' to avoid either the demise of the ward, or damage to certain individuals (staff as well as patients) in it. Special meetings are set up to restore communication, resolve staff disagreements, and reassert the normal policies and procedures. Usually within days the disturbance dies down as reparative forces appear. But generally the analysis of the processes of disintegration is clearer than of those of reintegration.

This process seems similar to that described by Rapoport (1956) as a general feature of therapeutic community life — regular oscillations in morale and effectiveness in response to the arrival and departure of staff and patients, seasonal factors, and external pressures on the community. Savalle and Wagenborg (1979) have observed a similar process in Holland. Both these papers suggest how these disturbances come to be resolved, and indeed can be consciously resolved in a way that can prove positively beneficial to community members. Both of them stress that such oscillations, far from being inherently destructive, are potentially valuable features of community life and hence to be accepted, if not actually encouraged.

However, the outcome is not always so agreeable since on occasions such disturbance may go beyond the resources of the institution or community to resolve, and hence threaten its future existence. In considering the point at which resolution fails and threatens a total breakdown, we can look further afield than therapeutic communities to see if we can discover some general patterns in institutional life. For example, we can look at failed communes, student protest, naval mutinies, non-western healing communities, and so on for ideas. The common element in these examples is that they are all residential groups with a specific task or purpose in hand which can only be achieved through the co-operative effort of all the members.

Sources of disturbance to community life may be external or

217

internal. It is clear that since residential groups have to survive within a society, however self-sufficiently, they must operate with some resources drawn from outside and if not with the positive approval of, at least without overwhelming hostility from, outsiders. For example, many communes have had difficulty in finding suitable land (in the nineteenth century) or property (in the twentieth century) on and in which to live. In addition they need to buy certain goods, particularly tools, machines, and so on with which to manufacture even the essentials of life: food and clothing. Not only do they require money for this but they must at least conduct themselves in a fashion which does not upset their environment, either morally (for example, sexual relations) or politically (for example, observing the law, paying taxes, registering births and deaths, and so on). Many communes in the nineteenth and twentieth ceturies studied by Kanter (1972), Hardy (1979), Rigby (1974a, 1974b) and others never got beyond these initial hurdles, or if they did, survived for only a short while. Therapeutic communities also must face these difficulties, heightened by their frequent dependence on public finance and the consequent scrutiny of their moral, political, or medical activities.

However, the internal life of communities and groups represents as great or even greater a threat than external pressures. The primary problem discussed earlier in this chapter is how to organize the group for its successful survival, how to involve and satisfy its members, how to get the necessary work done, make decisions, and so on. Failure in these areas may occur through a rapid turnover of members, splitting of the community into sub-groups or factions, the weakening of ideology or culture, loss of social control, and so on. The therapeutic communities are usually disturbed by the arrival and departure of new members (Rapoport, 1956; Hall, 1973), the development of uncommitted sub-groups (Parker, 1956; Sharp, 1975), loss of an accepted ideology (Kensington & Chelsea & Westminster Area Health Authority, 1976), or a breakdown in control (Almond, 1974).

In many cases communal groups which are functioning well manage to survive either external pressure, or internal disorganization. For example, it is well-known that increased external pressure can increase internal solidarity and strength — 'unity in the face of the enemy'. Again a community which has protective support from an outside agency, such as an umbrella organization or other similar communities, or is financially independent, may survive considerable internal crisis. For example, attempted mutinies or prison revolts, although temporarily destroying the internal organization, have often been quickly repressed through the intervention of reinforcements to

aid the particular ship or prison. Less dramatically, a poorly functioning community may stagger on without alarming its benign
supporters, as the religious group in Irish Murdoch's novel (1962),
*The Bell*, managed to. However, it is the combination of external
pressure and internal disorganization which is most deadly to the
survival of the group, and often these are linked when external
pressure prove too great and undermine the internal life of the
community. For example, nineteenth-century communes under
external financial pressure often concentrated on the business side of
their activities which ultimately subverted the ideals of the community
for shared property, communal work, and so on (Kanter, 1972).

As far as therapeutic communities are concerned, it is the combination of internal and external pressures which has proved most difficult to resist. For example, the Paddington Day Hospital (Kensington
& Chelsea Area Health Authority, 1976), early problems at the
Belmont Rehabilitation Unit (Parker, 1956), Chestnut Lodge (Stanton
and Schwartz, 1954), and the experiences of the Connolly unit
(Association of Therapeutic Communities, 1979), all exhibit this
combination. A similar process akin to the financial subversion already
mentioned, whereby staff need to develop psychotherapeutic skills
to advance their external careers have threatened to undermine the
internal ideals for shared (psychotherapeutic) work, was discussed
earlier in chapter 4.

A critical facet of this relationship between external and internal
problems is the way leadership functions to manage its boundary:

> A leader in this sense must be a Janus-like figure, capable of facing
> both ways at once and of taking into account the contradictions
> of his two views. Looking outwards he may be aware of oppor-
> tunities the enterprise should exploit; looking inwards he may see
> the drastic changes that such exploitation might require in the
> existing organisation and its staff. (Rice, 1963)

Punch (1974) has pointed out that 'anti-institutions' involve
themselves in a fundamental contradiction between setting up a new
way of life, with new rules or even no rules, in an environment and
with people who have in the past subscribed to conventional rules.
There is a constant danger here of contamination across the boundary
which is generally managed by powerful and charismatic leadership.
In addition, in communities (especially therapeutic communities) in
which spontaneity and self-awareness are valued, there is a constant

tendency for routinization to set in (Bloor, 1980), particularly in the face of repeated problems or patients — 'we have seen this before and know how to deal with it'. A common method of trying to avoid such routines is to dispense as far as possible with a highly structured organization and rely on the personal charisma of the leader to integrate and direct the community process. This gives the necessary space to other members to be spontaneous.

Of course, this excessive dependence on leadership necessarily implies a danger for any community if the burden becomes too great for the leader (Almond, 1974; Hobson, 1979), or more often when the issue of succession arises (Hardy, 1979), as we have suggested earlier in this chapter.

Crisis does not of course necessarily lead to collapse. The resolution of crisis due to external pressures is a result of one of two processes. First, the pressure may be successfully resisted by mobilizing internal strength or external support. If a community is under suspicion from its immediate neighbours, they can be invited in to see for themselves the good work and ordered life which is really taking place. More often publicity is the key to success and many communes or therapeutic communities actively pursue some kind of public relations exercise in the face of such a threat.

The alternative is to accommodate to the external demands. For example, the initial cause of the collective disturbance at Chestnut Lodge described by Stanton and Schwartz (1954) was the need to accommodate financial constraints. In effect 25 per cent of the patients who could not pay their fees were to be given limited time in hospital. While solving the financial problem, this of course seriously compromised the ideals of the hospital.

The internal resolution of crises depends on the nature of the disturbance. In Kanter's (1972) terms the general problem will be to regain the commitment of members to the ideals and activities of the whole group. For example, a sudden and disturbing influx of newcomers may require special efforts to reconfirm the culture and legitimacy of group life. Splitting into sub-groups or the blocking of communications are often dealt with only when such problems become recognized and accepted as the responsibility of members themselves rather than projected elsewhere. Reparative forces stemming from guilt or fear of collapse then quickly reassert the primacy of the group. These experiences as Rapoport (1956) suggests may even be beneficial, serving to instruct members on the dynamics of the community, and reconfirming the viability and intrinsic worth of the enterprise.

220

Despite the common observation that internal disorganization and resolution are group processes, many groups react by expelling individuals felt to be the source of the trouble. For example mutinies (Wintringham, 1936), prison riots (Fitzgerald, 1977) and student protests (Kidd, 1969) almost always result in the rejection of 'ringleaders' and their demands. A similar reaction occurs in therapeutic communities (Hinshelwood, 1979), which while on occasions a practical necessity, carries with it the danger of avoiding the real nature of the disturbance in favour of explanation in terms of individual pathology.

The combination of external and internal crises has generally proved most fatal. For example, the mutiny on board the 'Potemkin' in the 'dress rehearsal' 1905 revolution in Russia failed; but by 1917, general military discipline was so weak that the 'Aurora' mutiny not only succeeded but rapidly spread to encompass the whole Russian fleet within two weeks (Wintringham, 1936).

The experience of therapeutic communities here is varied. Those that have survived appear to have done so in one of two ways. First, the external and internal threat may happen sequentially, as was the case for Chestnut Lodge. Here the internal disturbance occurred as a result of accommodating the external (financial) threat. The hospital only had to deal with one at a time. Second, the reverse process may occur whereby internal disorganization and acting out provoke external pressure. In this case, for example described by Parker (1956), the external threat ironically provided the incentive to resolve the internal problems.

Just as dependence on charismatic leadership is a source of potential crisis, so it also provides a common solution to the combination of external and internal difficulties. Melvyn Rose (1978) has argued that 'from time to time . . . the group becomes overwhelmed with the weight of the task. This is when they ask for inspiration and leadership. Democracy, independence, adolescent power don't matter for a while.' Crisis is the seedbed for a resurgence of powerful leadership. Student protests have frequently brought remote vice-chancellors out of their offices and onto the campus. However, crisis may also stimulate new leadership in the face of the ineffectiveness of the existing leader. This may, of course, be welcomed and help the group to survive. Unfortunately, it can also generate rivalry and split the group even further at a time of difficulty. Kanter (1972) describes how the New Harmony Community in nineteenth-century America suffered such a leadership rivalry with the result that the community split into two, the new leadership moving away with one-third of the

221

members. However, this operated it seems as a successful cleansing of the old community which recaptured the cohesion of earlier years.

## Crisis and collapse

The way groups and communities finally break down under various crises can be elucidated through a typology of collapse, modelled on the social organization of 'death work' in American hospitals (Sudnow, 1967). In this study he observes that the moment of death is not a self-evident fact, and he distinguishes three aspects. First, there is biological death, when the organism in fact ceases to function. Second, there is clinical death, when medical staff recognize and confirm biological death (some five minutes after the heart stops). Third, there is social death, when people in the patient's environment stop relating to him as a person. This is a useful distinction to consider for the possible breakdown of therapeutic communities. It helps us to appreciate different types of survival — is a therapeutic community which has declined into a routinized authoritarian group still alive? Or does its failure have to be acknowledged by the staff in it? Or perhaps it only really dies when its environment, for example the health service administration, closes the books on it?

It can be suggested that a completely failed therapeutic community will die in all three ways Sudnow (1967) suggests: biological — when a therapeutic community actually stops working and becomes either ineffective or a positive harm to its members; clinical — when the staff or leadership of a therapeutic community come to realize that it has stopped working; social — when significant aspects of the therapeutic community's environment begin to relate to it as if it were dead, for example not referring patients, withdrawing finance, and so on.

Sudnow (1967) makes the important point that these three processes are not necessarily sequential but that social death may occur before biological death. For example, nursing staff sometimes stop treating a dying patient as a person although the patient is still bilogically and clinically alive. Sudnow relates the case of a patient admitted for an emergency operation whose wife was told his chances of survival were slim, whereupon she stopped visiting him. After two weeks he improved dramatically, was discharged, and returned home to find his clothing and personal effects removed, arrangements made for his burial, and a new man installed with his wife. Shocked, he left the house, drank heavily, had a heart attack, returned to the hospital, and subsequently died. In this case we could argue that social death led to biological and clinical death. However, the normal sequence is, of course: biological; clinical; social. These may be seen as a progression or career of dying. This career can sometimes be arrested: for example, when the heart stops and is revived, only the first stage is reached. If clinical death is reached then the social environment may still deny this reality, where, for example, family members still relate to the corpse as if it existed as a person.

If we now apply this model to therapeutic communities we can see diagrammatically in figure 6.2 how these stages might be reached in the cycle of oscillation described by Rapoport (1956):

*Figure 6.2* Tension and the death of therapeutic communities

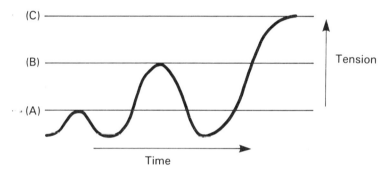

At level 'A' the peak of tension just reaches the point at which biological death may occur. The therapeutic community is ceasing to work and in danger of being positively harmful. At level 'B', the therapeutic community has stopped working, is operating socio-pathologically, and is acknowledged by the staff to be in danger of clinical or official death. At level 'C', the level of disorganization has reached the point at which social death is imminent whereby the therapeutic community is in danger of being closed down and recognized as dead by its environment.

Breakdown under external pressures is analogous to the patient whose wife effectively kills him before he physically dies. This is so disturbing that he does ultimately die. Communes have often suffered this fate, where the pressure is commonly financial. Therapeutic communities, for example a special ward in a mental hospital, have also been closed down or effectively starved of both staff and patients until they collapse.

223

The most common reason for breakdown however is generally as a result of internal disorganization, where a community proceeds from biological to social death. For example successful mutiny, as on board HMS 'Bounty', or at the Paddington Day Hospital, arrested the activity of the group as it was then constituted (biological death), which was then recognized by those in authority (clinical death), and ultimately sanctioned by the outside environment (social death). Obviously in other cases, death was halted at the biological stage, and the process reversed (Rapoport, 1956) by a reassertion of the authority structure. It is also possible that this career of dying actually gets stuck. For example in Kanter's (1972) terms, commitment to the group may be substantially weakened by the development of uncooperative sub-groups, rejection of the dominant ideology, or breakdown of social control. However this is denied by the staff or leadership such that biological death is not followed by clinical or social recognition. We might suggest that such a community had become comatose and essentially inactive, while officially alive.

Obviously in moving from biological to social death, we are moving across the boundary of the system. And as we have seen the group may die from the outside or from the inside in different circumstances. However, it is only when both processes have operated together that a community is totally finished. Moreover, if we accept that strong, often charismatic, leadership is an essential part of successful communities, as Almond (1974) and Rigby (1974a, 1974b) have argued most forcefully, then it is not surprising that failure of leadership is one of the commonest causes of breakdown. Added to this the crucial strategic position of the leader in terms of boundary management, and the necessity (for total collapse) of the co-ordination of 'biological' and 'social' death on either side of the boundary, it is probably safe to say that even if the causes of crisis originate elsewhere, the fact of collapse is almost always marked by leadership failure.

It is evident that the stability of institutions like the therapeutic community, but also others from prisons to navel ships, depends upon a combination of internal cohesion and external support. Within limits these may well vary independently but in the extreme they appear to be causally linked. Indeed they have to be before the complete demise of an institution occurs. This event is not a single, clearcut occrrence, but appears to involve cessation of both the function of the institution and the interpretation of this state by its members and external agencies. A key figure connecting these various factors is the institution's leader, who plays a vital part in mobilizing responses to internal and external disturbances. The ability to understand these processes and hence devise strategies to deal with them seems to be important for the continued existence of the institution or community. The extent to which this quality resides in the person of the leader, or his followers, or the relationship between them seems to vary. However, there is no doubt that ultimately even an effective leader will be unable to resist the combined impact of internal disorganization and external pressure.


## CONCLUSION

In this chapter a sociological account of the therapeutic community has been offered. Such an account must include the views of therapeutic community practitioners but it must also attempt to elucidate the structure and processes which can explain the origin, development, and fate of therapeutic communities. Consequently the chapter begins with a discussion of the therapeutic community in its own terms and subjects that model to the criticism that it leaves too much unexplained. The rest of the chapter explores the therapeutic community's own aspirations for scientific innovation, and for social change, by examining the sociological literature dealing with both those areas with a view to fitting the therapeutic community to existing models. There is no doubt that this exercise sheds considerable light on this area.

Rawlings (1981) recalls that research workers in therapeutic communities are regularly asked two questions: what is a real therapeutic community? and does it work? Her answer is, in ethnomethodological terms, reminiscent of Lewis Carrol: it is as real as its practitioners define it to be, and it works in so far as it is defined as working. In other words, the research worker turns the question back on the questioner. While respectful of the ethnomethodological project, and thus mindful of the hidden assumptions in therapeutic community practices, answers to these two questions can be given. The therapeutic community is both a scientific innovation within psychiatric medicine, and a social movement to change residential psychiatric practice, therapeutic education, and the treatment of the addictions. In both of these aspects it has worked with some, but not complete, success. It is and can be demonstrated to be a successful treatment. It has also substantially changed ideas and practices in the fields of psychiatry, education, and the addictions, although its fortunes here ebbed and flowed in response to factors outside its control.

This dual nature of the therapeutic community explains to some extent the disagreements which have appeared both within and without the movement as to whether therapeutic communities are 'really' radical, or 'really' a sophisticated means of social control. They are, it seems, both.

# References

Ahmed, P.I. and Plog, S.C. (eds), 1976, *State Mental Hospitals, what happens when they close*, New York: Plenum Medical Book Co.

Ahrenfeld, R.H. (1958), *Psychiatry in the British Army in the Second World War*, London: Routledge & Kegan Paul.

Almond, R.H. (1974), *The Healing Community*, Northvale, NJ: Jason Aronson.

—— 1983, 'Concepts and new developments in milieu treatment', in Gunderson, J.G. *et al* (eds), *Principles and Practice of Milieu Therapy*, Northvale, NJ: Jason Aronson.

Althusser, L., (1979), *For Marx*, London: Verso.

Anderson, O.W. (1968), *The Uneasy Equilibrium, Private and Public Financing of Health Services in the United States, 1875–1965*, New Haven, Connecticut: College and University Press.

Antze, P. (1979), 'The role of ideologies in peer psychotherapy groups', in Lieberbaum, M. and Borman, C.D. (eds), *Self-Help Groups for Coping with Crisis*, Jossey-Bass.

Argyle, M. (1976), 'Personality and social behaviour', in Harré, R. (ed.), *Personality*, Oxford: Basil Blackwell.

Arthur, C. (1980), 'Personality and the dialectic of labour and property. Locke, Hegel, Marx', *Radical Philosophy*, no. 26.

Association of Therapeutic Communities (1979), *Love and Hate in the Therapeutic Community*, ATC Bulletin, no. 28 (supplement).

Baldock, J. and Prior, D. (1981), 'Social workers talking to clients: a study of verbal behaviour', *British Journal of Social Work*, vol. 11:19–38.

Banks, J.A. (1972), *The Sociology of Social Movements*, London: Macmillan.

Banton, M. (1965), *Roles*, London: Tavistock Publications.

Baron, C. (1984), 'The Paddington Day Hospital: crisis and control in a therapeutic institution', *International Journal of Therapeutic Communities*, vol. 5:157–70.

—— (1987), *Asylum to Anarchy*, London: Free Association Books.

Barton, R. (1959), *Institutional Neurosis*, Bristol: Wright.

Baruch, G. and Treacher, A. (1978), *Psychiatry Observed*, London: Routledge & Kegan Paul.

Bateman, J.F. and Dunham, H.W. (1948), 'The state mental hospital as a specialised community experience', *American Journal of Psychiatry*, vol. 105.

Bazeley, E.T. (1928), *Homer Lane and the Little Commonwealth*, London: George Allen and Unwin.

Bebbington, A.C. (ND), 'The experimental evaluation of social intervention', PSSRU discussion paper 93, University of Kent at Canterbury.

Bebbington, A.C. (1978), 'Re-analysis of the Goldberg data: use of covariance analysis to improve precision for testing effects', PSSRU discussion paper 84/2, University of Kent at Canterbury.

Belknap, I. (1956), *Human Problems of a State Mental Hospital*, New York: McGraw Hill.

Bell, M.D. and Ryan, E.R. (1985), 'Where can therapeutic community ideals be realised? An examination of three treatment environments', *Hospital and Community Psychiatry*, vol. 36, no. 12:1286–91.

Berger, P. and Luckman, T. (1967), *The Social Construction of Reality*, London: Allen Lane.

Bergin, A.E. and Lambert, M.J. (1978), 'The evaluation of therapeutic outcomes', in Garfield, S.L. and Bergin, A.E. (eds), *Handbook of Psychotherapy and Behaviour Change: an Empirical Analysis*, 2nd edn, New York: John Wiley.

Berke, J.H. (1982), 'The Arbours Centre', *International Journal of Therapeutic Communities*, vol. 3, no. 4:248–61.

Bierenbroodspot, P. (1980), 'The therapeutic community: its model, its possible aid to community mental health', *International Journal of Therapeutic Communities*, vol. 1:24–37.

Bion, W.R. (1960), *Experiences in Groups*, London: Tavistock Publications.

—— (1962), 'A theory of thinking', *British Journal of Psycho-Analysis*, vol. 43:306.

Bittner, E. (1969), 'Radicalism and the organisation of radical movements', in McLaughlin, B. (ed.), *Studies in Social Movements*, New York: Free Press.

—— (1979), 'The concept of organisation', in Turner, R. (ed.), *Ethnomethodology*, Harmondsworth: Penguin Books.

Blau, P.M. (1970), 'Critical remarks on Weber's theory of authority', in Wrong, D. (ed.), *Max Weber*, Englewood Cliffs: Prentice-Hall.

Bloch, S. and Crouch, E. (1985), *Therapeutic Factors in Group Psychotherapy*, Oxford: Oxford University Press.

Bloor, M.J. (1980), 'The nature of therapeutic work in the therapeutic community — some preliminary findings', *International Journal of Therapeutic Communities*, vol. 1:80–91.

—— (1986), 'Social control in the therapeutic community: re-examination of a critical case', *Sociology of Health & Illness*, vol. 8:305–24.

Bloor, M.J. and Fonkert, J.D. (1982), 'Reality construction, reality exploration, and treatment in two therapeutic communities', *Sociology of Health and Illness*, vol. 4:123–40.

Bloor, M.J., McKeganey, N.P., and Fonkert, J.D. (1988), *One Foot in Eden*, London: Routledge.

Bottoms, A.E. and McClintock, F.H. (1973), *Criminals Coming of Age*, London: Heinemann.

Brannigan, A. (1981), *The Social Basis of Scientific Discoveries*, Cambridge: Cambridge University Press.

Bridgeland, M. (1971), *Pioneer Work with Maladjusted Children*, London: Staples Press.

—— (1985), 'Editorial', *International Journal of Therapeutic Communities*, vol. 6, no. 4:179–80.

Briggs, D. (1972), 'Chino, California', in Whiteley, J.S. *et al*, *Dealing with Deviants*, London: Hogarth Press.

Brooks, R. (1972), *Bright Delinquents*, Slough: NFER.

Cantril, H. (1941), *The Psychology of Social Movements*, New York: John Wiley.

Carstairs, G.M. (1974), 'Introduction' to Clark, D.H., *Social Therapy in Psychiatry*, Harmondsworth: Penguin Books.

Castel, R. (1976), *L'ordre psychiatrique: l'age d'or de l'alienisme*, Paris: Editions Minuit.

Caudill, W. (1958), *The Psychiatric Hospital as a Small Society*, Cambridge, Mass.: Harvard University Press.

Cherniss, C. (1980), *Staff Burnout, Job Stress in the Human Services*, Newbury Park, CA: Sage.

Christian, A. and Hinshelwood, R.D. (1979), 'Work groups', in Hinshelwood, R.D. and Manning, Nick (eds), *Therapeutic Communities*, London: Routledge & Kegan Paul.

Churchill, W.S. (1951), *The Second World War*, vol. 4, London: Cassell.

Clark, A.W. and Walker, R.M. (1984), 'The continuing influence of the therapeutic community concept', *International Journal of Therapeutic Communities*, vol. 5, no. 3:140–56.

Clark, D.H. (1964), *Administrative Psychiatry*, London: Tavistock Publications.

—— (1965), 'The therapeutic community, concept, practice and future', *British Journal of Psychiatry*, vol. III:947–54.

—— (1973), 'Therapeutic community developments at Fulbourn Hospital, 1971–1973', unpublished paper, ATC conference.

—— (1974), *Social Therapy in Psychiatry*, Harmondsworth: Penguin Books.

—— (1977), 'The therapeutic community', *British Journal of Psychiatry*, vol. 131:553–64.

—— (1987), personal communication.

Clarke, R.V.G. and Cornish, D.B. (1972), *The Controlled trial in Institutional Research*, London: HMSO.

Clarke, R.V.G. and Sinclair, I. (1973), *Towards More Effective Treatment Evaluation*, Luxembourg: Council of Europe.

Cohen, G.A. (1978), *Karl Marx's Theory of History, A Defence*, Oxford: Oxford University Press.

Coleman, J.S. (1975), 'Methods and results in the IEA studies of the effect of school on learning', *Review of Educational Research*, vol. 45:355–86.

Coleman, J., Katz, E., and Menzel, H. (1957), 'Diffusion of an innovation among physicians', *Sociometry*, vol. 20:253–70.

Conrad, P. and Schneider, J. (1980), *Deviance and Medicalisation, from Badness to Sickness*, St Louis: C.V. Mosby.

Copas, J.B. and Whiteley, J.S. (1976), 'Predicting success in the treatment of psychopaths', *British Journal of Psychiatry*, vol. 129:388–92.

Coser, L.A. (1974), *Greedy Institutions*, New York: Free Press.

Coser, R.L. (1969), 'Role distance, sociological ambivalence, and transitional status systems', in Coser, L.A. and Rosenberg, B. (eds), *Sociological Theory*, London: Macmillan.

Coward, R. and Ellis, J. (1977), *Language and Materialism*, London: Routledge & Kegan Paul.

Crockett, R. (1966), 'Authority and permissiveness in the psychotherapeutic community: theoretical perspectives', *American Journal of Psychotherapy*, vol. XX, no. 4:669–76.

—— (1985), 'On Claire Baron's paper "The Paddington Day Hospital: crisis and control in a therapeutic institution" ' *International Journal of Therapeutic Communities*, vol. 6, no. 2:109–14.

Crockett, R., Kirk, J.B., Manning, N., and Millard, D.W. (1978),

'Community time structure', *Association of Therapeutic Communities Bulletin*, no. 25:12-17.

Cumming, J. and Cumming, E. (1956), 'The locus of power in the Large Mental Hospital, *Psychiatry*, vol. 19:361-70.

—— (1957), 'Social equilibrium and social change in the large mental hospital', in Greenblatt, M. *et al.* (eds), *The Patient and the Mental Hospital*, New York: Free Press.

—— (1962), *Ego and Milieu*, New York: Atherton Press.

Curle, A. (1947), 'Transitional communities and social reconnection', *Human Relations*, vol. 1, no. 1.

Davies, M. (1969) *Probationers in their Social Environment*, London: HMSO.

Davies, M.S. (1970), 'That's interesting! Towards a phenomenology of sociology and a sociology of phenomenology', *Philosophy of Social Science*, vol. 1:309-44.

Day, R. and Day, J. (1977), 'A review of the current state of negotiated order theory', *Sociological Quarterly*, vol. 18:126-42.

Dear, M.J. and Taylor, S.M. (1982), *Not on our Street*, London: Pion Limited.

De Leon, G. (1983), 'The next therapeutic community: autocracy and other notes toward integrating old and new therapeutic communities', *International Journal of Therapeutic Communities*, vol. 4, no. 4:249-61.

—— (1985), 'The therapeutic community: status and evolution', *The International Journal of the Addictions*, vol. 20:823-44.

—— (1973), 'The Phoenix House therapeutic community: changes in psychopathological signs', *Archives of General Psychiatry*, vol. 28:131-5.

De Leon, G. and Zeigenfuss, J.T. (eds) (1986), *Therapeutic Communities for Addictions*, Austin, Texas: Chaıles C. Thomas.

Denber, H.C.B. (1960), *Research Conference on the Therapeutic Community*, Watsonville, CA: Blackwells.

De Waele, J.P. and Harré, R. (1976), 'The personality of individuals', in Harré, R. (ed.), *Personality*, Oxford: Basil Blackwell.

Dicks, H.V. (1970), *50 years of the Tavistock Clinic*, London: Routledge & Kegan Paul.

Doyal, L. and Gough, I. (1984), 'A theory of human needs', *Critical Social Policy*, Issue 10, vol. 4, no. 1:6-38.

Dunham, W. and Weinberg, S.K. (1960), *The Culture of the State Mental Hospital*, Detroit, MI: Wayne State University Press.

Edelson, M. (1970), *Sociotherapy and Psychotherapy*, Chicago: University of Chicago Press.

Etzioni, A. (1975), *A Comparative Analysis of Complex Organisations*, Glencoe, Illinois: Free Press.

Fairweather, G. (ed.), (1964), *Social Psychology in Treating Mental Illness*, New York: John Wiley.

Festinger, L., Rieken, H.W., and Schachter, S. (1956), *When Prophecy Fails*, New York: Harper & Row.

Finch, J. (1984), 'Community care: developing non-sexist alternatives', *Critical Social Policy*, vol. 9:6-18.

Finch, J. and Groves, D. (eds) (1983), *A Labour of Love: Women, Work, and Caring*, London: Routledge & Kegan Paul.

Fishbein, M. (1967), 'A behaviour theory approach to the relations between beliefs about an object and the attitude toward an object', in Fishbein, M. (ed.), *Readings in Attitude Theory*, New York: John Wiley.

—— (1971), 'The search for attitudinal behavioural consistency', in Cohen, J. (ed.), *Behavioural Science Foundations of Consumer Behaviour*, New York: Free Press.

Fitzgerald, M. (1977), *Prisoners in Revolt*, Harmondsworth: Penguin.

Foucault, M. (1967), *Madness and Civilization*, London: Tavistock Publications.

Foudraine, J. (1974), *Not Made of Wood*, London: Quartet Books.

Fowler, R. (1979), *Language and Control*, London: Routledge & Kegan Paul.

Franklin, M. (1968), 'The meaning of planned environmental therapy', *Studies in Environment Therapy*, vol. 1:93–101.

Freeman, T. (1952), in M. Jones *et al*, *Social Psychiatry*, London: Tavistock Publications.

Freud, S. (1922), *Group Psychology and the Analysis of the Ego*, London: Hogarth Press.

Geras, N. (1983), *Human Nature*, London: Verso.

Giddens, A. (1985), *The Constitution of Society: Outline of the Theory of Structuration*, Oxford: Polity Press.

Gillespie, D.P. (1983), 'Conservative tactics in social government organisations', in Freeman, J. (ed.), *Social Movement of the Sixties and Seventies*, Harlow: Longman.

Glaser, F. (1977), 'The origins of the drug-free therapeutic community — a retrospective history', in Vamos, P. and Brown, J.E. (eds), *Proceedings of the 2nd World Congress of Therapeutic Communities*, New York: Portage Press.

Goffman, E. (1961), *Asylums: Essays on the Social Situation of Mental Patients and Other Inmates*, Harmondsworth: Penguin Books.

—— (1971), *The Presentation of Self in Everyday Life*, Harmondsworth: Pelican Books.

Goodwin, B. and Taylor, K. (1982), *The Politics of Utopia*, London: Hutchinson.

Gouldner, A.W. (1980), *The Two Marxisms*, London: Macmillan.

Gralnick, A. (1969), *The Psychiatric Hospital as a Therapeutic Instrument*, New York: Brunner/Mazel.

Gramsci, A. (1971), *Selections from the Prison Notebooks*, London: Lawrence & Wishart.

Graycar, A. (1984), *Non-government Welfare Organisations in Australia: a national clarification*, Social Welfare Research Centre, Sydney, report no. 51.

Greenblatt, M., Brown, E.L., and York, R.H. (in coll. with Hyde, R.W.) (1955), *From Custodial to Therapeutic Care in Mental Hospitals*, New York: Russell Sage.

Greenblatt, M., Levinson, D.J., and Williams, R.H. (eds), (1957), *The Patient and the Mental Hospital*, New York: Free Press.

Gross, N., Mason, W.S., and McEacheran, A.W. (1958), *Explorations in Role Analysis*, New York: John Wiley.

Grove, Bob (1985), 'Negotiation and social order in the therapeutic community', PhD thesis, University of Bristol.

Grunberg, S. (1979), 'Thinking and the development of structure in a community group', in Hinshelwood, R.D. and Manning, Nick (eds), *Therapeutic Communities*, London: Routledge & Kegan Paul.

Guindon, J. (1969), 'Le processus de rééducation du jeune delinquent par l'actualisation des forces du moi', unpublished paper, Montreal: Centre de recherche en relations humaines.

Gumpe, P., Shoggen, P., and Redl, F. (1957), 'The camp milieu and its immediate effects', *Journal of Social Issues*, vol. 13, no. 1: 40-6.

Gunderson, J.G., Will, O.A., jr, and Mosher, L.R. (eds) (1983), *Principles and Practice of Milieu Therapy*, Northvale, NJ: Jason Aronson.

Gunn, J., Robertson, G., Dell, F. and Way, C. (1978), *Psychiatric Aspects of Imprisonment*, London: Academic Press.

Guttentag, M. (1971), 'Models and methods in evaluating research', *Journal of Theory in Social Behaviour*, vol. 1.

Habermas, J. (1971), *Toward a Rational Society*, London: Heinemann.

—— (1972), *Knowledge and Human Interests*, London: Heinemann.

Hagstrom, W.O. (1965), *The Scientific Community*, New York: Basic Books.

Hall, J.R. (1973), 'Structural characteristics of a psychiatric patient — community and the therapeutic milieu', *Human Relation*, vol. 26, no. 6:787-809.

Halmos, P. (1965), *The Faith of Counsellors*, London: Constable.

Hardy, O. (1979), *Alternative Communities in Nineteenth Century England*, Harlow: Longman.

Harré, R. (1979), *Social Being*, Oxford: Blackwell.

Harré, R. and Secord, P. (1972), *The Explanation of Social Behaviour*, Oxford: Blackwell.

Hartshorne, H. and May, M.A. (1928), *Studies in the Nature of Character: Studies in Deceit*, London: Macmillan.

Hatch, S. and Mocroft, I. (1979), 'The relative cost of services provided by voluntary and statutory organisations', *Public Administration*, vol. 57:397-405.

Held, D. (1980), *Introduction to Critical Theory*, London: Hutchinson.

Hinshelwood, R.D. (1978), 'Psychotherapy and the ''community personality'' ', unpublished paper given at the Anglo/Dutch Conference on Therapeutic Communities, Windsor.

—— (1979), 'Hate and love in the staff team', *ATC Bulletin*, no. 28 (supplement).

—— (1981), 'Reemergence of the therapeutic community', *American Journal of Psychiatry*, vol. 138, 1130-1.

—— (1987), *What Happens in Groups*, London: Free Association Books.

Hinshelwood, R.D. and Grunberg, S. (1979), 'The large-group syndrome', in Hinshelwood, R.D. and Manning, Nick (eds), *Therapeutic Communities*.

Hinshelwood, R.D. and Manning, Nick (eds) (1979), *Therapeutic Communities*, London: Routledge & Kegan Paul.

Hinton, N. and Hyde, M. (1982), 'The voluntary sector in a remodelled welfare state', *Year Book of Social Policy 1980-1*, London: Routledge & Kegan Paul.

Hobson, R.F. (1979), 'The messianic community', in Hinshelwood, R.D. and Manning, Nick (eds), *Therapeutic Communities*.

Holland, R. (1977), *Self and Social Context*, London: Macmillan.

Hollander, R. (1981), 'Moral treatment and the therapeutic community',

231

*Psychiatric Quarterly*, vol. 53, no. 2:132–8.

Hood, R. and Sparks, R. (1970), *Key Issues in Criminology*, London: Weidenfeld & Nicholson.

Ingleby, D. (1972), 'Ideology and the human sciences', in Pateman, T. (ed.), *Counter Course*, Harmondsworth: Penguin Books.

—— (1983), 'Mental health and social order', in Cohen, S. and Scull, A. (eds), *Social Control and the State*, Oxford: Martin Robertson.

—— (1986), 'Development in social context', in Richards, M.P.M. and Light, P. (eds), *Children of Social Worlds*, Cambridge, Mass.: Harvard University Press.

Jackson, J.A. (ed.) (1972), *Role*, Cambridge: Cambridge University Press.

Jacoby, R. (1975), *Social Amnesia*, Boston, MA: Beacon Press.

Jansen, E. (ed.) (1980), *The Therapeutic Community*, London: Croom Helm.

Jones, K. (1972a), *A History of the Mental Health Services*, London: Routledge & Kegan Paul.

—— (1972b), 'The 24 Steps: an analysis of institutional admission procedures', *Sociology*, vol. 6:405–15.

—— (1975), 'The reorganisation of institutional care', in Butterworth, E. and Holman, R. (eds), *Social Welfare in Modern Britain*, London: Fontana.

Jones, M. (1952), *Social Psychiatry*, London: Tavistock Publications.

—— (1968), *Social Psychiatry in Practice*, Harmondsworth: Penguin Books.

—— (1976), *The Maturation of the Therapeutic Community*, New York: Human Sciences Press.

—— (1979), 'Therapeutic communities, old and new', *American Journal of Drug and Alcohol Abuse*, vol. 6, no. 2:137–49.

—— (1982), *The Process of Change*, London: Routledge & Kegan Paul.

—— (1984), 'Why two therapeutic communities?', *Journal of Psychoactive Drugs*, vol. 16, no. 1:23–6.

Jones, M. and Rapoport, R.N. (1955), 'Progress report to the Nuffield Foundation and project advisors', unpublished ms.

Kanter, R.M. (1972), *Commitment and Community*, Cambridge, Mass.: Harvard University Press.

Kennard, D. (1979), 'Limiting factors: the setting, the staff, the patients', in Hinshelwood, R.D., and Manning, Nick (eds), *Therapeutic Communities*.

—— (1983), *An Introduction to Therapeutic Communities*, London: Routledge & Kegan Paul.

Kensington & Chelsea & Westminster AHA(T) (1976), *Report of the Committee of Enquiry Concerning the Day Hospital at the Paddington Centre for Psychotherapy*.

Kesey, K. (1973), *One Flew over the Cuckoo's Nest*, London: Picador (Pan Books).

Kidd, H. (1969), *The Trouble at LSE, 1966–1967*, Oxford: Oxford University Press.

King, C.W. (1956), *Social Movements in the United States*, New York: Random House.

Kiresuck, P.J., (1976), 'Goal-attainment seeking at a county mental health service', in Makson, E.W. and Allen, D.F. (eds), *Trends in Mental Health Evaluation*, Lexington, MA: Lexington.

Kittrie, N.N. (1971), *The Right to Be Different: Deviance and Enforced*

*Therapy*, Baltimore, MD: John Hopkins Press.

Kramer, R.M. (1981), *Voluntary Agencies in the Welfare State*, University of California Press.

Kräupl Taylor, F. (1958), 'A history of group and administrative therapy in Great Britain', *British Journal of Medical Psychology*, vol. 31:153–73.

Krech, D., Crutchfield, R.S., and Ballachey, E.L. (1962) *Individual in Society*, New York: McGraw-Hill.

Kreeger, L. (ed.) (1975), *The Large Group*, London: Constable.

Kuhn, T. (1962/1970), *The Structure of Scientific Revolutions*, Chicago: University of Chicago Press.

Laing, R.D. (1967), *The Politics of Experience and the Bird of Paradise*, Harmondsworth: Penguin Books.

Lees (referenced as Kirk), J.D. and Millard, D.W. (1979), 'Personal growth in the residential community', in Hinshelwood, R.D., and Manning, Nick (eds), *Therapeutic Communities*.

Leff, J. (1973), personal communication.

Lemaire, A. (1979), *Jacques Lacan*, London: Routledge & Kegan Paul.

Levinson, D.J. (1969), 'Role, personality, and social structure', in Coser, L.A. and Rosenberg, B. (eds), *Sociological Theory*, London: Macmillan.

Lewis, A. (1952), 'Introduction', in Jones, M. *et al.*, *Social Psychiatry*, London: Tavistock Publications.

Lewis, Sir T. (1919), *The Soldier's Heart and Effort Syndrome*, London: Shaw & Sons.

Linton, R. (1936), 'Status and role', in Coser, L.A. and Rosenberg, B. (eds), *Sociological Theory*, London: Macmillan.

Lofland, J. (1985), *Protest, Studies of Collective Behaviour and Social Movements*, New Brunswick, NJ: Transaction Books.

Lord, F.M. (1963), 'Elementary models for measuring change', in Harris, C.W. (ed.), *Problems in Measuring Change*, Madison, WI: University of Wisconsin Press.

Lukacs, G. (1971), *History and Class Consciousness*, London: Merlin Press.

McAdam, D. (1983), 'The decline of the civil rights movement', in Freeman, J. (ed.), *Social Movements of the Sixties and Seventies*, Harlow: Longman.

McCarthy, J.D. and Zald, M.N. (1977), 'Resource mobilization and social movements: a partial theory', *American Journal of Sociology*, vol. 82:1212–41.

Macdonald, K.I. (1977), 'Path analysis', in O'Muircheartaigh, C.A. and Payne, C. (eds), *Model Fitting*, New York: John Wiley.

Mahony, N. (1979), 'My stay and change at the Henderson therapeutic community', in Hinshelwood, R.D. and Manning, Nick (eds), *Therapeutic Communities*.

Main, T. (1946), 'The hospital as a therapeutic institution', *Bulletin of the Menninger Clinic*, vol. 10:66–70.

—— (1957), 'The ailment', *British Journal of Medical Psychology*, vol. 30:129–45.

—— (1975), 'Some psychodynamics of large groups', in Kreeger, L. (ed.), *The Large Group*, London: Constable.

—— (1977), 'The concept of the therapeutic community: variations and vicissitudes', *Group Analysis*, vol. X, no. 2.

Manning, Nick (1975), 'Factors affecting referrals to therapeutic communities', *Association of Therapeutic Communities Bulletin*, no. 17:7-10.

—— (1976), 'Innovation in social policy — the case of the therapeutic community', *Journal of Social Policy*, vol. 5, part 3:265-79.

—— (1977), 'Referrers survey', unpublished paper.

—— (1980), 'Collective disturbance in institutions: a sociological view of crisis and collapse', *International Journal of Therapeutic Communities*, vol. 1:147-58.

Manning, Nick, and Blake, R. (1979), 'Implementing ideals', in Hinshelwood, R.D. and Manning, Nick (eds), *Therapeutic Communities*.

Manning, Nick and Rapoport, R.N. (1976), 'Rejection and reincorporation: a case study in social research utilisation', *Social Science and Medicine*, vol. 19:459-68.

Marcuse, H. (1964), *One-Dimensional Man*, London: Routledge & Kegan Paul.

—— (1966), *Eros and Civilisation*, Boston, MA: Beacon Press.

Martin, D.V. (1962), *Adventure in Psychiatry*, Oxford: Cassirer.

Marx, K. (1951), 'Theses on Feuerbach', in Marx, K. and Engels, F., *Selected Works, Vol. 2*, Moscow: Foreign Languages Publishing House.

—— (1961), 'Economic and philosophical manuscripts', in Fromm, E., *Marx's Concept of Man*, New York: Frederick Ungar & Co.

—— (1976), *Capital, Vol. 1*, Harmondsworth: Penguin Books.

Mauss, M. (1954), *The Gift*, New York: Free Press.

Mead, G.H. (1934), *Mind, Self and Society*, Chicago: University of Chicago Press.

—— (1938), *The Philosophy of the Act*, Chicago: Chicago University Press.

Medawar, P.B. (1969), *Induction and Intuition in Scientific Thought*, London: Methuen.

Menninger, W.C. (1947), 'Psychiatric experience in the war, 1941-1946', *American Journal of Psychiatry*, vol. 103.

Menzies, I. (1960), 'A case study in the functioning of social systems as a defense against anxiety', *Human Relations*, vol. 13:95-121.

Merton, R.K. (1961), 'Singletons and multiples in scientific discovery', *Proceedings of the American Philosophical Society*, VC, 5:470-86.

—— (1968), *Social Theory and Social Structure*, New York: Free Press.

—— (1969), 'The role-set: problems in sociological theory', in Coser, L.A. and Rosenberg, B. (eds), *Sociological Theory*, London: Macmillan.

Michels, R. (1949), *Political Parties*, New York: Free Press.

Millard, D.W. (1983), 'The therapeutic community in the seventies', unpublished paper, Dept. Applied Social Studies, University of Oxford.

Miller, D.H. (1957), 'The etiology of an outbreak of delinquency in a group of hospitalised adolescents', in Greenblatt, M., Levinson, D., and Williams, R.H. (eds), *The Patient and the Mental Hospital*, New York: Free Press.

Miller, P. and Rose, M. (1986), *The Power of Psychiatry*, Oxford: Polity.

Mills, C.W. (1970), *The Sociological Imagination*, Harmondsworth: Penguin Books.

Mischel, W. (1968), *Personality and Assessment*, New York: Wiley.

Molina, V. (1978), 'Notes on Marx and the problem of individuality', in CCCS, *On Ideology*, London: Hutchinson.

Mood, A. (1971), 'Partitioning variance in multiple regression analyses as a tool for developing learning models', *American Education Research Journal*, vol. 8:191-202.

Moos, R.H. (1974), *Community Oriented Programs Environment Scale*, Palo Alto, CA: Consulting Psychologists Press.

— (1980), 'Evaluating the environments of residential care settings', *International Journal of Therapeutic Communities*, vol. 1:211-25.

Morrice, J.K.W. (1972), 'Myth and the democratic process', *British Journal of Medical Psychology*, vol. 45:327-31.

— (1979), 'Basic concepts: a critical review', in Hinshelwood, R.D. and Manning, Nick (eds), *Therapeutic Communities*.

Morris, T. and Morris, P. (1963), *Pentonville*, London: Routledge & Kegan Paul.

Mulkay, M. (1972), *The Social Process of Innovation*, London: Macmillan.

— (1979), *Science and the Sociology of Knowledge*, London: Allen & Unwin.

Myerson , A. (1939), 'Theory and principles of the "total push" method in the treatment of chronic schizophrenia', *American Journal of Psychiatry*, vol. 95.

Namboodiri, N.K., Carter, L.F., and Blalock, H.M. (1975), *Applied Multivariate Analysis and Experimental Designs*, New York: McGraw-Hill.

Niv, A. (1980), 'Organisational disintegration: roots, processes and types', in Kimberly, J.R., Miles, R.H., and Associates (eds), *The Organisational Life Cycle*, San Francisco, CA: Jossey-Bass.

Nunnally, J.C. (1975), 'The study of change in evaluation research: principles concerning measurement, experimental design, and analysis', in Struening, E. and Guttentag, M. (eds), *Handbook of Evaluation Research, vol. 1*, Newbury Park, CA: Sage.

Olson, M., jr (1965), *The Logic of Collective Action*, Cambridge, Mass.: Harvard University Press.

Parker, S. (1956), 'Disorganisation in a psychiatric ward: the natural history of a crisis', unpublished paper, Henderson Hospital.

— (1958), 'Changes in the administration of psychotherapy during a collective upset', *Human Organisation*, vol. 16, no. 4:32-7.

Parker, T. (1971), *The Frying Pan: a Prison and its Prisoners*, London: Panther.

Parkin, F. (1982), *Max Weber*, London: Tavistock Publications.

Paul, G.L. (1967), 'Strategy of outcome research in psychotherapy', *Journal of Consulting Psychology*, vol. 31, no. 2.

Pearson, G. (1975), *The Deviant Imagination*, London: Macmillan.

Perrow, C. (1965), 'Hospitals: technology, structure and goals', in March, J.G. (ed.), *Handbook of Organisations*, Chicago, Illinois: Rand McNally.

Perry, N. (1974), 'The two cultures of the total institution', *British Journal of Sociology*, vol. 25:345-55.

Price, R.H. and Moos, R.H. (1975), 'Towards a taxonomy of inpatient treatment environments', *Journal of Abnormal Psychology*, vol. 84, no. 3:181-8.

Punch, M. (1974), 'The sociology of the anti-institution', *British Journal of Sociology*, vol. 25:312-25.

—— (1977), *Progressive Retreat*, Cambridge: Cambridge University Press.

Rapoport, R.N. (1956), 'Oscillations and sociotherapy', *Human Relations*, vol. 9, no. 3:357–74.

—— (1970), 'A new era in psychiatry', *Social Science and Medicine*, vol. 3:407–12.

Rapoport, R.N. (1960), *Community as Doctor*, London: Tavistock Publications.

Rawlings, B. (1981), 'The production of facts in a therapeutic community', in Atkinson, P. and Heath, C. (eds), *Medical Work*, Aldershot: Gower.

—— (1984), 'On new ground: how therapists maintain belief in a radical ideology', unpublished paper, SCOS/EGOS Conference on Organisational Symbolism & Corporate Culture, Sweden.

Rees, J.R. (1943), 'Three years of military psychiatry in the United Kingdom', *British Medical Journal*, vol. 1.

—— (1945), *The Shaping of Psychiatry by War*, London: Chapman & Hall.

Reeves, F. (1983), *British Racial Discourse*, Cambridge: Cambridge University Press.

Reis, H.T. (1982), 'An introduction to the use of structural equations: prospects and problems', in Wheeler, L. (ed.), *Review of Personality and Social Psychology Vol. 3*, Newbury Park, CA: Sage.

Rice, A.K. (1963), *The Enterprise and its Environment*, London: Tavistock Publications.

Richards, M.P.M. (ed.) (1974), *The Integration of a Child into a Social World*, Cambridge: Cambridge University Press.

Richards, M.P.M. and Light, P. (eds) (1986), *Children of Social Worlds*, Cambridge, Mass.: Harvard University Press.

Richmond Inquiry (1983), *Health Services for the Psychiatrically Ill and the Developmentally Disabled*, Department of Health, New South Wales.

Rigby, A. (1974a), *Alternative Realities: a Study of Communes and their Members*, London: Routledge & Kegan Paul.

—— (1974b), *Communes in Britain*, London: Routledge & Kegan Paul.

Righton, P. (1979), 'Planned environment therapy: a reappraisal', *Studies in Environment Therapy*, vol. 3:9–16.

Roethlisberger, F.J. and Dickson, W.J. (1939), *Management and the Worker*, Cambridge, Mass.: Harvard University Press.

Rose, M. (1978), Unpublished paper, Anglo-Dutch workshop on therapeutic communities, Windsor.

Rosen, H. (1972), *Language and Class*, Bristol: Falling Wall Press.

Rosow, I. (1955), 'Research memorandum: patterns of patient referral to the Belmont Social Rehabilitation Unit', unpublished ms.

—— (1957), 'Factors in patient referral to an innovating psychiatric centre', unpublished ms.

Ross, E.A. (1908), *Social Psychology*, London: Macmillan.

Rossi, J.J. and Filstead, W.J. (eds) (1973), *The Therapeutic Community*, Pasadena, CA: Behavioural Publications.

Rossi, P.H., Freeman, M.E., and Wright, F.R. (1978), *Evaluation, a Systematic Approach*, Newbury Park, CA: Sage.

Roth, J.A. (1962), *Timetables*, New York: Bobbs Merrill.

Rothman, D. (1971), *The Discovery of the Asylum*, Boston, MA: Little Brown.

Rubel, J.G., Baker, K.G., Bratten, T.E., Hartwig-Thomson, L., and Smirnoff, A.M. (1982), 'The role of structure in the professional model and the self-help concept of the therapeutic community: different strokes for different folks', *International Journal of Therapeutic Communities*, vol. 3, no. 4:218–32.

Savalle, H. and Wagenborg, H. (1979), 'Oscillations in a therapeutic community', *ATC Bulletin*, no. 27:6–14.

Schoenberg, E. (ed.), (1972), *A Hospital Looks at Itself*, Oxford: Cassirer.

Schutz, A. (1964), *Collected Papers, Vol. II: Studies in Social Theory*, Dordrecht, Netherlands: Nijhoff.

Schwarz, M.S. (1957), 'What is a therapeutic milieu?', in Greenblatt, M. et al. (eds), *The Patient and the Mental Hospital*, New York: Free Press.

Scull, A.T. (1977), *Decarceration*, New York: Prentice-Hall.

Scull, A.T. (1979), *Museums of Madness, the Social Organisation of Insanity in 19th Century England*, London: Allen Lane.

Séve, C. (1978), *Man in Marxist Theory and the Psychology of Personality*, Brighton: Harvester Press.

Sharp, V. (1975), *Social Control in the Therapeutic Community*, Aldershot: Saxon House.

—— (1977), 'The research act in sociology and the limits of meaning: the understanding of crisis, care and control in a therapeutic community', *Australia and New Zealand Journal of Sociology*, vol. 13:236–47.

Shenker, B. (1986), *International Communities*, London: Routledge & Kegan Paul.

Shils, E.A. (1965), 'Charisma, order and status', *American Sociological Review*, vol. 30:199–213.

Shotter, J. (1976), 'Acquired powers: the transformation of natural into personal powers', in Harré, R. (ed.), *Personality*, Oxford: Basil Blackwell.

Silverman, D. (1970), *The Theory of Organisations*, London: Heinemann.

Simon, F.H. (1971), *Prediction Methods in Criminology*, London: HMSO.

Slater, P. (1977), *Origin and Significance of the Frankfurt School*, London: Routledge & Kegan Paul.

Smelser, N.J. (1962), *Theory of Collective Behaviour*, London: Routledge & Kegan Paul.

Social Services Committee (1985), *Community Care Vol. 1*, London: HMSO.

Spender, D. (1980), *Man Made Language*, London: Routledge & Kegan Paul.

Sprafkin, R.P. (1977), 'The rebirth of moral treatment', *Professional Psychology*, vol. 8:161–9.

Stanton, A.H. and Schwartz, M.S. (1954), *The Mental Hospital*, New York: Basic Books.

Stotland, E. and Kobler, A.L. (1965), *The Life and Death of a Mental Hospital*, Washington: University of Washington Press.

Strauss, A. (1978), *Negotiations*, San Francisco, CA: Jossey-Bass.

Strauss, A. et al. (1963), 'The hospital as a negotiated order', in Freidson, E. (ed.), *The Hospital in Modern Society*, New York: Free Press.

—— (1964), *Psychiatric Ideologies and Institutions*, New York: Free Press.

Strong, P.M. (1979), *The Ceremonial Order of the Clinic*, London: Routledge & Kegan Paul.

Suchman, E.A. (1967), *Evaluative Research*, New York: Russell Sage.

Sudnow, D. (1967), *Passing On: the Social Organisation of Dying*, New York: Prentice Hall.

Sugarman, B. (1974), *Daytop Village — A Therapeutic Community*, Orlando, Fl: Holt, Rinehart & Winston.

—— (1984), 'Towards a new, common model of the therapeutic community: structural components, learning processes and outcomes', *International Journal of Therapeutic Communication*, vol. 5, no. 2:77–98.

Sullivan, H.S. (1955), *Interpersonal Theory of Psychiatry*, London: Tavistock Publications.

Szasz, T. (1971), *The Manufacture of Madness, a Comparative Study of the Inquisition and the Mental Health Movement*, London: Routledge & Kegan Paul.

Tajfel, H. (ed.) (1982), *Social Identity and Intergroup Relations*, Cambridge: Cambridge University Press.

Thomas, W.I. and Znaniecki, F. (1918–1920), *The Polish Peasant in Europe and America*, New York: Dover Publications, facsimile edn, 1958.

Toch, H. (ed.), (1980), *Therapeutic Communities in Corrections*, New York: Praeger.

Trauer, T. (1984), 'The current status of the therapeutic community', *British Journal of Medical Psychology*, vol. 57: 71–9.

Treacher, A. and Baruch, G. (1981), 'Towards a critical history of the psychiatric profession', in Ingleby, D (ed.), *Critical Psychiatry*, Harmondsworth: Penguin Books.

Truax, C.B. and Carkuff, R.R. (1967), *Toward Effective Counselling & Psychotherapy*, Chicago: Aldine.

Turkle, S. (1981), *Psychoanalytic Politics*, London: Burnett Books.

Turner, J.C. (1982), 'Towards a cognitive redefinition of the group', in Tajfel, H. (ed.), *Social Identity and Intergroup Relations*.

—— (1987), *Rediscovering the Social Group*, Oxford: Basil Blackwell.

Turner, R.H. (1981), 'Collective behaviour and resource modification as approaches to social movements: issues and continuties', *Research in Social Movements, Conflict and Change*, vol. 4:1–24.

Ullman, C.P. (1967), *Institution and Outcome*, Oxford: Pergamon.

Walker, A. (ed.) (1982), *Community Care*, Oxford: Basil Blackwell & Martin Robertson.

Walter Reed Army Institute of Research (1958), *Symposium on Preventive and Social Psychiatry*, Washington: US Government Printing Office.

Walton, P. and Gamble, A. (1972), *From Alienation to Surplus Value*, London: Sheed & Ward.

Weber, M. (1947), *The Theory of Social and Economic Organisation*, Oxford: Oxford University Press.

—— (1949), *The Methodology of the Social Sciences*, Glencoe, Illinois: Free Press.

Wells, D. (1981), *Marxism and the Modern State*, Brighton: Harvester Press.

White Paper (1959), *Penal Practice in a Changing Society*, cmnd 645, London: HMSO.

White, R.K. and Lippitt, R. (1960), *Autocracy and Democracy*, New York: Harper & Row.

Whiteley, J.S., Briggs, D., and Turner, M. (1972), *Dealing with Deviants*, London: Hogarth Press.

Whiteley, J.S. and Collis, M. (1987), 'The therapeutic factors in group psychotherapy applied to the therapeutic community', *International Journal of Therapeutic Communities*, vol. 8, no. 1.

Whiteley, J.S. and Gordon, J. (1979), *Group Approaches in Psychiatry*, London: Routledge & Kegan Paul.

WHO (1953), *Technical Report Series*, Geneva: no. 73.

Wiles, Sir H. (1949), *2nd Report of the Standing Committee on the Rehabilitation and Resettlement of Disabled Persons*, London: HMSO.

Wilkins, L.T. (1964), *Social Policy, Action and Research*, London: Tavistock Publications.

Willer, D. (1967), *Scientific Sociology*, New York: Prentice-Hall.

Willis, P. (1977), *Learning to Labour*, Aldershot: Saxon House.

Wills, W.D. (1968), 'What do we mean by planned environment therapy?', *Studies in Environment Therapy*, vol. 1:102-8.

Wilmer, H.A. (1958), *Social Psychiatry in Action*, Austin, Texas: Thomas.

—— (1981), 'Defining and understanding the therapeutic community, *Hospital and Community Psychiatry*, vol. 32, no. 2:95-9.

Wilson, S. (1979), 'Ways of seeing the therapeutic community', in Hinshelwood, R.D. and Manning, Nick (eds), *Therapeutic Communities*.

Wing, J.K. (1972), 'Principles of evaluation', in Wing, J.K. and Hailey, A.M. (eds), *Evaluating a Community Psychiatric Service*, Oxford: Oxford University Press.

Wintringham, T.H. (1936), *Mutiny, Being a Survey of Mutinies from Spartacus to Invergordon*, Stanley Nott.

Wolfenden Committee (1978), *The Future of Voluntary Organizations*, London: Croom Helm.

Wood, P. (1941), *British Medical Journal*, vol. 1.

Youngman, M.B. (1979), *Analysing Social and Educational Research Data*, New York: McGraw-Hill.

Zald, M.N. and Ash, R. (1966), 'Social movement organisations: growth, decay and change', *Social Forces*, vol. 44:327-41.

Zeitlyn, B. (1967), 'The therapeutic community — fact or fantasy', *British Journal of Psychiatry*, vol. 113:1083-6.

Zubin, J. (1964), in Hoch, H.H. and Zubin, J. (eds), *The Evaluation of Psychiatric Treatment*, Orlando, FL: Grune & Stratton.

# Index

actions, personality as 85-8, 97
Ahmed, P.I. 184
Ahrenfeld, R.H. 17
alienation 83-6
Almond, R.H. 34, 49, 55-6, 58, 66, 218, 220, 224
Althusser, L. 84, 89-91
Anderson, O.W. 5
anti-psychiatry 42
Antze, P. 184
L'Arche 42, 53
Argyle, M. 76, 80
Army Psychiatric Services, UK 7-9, 18
Arthur, C. 84
Ash, R. 211, 215
Association of Therapeutic Communities (ATC) 34, 51-4, 61, 209-13, 219
asylums 1-6, 135-6
Australia 135-82; community care 136-7; evaluation of Richmond Fellowship therapeutic communities 156-82; Richmond Fellowship 139-42; therapeutic communities in the community 135-42; voluntary sector 137-9
authority 57-9, 203-4, 211

Baldock, J. 96
Ballachey, E.L. 75
Banks, J.A. 214
Banton, M. 101
Baron, C. 49, 123
Barton, R. 27-8, 152
Baruch, G. 6, 184
Bateman, J.F. 19
Bazeley, E.T. 39
Bebbington, A.C. 165
Belknap, I. 19
Bell, M.D. 44
Belmont Hospital, Industrial Neurosis Unit, *later* Social

Rehabilitation Unit, *later* Henderson Hospital 12-13, 48, 55, 99-134, 193; aims 99-100, 213; ideology 104-5; Jones's model, criticisms 100-3; leadership 66, 109, 205, 211; Rapoport's study 17; 27-8, 48, 55, 102-13, 120-3, 143, 184-8, 196-7; 1970s 110-25; referral patterns 125-34; social control 109-10
Berger, P. 143-5
Bergin, A.E. 108, 149-52
Berke, J.H. 42
Bernstein, Basil 95-6
Bierenbroodspot, P. 32
Bion, W.R. 8-9, 14-15, 17, 141, 193
Bittner, E. 22, 201-3
Blake, R. 44
Blau, P.M. 204
Bloch, S. 66-7
Bloor, M.J. 42, 46, 49, 145-7, 202, 220
Bottoms, A.E. 149-50
Brannigan, A. 188
Bridgeland, M. 39-41
Briggs, D. 42, 124
Brooks, R. 153
Brown, E.L. 24

Camphill communities movement 42, 53
Cantril, H. 198
capitalism 83-6, 90-7
Carkuff, R.R. 153
Carstairs, G.M. 19, 26
Cassel Hospital 12, 27, 193
Castel, R. 3
Caudill, W. 19, 186, 216
charisma, leadership 203-6, 219-20; and authority 66, 203-4; routinization of 60-2, 211-16

240

Lewis, Aubrey 12, 100, 102
Lewis, Sir T. 9
Linton, R. 70
Lippitt, R. 76
Lofland, J. 205
Lord, F.M. 165
Luckmann, T. 143-5
Lukacs, G. 85
Lunatics Act (1845) 4-5
Lunacy Act (1890) 5, 11

McAdam, D. 216
McCarthy, J.D. 200, 209
McClintock, F.H. 149-50
Macdonald, K.I. 166, 177, 179
Mahony, N. 122
Main, Tom 8-9, 12, 14; collapse
    of a community 27, 62;
    groups 64; model for
    therapeutic community 13,
    30, 35, 47-8, 75, 104, 119,
    202; and resources 66, 200
Manning, Nick: models of
    therapeutic communities 187;
    organization and charisma
    212; Rapoport study 196-7;
    social movement 60-1, 205,
    215-16; therapeutic
    community studies 30-1, 44,
    46, 131
Marcuse, H. 89, 96
Marlborough Day Hospital 63-4
Martin, Dennis 26
Marx, Karl 72, 83-6, 89-94, 97
material basis for social life
    82-9; capitalism 83-6;
    personality as actions 85-8,
    97
Maudsley Hospital 11-12
Mauss, M. 190
May, M.A. 76
Mead, G.H. 16, 77
Medawar, P.B. 188
Menninger, W.C. 17
Mental Health Act (1959) 11, 140
mental hospitals 192; USA 19-24
Mental Treatment Act (1930) 6
Menzies, I. 64, 122
Merton, R.K. 11, 70, 102, 184,
    190

Michels, R. 211, 213
military psychiatry 7-9, 17-18,
    20, 24
Mill Hill 9-11
Millard, D.W. 69, 156
Miller, D.H. 19, 216
Miller, P. 48
Mills, C.W. 184
Mischel, W. 41, 76
Mocroft, I. 139
Molina, V. 84, 91
Mood, A. 167, 179
Moos; R.H. 32, 42, 159
Moreno, J.L. 10
Morrice, J.K.W. 110, 120-1,
    203
Morris, T. and P. 27, 124
movement, social, therapeutic
    communities as 47-55, 60-1,
    198-225; charisma routinized
    211-16; crisis and collapse
    222-5; crisis and survival
    216-22; organization 201-11,
    218
Mulkay, M. 184, 188-90
Multi-phasic Environmental
    Assessment Procedure
    (MEAP) 159, 162-5
Murdoch, Iris 219
Myerson, A. 24

Namboodiri, N.K. 166, 173, 177
'negotiated order' theory 22-3,
    59-60
Neil, A.S. 39
New Harmony Community 221-2
Niv, A. 215
Northfield Hospital 8-9, 193
Nunnally, J.C. 165

Olson, M., Jr 200
organization theory 14, 57-8
organization of therapeutic
    communities 201-11, 218
origins of therapeutic
    communities 1-28; asylums
    1-6; Jones at Mill Hill 9-11;
    'new psychiatry' 6-17; post-
    war era 17-28; social sciences
    developments 14-17;